Horus Templar

and the

Case of the Vengeful Vigilant

E.L. WARD

Horus Templar and the Case of the Vengeful Vigilant is a work of fiction. Names, characters, places, and incidents either are the product of the author's imagination or are used fictitiously. Any resemblance to actual persons, living or dead, events, or locales is entirely coincidental.

ISBN: 978-1-7370436-4-5

Table of Contents

"What can I say on the subject of family? I've never had one. But of course, I've observed its effects on others for many centuries. Vulnerability, partiality. Empty tradition and sentiment. Vices long handed down. Yes, if there is one specially exorbitant mercy in my life, it must be that I was spared all such entanglements."

- Magormissahr, *Referendums on the World, Vol. 888*

Chapter 1

It was to be the first of many dismal days to follow. The sun lazed in some invisible fold of the cloud-filled sky, and the Phantom Light shared its bleary mood. The workhands of Jast-Madiir's Great Harbor felt those azure pre-dawn hours stretch on and on, while their pocket watches told them little white lies...

But the air was cool. It was crisp. And there were feet and hands and eyes astir that were too intent to notice any lethargy at work on the world around them. They moved purposefully. They moved discreetly. They were quickened by malice aforethought...

None of this, however, escaped the watchful eye of Harbormaster Fitzgerald. Shuffling over to the window in the dark cabin of an unassuming cargo barge, his grim gaze followed a trio of smartly-dressed Jackals, brashly marching up the long, long docks... in just the direction they ought not to be. Which is to say, they were marching in *his* direction.

Fitzgerald tried to reach what conclusions he could for himself, but hardly a moment passed before he was joined in the window. While he'd been watching the world, his military cohort – the army sergeant – had evidently been watching him...

"See something?" Sergeant Oregano asked.

Fitzgerald nodded at the window, never blinking. "Mesomelae, headed our way."

The sergeant's face slowly bunched up as he watched the pack approach. They looked *big*... even next to the muscled ship hands hefting cargo to and from, up and down. "Dianodes," he cursed. "How did they know? How *could* they know? We took every precaution."

A moment of silence followed Oregano's unanswerable questions.

"Might just be they're lawyers," Fitzgerald tried with a shrug. "We're never short of legal trouble in the ports. Smuggling... immigration. It could be nothing."

Scarcely had the Harbormaster finished assuaging the sergeant when the three Mesomelae reached the foot of their barge's ramp, where they abruptly stopped. The Humans in the cabin watched the Jackals look the whole ship over, even as one of them seemed to glance right back at them through the tinted glass.

"Lawyers indeed," Oregano scoffed. "And I'll be a jelly's uncle." He turned Fitzgerald roughly by his shoulders, sneering down at him like he would a clumsy cadet. "Get out there and find them out!" he commanded with a shove. Then he crossed the cabin.

"What about you?" Fitzgerald inquired weakly.

"I'll round up the others," he answered, throwing a plain, tattered cloak over his uniform.

"But..." Fitzgerald began. Oregano shot him another look. Nevertheless, he decided to complete his thought. "I mean... you're an officer. Wouldn't your very appearance likely scare them off?"

"We don't want to *scare them off*, Fitzgerald." Oregano slipped a flintlock into a deep pocket. "We want *them*. Dead or alive. Now get out there!"

* * *

Fitzgerald shivered and drew his hands up into his sleeves as he walked down the long, shallow ramp, alone and exposed. Whatever the sergeant might want, he couldn't help hoping that his *own* appearance and authority as a Harbormaster might be enough to ward the villains away. Assuming, of course, that they *were* villains. There remained a faint shadow of a chance that these Mesomelae had legitimate business. He never thought he'd see the day when he prayed he was about to have a chat with a trio of lawyers. Tall, meaty lawyers, he noted. No more than half-way down the ramp, he was already looking up into beady eyes, jagged ears, and sleek snouts. There was no mistaking a predatory aspect about them. But then, he had to remind himself: That would still hold true, even if they *were* only lawyers...

"Good morning, gentlemen," Fitzgerald called out, fighting the reflex to draw a Pi symbol in front of himself, lest he be jinxed. "Can I help you?"

"I certainly hope so," said the Mesomela in the middle. "No one else this morning has been any help at all. We've been asking after the Harbormaster for the last half-hour. He's not been at his post, nor can anyone seem to shed any light on his whereabouts." He cocked a brow. "I call that very odd."

"I'm... I'm the Harbormaster here," Fitzgerald admitted, rather taken aback to discover they were looking for *him*. "May I ask who's calling?"

The three of them flashed badges. "Jasta, Panzer and Mikoyen," the middle Jackal answered, pointing first at himself, then his two compatriots. "We run a private law practice. But we've been contracted by the District

Attorney to inspect this stretch of the port. I regret to inform you... we've already found some troubling discrepancies."

Fitzgerald set his jaw. Even with some assurance that these men were indeed lawyers, he didn't feel at all assured. "Discrepancies? What discrepancies?"

'Jasta' flashed a toothy grin. "As luck would have it, this very barge," he answered, nodding past Fitzgerald. "Neither the ship itself, nor its cargo manifest can be found on any of the registries. It's a ship that doesn't belong. And yet, here we find our elusive Harbormaster. One might also find *that* rather odd, don't you think?"

Again, Fitzgerald found himself staggered by the unexpected trajectory of the whole conversation. Not only did these Mesomelae convincingly assert they had a legitimate reason to be here, but they even dared suggest that *he* did not. They were indeed sure of themselves, which made it much harder to be sure of himself. Fortunately, in that moment, he heard the steps of his 'deck hands' casually approaching the scene from behind him, and he rallied some confidence. "Why no, Sir; I don't think so at all. As Harbormaster, this barge is my responsibility, whether it's on the registry or not. *Particularly* if it's not. As such, may I politely suggest that you leave this matter in my hands and be on your way now."

The three Jackals exchanged glances, before Jasta returned to Fitzgerald. "I'm sorry, Mr. Harbormaster... but that's not the way these things work." He reached into his jacket and took out a folded sheet of paper. "This is a search warrant, notarized by the District Attorney's office, authorizing an investigation of this ship and its contents. You have been served."

Fitzgerald accepted the paper, utterly bewildered... having to ask himself whether this could all be a big mix-up. Had the authorities been *too* secretive about the shipment? Was it even just possible this warrant was being served simply because one hand didn't know what the other was doing? Or was this still nothing more than an incredibly elaborate ruse to get them on the ship?

Either way, they were bound to be disappointed...

"Now wait just a minute," he began. "I know how this must look... believe me. I understand your responsibilities. I understand the legally binding nature of this document. But even if Mr. Blackforest *himself* came here to serve this warrant, I would still have to deny him access. This is a highly privileged matter. *Very* highly privileged. Do you understand?"

"I'm not sure I do," Jasta replied, before looking out crossly at the men in long coats joining them at the foot of the ramp. "But perhaps you mean to have your ruffians explain it to me?"

"The only 'ruffians' here are you people," Sergeant Oregano retorted, fanning out with the rest of his plain-clothes troop. "Don't think we can't see right through the phony lawyer bit."

"Phony?" Jasta questioned, his jowls tightening over his fangs. "I only just explained to your Harbormaster: We've been legally empowered by the top brass of St. Argonsburg."

"Papers can be forged," Oregano said with a shrug.

The large canine sized him up. "I suppose that's true. Still, we *have* papers. Where are yours? Who do *you* purport to be? For all we know, you're nothing more than a thug with a big mouth. Give us one reason we should even be having this conversation."

Oregano shook his head. "I don't have to prove anything to you. You say I don't belong here... I say you don't. The only difference is: I know I'm not bluffing. That's enough for me."

The 'lawyers' glowered. "Nothing at all to show for yourself, eh? Alright. But we'll have to insist on a name, at least. You leave us no choice but to draw up charges against you for Obstruction of Justice."

The sergeant laughed. "You play the part well... I'll grant you that. You want to know what gives me a right to be here? You want a *name*?" He drew aside his cloak, revealing part of his uniform. "How about a rank and serial number to match?"

BANG!

Oregano went down as the imposters bolted. They got the drop on the soldiers in their way and plowed right through them, fleeing full-speed for the coast. They were several yards distant before any fire was returned. The soldiers' shots went wide. They were only fortunate to miss the startled bystanders, who were immediately stirred up into a panic...

"After them!" Oregano bellowed from the ground, pulling his wounded leg up for examination. "Don't let them get away!"

"Are you alright?" Fitzgerald asked reflexively, crouching by the sergeant. "Is there anything I can do to help?"

"Raise the alarm, you fool!" Oregano growled. "Don't worry about me."

"Of course!" Fitzgerald replied, nodding and leaping back to his feet in one flurried action. "Right away!" He ran for the nearest bell.

Oregano muttered endless curses under his breath as he broke off a loose piece of planking from the dock. He bit the sleeve of his cloak and tore a big strip down the seam. The groans of agony that followed were muted out by the terror and confusion all around... and by the sudden ringing in the bell tower. A ringing that carried for leagues...

* * *

Unbeknownst to the sergeant or the Harbormaster, a bell of a different sort lay strategically positioned below the covering of the sea, sheltering a second team of Mesomela agents, whose waiting ears easily detected the clanging of the alarm far above. Silently, they took their cue, slipping out from under the diving bell in synchronous, paddling for the surface. They emerged at the stern of the barge, with no need of grappling hooks to make their ascent. Their sharp claws anchored them to the wooden hull as they clambered for the top deck...

But just as they were making their way up the paneling alongside the rear portholes – the easiest part of the climb – Seth got overconfident and careless. He fumbled, and nearly came peeling off the side of the ship...

Just in time, Khonshu reached back and caught Seth's wrist in a flash of action. Also flashing – Seth noted – was that stupid grin of his. That insufferable, smug grin that told you he was the golden boy, and he knew it. Anchored again, Seth ground his teeth and resumed his climbing...

Without a sound, the tiny, padded feet of the three Mesomelae alighted their collective half-ton of weight on the deck. They scrambled along the cover of the bulwark, angling for the lower levels... for the cargo hold. Their brethren's bit about the registries was no bluff: There was no official record of the barge, let alone its freight. Nevertheless, the Vigilants knew full well what they were looking for...

Unavoidably, the stairway down from the poop deck left them momentarily exposed. Khonshu, still basking in his element, dropped his grin in an instant when Weneg suddenly froze in place just ahead of him. He followed his gaze, seeing a woman, far off on the dock, staring back at them with narrowed, judgmental eyes. Their hearts stopped, waiting to hear a shrill call between strokes of the bell...

But after a long, tense moment, she dutifully turned up her nose and continued on in a huff...

"What's the hold up, old man?" Seth whispered hoarsely from the back.

"She saw us," Weneg answered. "A lady on the dock."

"Yeah, and she kept moving," Seth sighed. "If we don't do likewise, we'll be spotted again. Chop-chop! And no more mistakes!"

"No more mistakes," Khonshu repeated in a whimsical voice as they sped down the stairs. "Why Seth, I do believe that should be your mantra from now on."

"Quiet," Weneg cautioned, while Seth fumed for something to riposte with.

Clandestinely, they rounded the cabin, quickly springing below deck...

Upright now, but no less cautious, the infiltrators passed empty, unguarded crew quarters on their way to the hold. The barge was still awaiting a carefully vetted crew to make its voyage far to the east, and south... to the cursed and appropriately blasted lands of their Enemies, the Berlie Beirels. And for the moment, the compliment of soldiers patrolling the ship had been, apparently, emptied... drawn off in pursuit of their brethren's bold diversion. Everything was going to plan. *Better* than to plan, it appeared...

Finally, they reached their destination, completely unopposed. They stopped short in the doorway... fearing that the cargo area might – of all places – still have a guard or two. But it was more than just caution that held them back for a moment. They were each a bit amazed to see a mere four chests in the middle of the vast, dark space...

But after a listen and a sniff, and well satisfied the coast was clear, Seth was the first to enter. He lifted the lid of a chest, retrieving a phial with a long neck and a bulb that filled his fist. He looked back questioningly. "This is it? Four cases of *this*?"

"Don't be too quick to scoff," Weneg replied, as he and Khonshu entered the hold. "Just one of those has magic enough for a whole squad of sorcerers."

Seth turned his skeptical expression back on the bottle. But a grin quickly curled his jowls, and he gave the elixir a couple little tosses in his clawed grip. "Supposing... supposing we were to lift a few of these? Or maybe we split one three ways, here and now."

"I'd think twice before I trifled with it," Weneg said, lifting another lid. "Do you know what would happen if you got the dosage wrong? Even a *little* wrong?"

"It'd mean my death, by the sound of it."

"Worse than that," Khonshu boded. He smashed a phial on the lip of the chest. "This is no time to change the script anyway. Let's do what we came here for."

Seth's thick snout rippled as he bared fangs. "Fine." He threw his phial on the ground.

The three of them quickly busied themselves taking and smashing the elixirs in pairs, until the room was filled with an overpowering fragrance... sweet, and a little pungent... a bit like old oranges. Steam rolled off the dark-stained floorboards as the alchemical mixtures ate the varnish off the wood before leaking down into the bilge. Between crashes, they could hear the stuff bubbling in the rancid water beneath their feet.

Finally, Seth got the bright idea to overturn his entire chest. But even with his unparalleled bulk and strength, the chest toppled a bit slower than he meant it to. A few phials broke, but most simply rolled out across the floor...

"Oh, brilliant," Khonshu chuckled. "Fine time to discover your gentle side, Big Guy."

"Why you little...!" Seth stammered, none too quick on the draw. "Come over here and I'll show you my gentle side!"

Weneg gave a long sigh. "This is the last time I babysit the two of you. No more bright ideas... no more smart remarks. Alright?"

"And *no more mistakes*," Khonshu added, reprising his grin.

Seth only growled, reaching down for more magic to smash...

It wasn't long before the whole place reeked of over three chests worth of wasted elixirs. Weneg and Khonshu had their cases emptied out in plenty of time to help Seth round up his stragglers, which had rolled across the floor in every direction. Khonshu watched with amusement as Seth scanned for more phials under each arm, overlooking one that had made it almost all the way to the hold's entryway...

"You missed one," he was happy to point out.

"Yeah, yeah," Seth grumbled, following Khonshu's extended claw... crossing the empty space. The other two resumed their own searches...

But just as Seth began to reach down for the wayward phial, there was a clumsy flurry of sounds in the doorway. Khonshu and Weneg's eyes darted back up to see a man with one leg in a makeshift splint standing with a flintlock pistol pointed right up Seth's nose...

"Hold it; all of you," Sergeant Oregano commanded. He rattled the flintlock in Seth's face. "You: turn around. Hands up."

Seth cautiously obliged. Everyone remained still and silent...

"An excellent ruse, gentlemen," Oregano went on. "I badly misread your playbook. But your 'lawyer' friends made one big mistake, too. If they wanted to take me off the board, they should've shot to kill."

"Well, it doesn't matter now," Khonshu fired back. "We completed our mission. You're too late to stop us."

"He's right," Weneg explained. "Your Czarina's cargo is lost, along with the trade she meant to make. You've already failed. Do you really think our lives will be enough to ransom yours? Rather than hinder us, you ought to come *with* us. Your life is forfeit if you go back..."

Oregano shook his head. "You let *me* worry about that. I'm no deserter. At least one of you is coming in with me. And when we get you to squeal on the rest of your meddlesome little club, then we'll see what the Czarina thinks of me..."

Suddenly, Khonshu sprang for the starboard wall. Oregano reached out to trace his flight with the pistol, but this quickly proved his undoing. In a flash of simultaneous action, Seth caught Oregano by the wrist. *BANG*! The pistol went off ineffectually. And with one great heave, Seth threw the man over his shoulder. Oregano landed on the deck with a horrible crunch...

They all paused, as if stunned, waiting to see if the Sergeant would stir. But even after Seth nudged his prone form with his little foot, Oregano remained motionless on the ground...

"Well, great going there, Seth," Khonshu scolded him at length. "I swear, of all the clumsy, ham-fisted..."

"Hey!" Seth protested. "*You* made the move, Hotshot! What did you want me to do, then? Let him blast you?"

"He *missed*! You *made* him miss! What possible threat did he pose after that? You didn't have to snap him like a twig!"

The big, bulky Mesomela wore a genuine face of one unfairly accused. "Wh... I mean... it wasn't exactly on purpose! I didn't realize they were *that* fragile!"

"Oh, good... plead ignorance. Because I'd have to accept *that* coming from you, wouldn't I?"

Seth's wounded expression gradually began to shift into a look of disgust. "What are you so sore about, anyway? It's not like these Jast-Madiirans are innocent. They've been arming the Enemy! That's the whole reason we're here! Warships... mercenaries... now magic. Maybe it's about time one of them got what they have coming."

Khonshu shook his head. "That wasn't your call to make. We all accepted greater risk to avoid collateral damage. But every time the Stentor asks for a scalpel, you reach for the rusty hacksaw! You *know* how carefully he planned this. You know this isn't what he wanted."

By now, Seth looked mad enough to spit. He drew himself up and marched on smaller Khonshu, who watched unmoved. He leveled a big claw at his face...

"Listen, Fancy Son. Just because you're the Stentor's favorite doesn't give you the right to speak for him. I did what I was trained to do, and I saved your precious little hackles. One might think you'd be grateful. But I guess the only thing you know how to be is a brat. Wonder I don't put you on the floor, too."

"Why don't you try it and *see* who ends up on the floor?"

"Enough!" Weneg interjected. "You two are insufferable. No shame, no sense of reality... only raging egos. We have to get out of here before we're found again!"

Seth and Khonshu returned their stern glances, each daring the other to be the first to step down. Until finally, Seth clicked his jowls. "Yeah... I guess we do."

Khonshu grinned, gesturing with a slight bow to the doorway. Seth mangled a grumble between his grinding fangs, but followed Weneg's lead. Cautiously, they all issued out. It wasn't until they were halfway down the hall that Khonshu remembered something urgently...

"Wait!"

Weneg and Seth exchanged a look. "What is it now?" Seth asked.

"The last phial! The one you went for when you were jumped! We never took care of it. I..." Khonshu had another thought, just then... one he couldn't reconcile. "I don't even remember seeing it on my way out..."

"You mean, this phial?" a muffled voice asked from within the hold. Khonshu, Weneg and Seth all slowly peered back the way they'd come, watching a broken Sergeant Oregano roll himself back over, propping up on one arm to face them. In his other hand, he held the phial, mockingly sloshing it around. They all froze. The cork had been pulled...

"You counted me out a bit too soon again," Oregano quipped, his breathing labored. "It *is* too late to stop you. And it's clear I'm not long for this world. But at least I'll go out knowing this all blew up in your face..." With a hitch, he forced the elixir down his gullet in great draughts...

Khonshu had to catch himself mid-leap. There was no stopping the sergeant this time. He doubled back, waving his comrades on...

"Run! *Run*!!"

They all took off full-speed through the corridor, with no time to sneak so much as a peak at the transformation in progress behind them. All they knew of Oregano's fate was the brief flicker of orange-hot light just before they turned and charged up the stairs. Then, the searing wave of heat that overtook them on the climb...

And finally, just as Khonshu watched Seth and Weneg leap for the dock, there was the explosion...

Chapter 2

Joy. Anxiety. Hopeful anticipation. Certain doom. The courtroom was an electrically charged melting pot of conflicting emotions. Not one, but *two* lives hinged on the impending verdict. And not only that – the witnesses, jurors, and honored guests all had a stake in this thing. Maybe not the least Horus Templar himself, in whom the two young dreamers had entrusted their hopes, and their futures.

He'd fared well enough so far. After two full days in court, the prosecution had yet to throw anything more volatile into the mix than the tired old parade of gossipy friends and co-workers, with just a few jealous would-be suitors sprinkled on top. And while this wasn't the sort of case Horus worked all that often, he understood its operatic formula by now, and had little trouble impeaching one dissenting voice after another...

Still, the tension in the room was not at all lost on him. He knew his opponent was holding an ace up his sleeve... a climatic testimony that would surely spoil everything, if Horus could poke no holes in it...

Finally, Judge Beatrice emerged from her chambers, standing beside her seat at the bench. Everyone in the room crisply and silently came to their feet.

"The court will come to order," she said. "Day three of Stephano and Victoria vs. Imperium in Exilium is now in session." Her gavel rapped the sound block three times as she sat down, prompting the entire assembly to return to their seats. "The prosecution will call its next witness."

Attorney Marc-Antonius Sudstein stood back up, leaning deviously over his desk with one hand resting flat on the board, and the other curled behind his back in a tight fist. "I call Thornton Darby to the stand," he announced.

Horus' brow rose. This was it... they'd come to Sudstein's crescendo at last. He snuck a glance at his clients just in time to see Stephano take Victoria's clawed hand in his. Then he looked out into the sea of other Mesomela faces, spotting Darby as he stood and pulled out the folds of his jacket with a gruff flourish.

After swearing in and taking the stand, Darby crossed his arms and assumed his surliest expression. To Horus, he certainly appeared to be play-acting. Whether he could convince the jury of this, however, was another matter. After all, suits like this always ran a bit on the dramatic side...

"Now, Mr. Darby..." Sudstein began.

"Please, call me Thornton," Darby interjected.

"Alright. Now, Thorton..."

"Thor**n**ton, Thor**n**ton!" Darby corrected rather insistently. "It's pronounced 'Thor**n**ton'."

Horus shook his head. The fellow was most definitely a '*Thorn*ton'...

"My apologies, Mr. Thor**n**ton," Sudstein nearly sighed. "Now, I understand that you have testimony most damaging to the suitability of Mr. Stephano and Ms. Victoria's petition. Would you please relate to the court the conversation that you shared with me?"

"Yes," Darby replied, nodding. "It was a chat I had with Mother, over a year back..."

Sudstein held up a hand. "One moment, Mr. Thornton. I see that we're already getting ahead of ourselves. Would you please begin by explaining your relationship with the defendants."

"I'm Ms. Victoria's brother," he revealed, his jowls tightening contemptuously as he leveled a look at Stephano. "As for her little friend over there... I don't claim him."

"And that would mean the woman you spoke with is also the mother of Ms. Victoria... a one Clarissa Donovan... is that correct?"

"Obviously," Darby huffed.

"*Indeed*," Sudstein huffed back. "Now, as for this conversation you had with Mrs. Donovan: What were the two of you talking about?"

Darby reached out and pointed. "It was *him*. We were discussing *him*."

"Very good. Let the record show that Mr. Thornton has identified the defendant, Mr. Stephano."

"So ordered," Judge Beatrice said.

"And what specifically about him was being discussed?" Sudstein continued.

"Well, it was just after he and Victoria started dating," Darby explained. "Maybe a few days before Mother was put on the Pygmy Mountain case."

"You're referring to the closed-court suit in Maenea that Mrs. Donovan is currently working? The one that has already been established by earlier testimony as having her detained, and unable to be in attendance for this hearing?"

"Um... *yeah*," Darby answered with attitude. "How many Pygmy Mountain cases do you think she's worked?"

"You'll forgive me wanting to ensure the record reads clearly, Mr. Thornton," Sudstein riposted. "Now, please: What did Mrs. Donovan relate to you regarding Mr. Stephano?"

Darby grinned, having come to the bomb he'd been waiting to drop. "She said she didn't approve of him. She said Victoria could do a lot better."

Everyone in the courtroom gasped and murmured. Judge Beatrice was forced to employ her gavel.

"So, the mother of the would-be bride disapproves," Sudstein summed it up, when the crowd noise had at last simmered down. "Is there anything more you have to tell us, Mr. Thornton?"

"Well, what more do you want? I can't think of a weightier opinion than Mother's. And she said *nay*. The implications seem clear enough."

"Yes, perhaps they do at that," Sudstein said, turning away from the bench. "You may cross-examine, Mr. Templar."

Horus stood, making no motion for the witness stand. Instead, he only looked up at the Judge. "Your Honor, I protest the very admission of this hearsay testimony from Mr. Thornton. I move that it be stricken."

"And I object!" Sudstein chimed. "Thornton was a party in the conversation he introduced. It can scarcely be considered hearsay!"

"But it *is* uncorroborated..." Horus challenged. "And not best evidence. If Mrs. Donovan would indeed seek to annul this marriage proposal, let her do so in person, in her own words."

"Objection!" Sudstein insisted.

Judge Beatrice waved down the flustered junior prosecutor. "That's quite alright, Mr. Sudstein..." She turned back on Horus with narrow eyes, holding up her lorgnette. "The defense must understand that what he asks is quite impossible. Mrs. Donovan is currently incommunicado... abroad and otherwise engaged with a highly sensitive conservation lawsuit. She could not be present. It is highly doubtful that she was even permitted to receive her invitation."

"I do understand, Your Honor," Horus answered. "However, I maintain that Thornton Darby's testimony should not be permitted to stand, thus unsubstantiated. For by his own admission, he knows as well as anyone the power that a mother wields to sway the jury in a marriage case. This alleged conversation of his could be entirely fictitious! A convenient story he invented to give credence to his own disapproval of Mr. Stephano as a future brother-in-law."

"A *story*?!" Darby fumed. "Well of all the nerve!"

The Judge rapped her gavel. "Enough." She turned to Horus again. "The concerns of the defense are noted. However, the court does *not* intend to dismiss any opinion of the bride-mother with bearing on this case, be it earnestly offered. But now, if you have reason to believe that this witness' testimony is, indeed, fallacious, then I'm afraid the burden of proof lies with you. You will have to impeach it with your cross-examination."

Horus inclined his head solemnly. "Very well, Your Honor." He kept a low gaze and slow pace as he approached the stand, deep in thought. "Now, Mr. Thor***n***ton..."

"...That's Mr. *Darby* to you."

"Just as well. Mr. Darby, I couldn't help noting that the prosecution was content with a mere summary of this conversation you and your mother were supposed to have had. You presume to condense the whole substance of her words into a flat disapproval of Mr. Stephano. I say it should be for the *jury* to decide what she meant to say. Tell me, what were Mrs. Donovan's exact words? What were yours? Let's have the conversation in its entirety."

Darby shifted in his seat. "I... Well... I mean, you can't expect me to remember all that *exactly*. It happened months ago!"

"Why yes, of course," Horus mused. "Mrs. Donovan has been out-of-country for quite some time, hasn't she? In fact, I seem to recall earlier testimony that suggested her departure *predated* the start of Mr. Stephano and Ms. Victoria's courtship. Is that not accurate?"

Darby's eyes darted all around. "Uh, yes... I mean, *no*! Confound your misleading double-negatives!"

Horus shook his head. "But I used no double-negative, Mr. Darby. A double-negative would've been to ask: 'Is that not, *not* accurate?'"

"You're trying to confuse me!"

"Then let me be more clear. Did Mrs. Donovan leave the country *before* the defendants' relationship began, or *after*?"

"After! It was after! They'd been dating a little while before she left."

"Really? Then just how much overlap was there, Mr. Darby? Weeks? Days? *Hours*?"

"Something like two or three days... I don't know!" Darby answered, waving his hand around in the air. "What does it matter?"

"It would seem to matter a very great deal. We know Mrs. Donovan was scheduled to sail on Novtober 39th. Yet it was specifically reported by Ms. Victoria's coworker, Mrs. Forrester, that the defendants' first date did not occur until Novtober *41*st! Those two or three days seem to be working in the wrong direction for you, Mr. Darby. How do you explain that?"

"M...Mrs. Forrester must've mixed up her days. I'm sure their first date was earlier than that."

Horus looked over at the court recorder. "We also have the name of the restaurant where Mr. Stephano reserved seats for the date in question. Perhaps we ought to review *their* records?"

"Um..." Darby stammered, looking ready to pant under the pressure. "No... I remember now! Mrs. Forrester was right. Mother just didn't sail on time. She was... ill."

"Interesting..." Horus quipped, raising a brow. "And very lenient of the Maenean government to excuse her tardiness. So then, you must've spoken with her in the hospital?"

"That's right."

"Which hospital?"

"Oh, uh..." Darby went blank, before finally shaking his head with a shrug. "I don't recall. Must've slipped my mind."

"Well, no matter. Let's see if we can't help jog your memory. What sort of hospital was it? A surgical hospital? Outpatient clinic?"

"Don't come at me with all that advanced medical jargon! It was just any old general hospital!"

Horus took a step back from the stand – grimacing – letting a contemptuous silence build. "Mr. Darby, I'm afraid I find your entire story highly circumspect. You've flatly refused to offer any precise details. You've contradicted earlier testimony. You've contradicted *yourself*. How should the jury be expected to receive such a dubious account? Why should they believe what you say, if you remember nothing?"

Darby couldn't seem to answer. But just as Horus began to walk away, he called out. "But I *do*! I do now! I remember what she said! It was... it was something like: 'All my children have one life to live, and as surely as the world turns, I want only the best for them all. And Stephano is *not* the best for Victoria!'"

The whole crowd muttered their astonishment a second time.

Horus was still, making no sign. Yet inside, he deflated. Despite his best efforts, the court was obviously still caught up in the scandal. What more could he do?

"Alright, then, Mr. Darby..." he began, slowly turning back. "Let us for the moment examine another question. You've asserted knowledge of your mother's opinion. But what of your own? What do you personally think of Mr. Stephano?"

This question noticeably diminished Darby's resurgent confidence. He looked up at the Judge. "Must I answer that?"

"I believe the question is suitable," Judge Beatrice replied. "Counsel is within his right to demonstrate bias."

Darby's jowls contorted as he took his time weighing his response. Until finally, he smiled. "Alright... I admit: Maybe I don't like him very much. But if I don't, it's only because I'm a good son, who minds what his mother says."

"Then your mother must've somehow neglected to warn you about the seriousness of perjury!"

"Objection!" Attorney Sudstein called out. "Your Honor, I think this badgering has gone on quite long enough. Mr. Thornton is a model citizen, having served honorably in the profession of Rich Young Heir for many years. He is honest, as well as respectable. These ad-hominem attacks from Mr. Templar are entirely unwarranted."

"The prosecution will have to excuse me failing to take such personalities into account," Horus fired back. "But I submit that even an honest and respectable man may be driven to some manner of trickery, if he feels the need is great enough."

Judge Beatrice gave her sound block a few taps. "In any event, we *are* straying afield, Mr. Templar. The court is not the place for these philosophical meanderings and hostile insinuations. You will confine yourself to proper examination, Counselor."

Horus shot a stern look at a smug Mr. Darby before returning to the Judge. "The defense has nothing further on cross for this witness, your Honor."

Sudstein stood back up. "Nor does the prosecution seek to recross. Furthermore, the State rests its case."

"Very well," Beatrice said with a nod. "Does the defense intend to present a case, Mr. Templar?"

"Most assuredly, it does." Horus smirked as he watched Darby begin to withdraw from the stand. "For my first witness, I call Mr. Thornton Darby."

Darby blanched. "But... you said you had nothing more...?"

"...On *cross* examination. That's right. Now we begin with *direct* examination."

"The court reminds Mr. Darby that he is still under oath," Beatrice recited.

"Imagine that; I haven't even left my seat," Darby muttered just a little too loud, settling back into the chair.

"Now, before we begin in earnest..." Horus segued, interlacing his fingers as he returned to the stand, "...I offer you one final chance to retract the testimony earlier given to the prosecution."

"Ha!" Darby exclaimed. "And just what in the world would make me want to do that?"

Horus spun and returned to his desk. And then, with only the slightest internal flutter, he snatched up a piece of paper. Turning back, he examined the document in his hands silently for a long time, almost cherishing it. "Tell me, Mr. Darby: Are you familiar with the finer points of procedure regarding closed court sessions, such as your mother's?"

Darby winced. "I'm... that is... what's there to know? No one goes in or out. No contact with the outside world."

"That's a fine summary... in *general,*" Horus replied. "However, it may interest you to know that not all countries enforce their incommunicado policies in the same fashion, or to the same degree. Some are less strict than others. Particularly, you may be surprised to learn there are a few countries that allow participants in such cases some access to the *postal* service – both incoming and outgoing – when facilitated by special court-appointed censors."

The witness was wide-eyed and speechless. "That... that *is* quite surprising," he said in a low, weak voice. "W...what of it?"

Here, Horus took special care to hold his treasured paper up again, even giving it a little snap. "Supposing I were to tell you that your mother is not – in fact – entirely unreachable at present. Supposing I were to tell you that – upon assumption of my duties in this case – I took the liberty of reaching out to her personally." He rolled up the paper, waving it in one hand. "Supposing I were to present to you personal correspondence – signed and notarized by Mrs. Donovan, your mother – giving her blessing to the very union you claim she found unsuitable. Would you then consider retracting your testimony?"

For a time, Darby was utterly frozen. Then, at last, he made a sound... barely audible. It was... a *whimper.* His eyes moistened, and trembled. And before long, he looked ready to break down and curl up with a security blanket...

"Oh, Mumzy..." he mumbled. *"Forgive me. I never meant to... I never dreamed that..."*

"Speak up, Mr. Darby," Horus coached him. "What is it you have to say for yourself?"

"I... I retract my testimony," he stammered, making everyone gasp. "I admit I made the whole thing up. I never liked Stephano. Between his base-jumping accident, the bouts of amnesia, and that troublemaking identical twin brother of his, I just thought he'd bring too much drama to the family. But I'm only the *brother* of the bride. I wasn't even offered a seat on the jury. I knew no one would give a hoot what *I* thought. No one except... except for maybe Mother. Our dear, dear mother. But I never got an opportunity to talk it over with her. I had no chance... except one. Just this one chance that I might be able to pass my opinion off as hers. But I never once stopped to think she might..." He looked up, then, with pleading eyes, searching out his sister and Stephano, huddled together at the defense table. "I'm sorry. So sorry to both of you."

Horus watched as Victoria fell into Stephano's reassuring embrace, the two of them overcome with relief. He turned back to the witness stand. "Well done, Mr. Darby... well done." Then, he addressed the court. "Your Honor, the defense rests its case."

"Very well." Judge Beatrice stood. "We will proceed immediately to arbitration. Is the jury prepared to deliver a verdict?"

The jury – an assortment of cousins and siblings, aunts and uncles, and the three available parents – conferred briefly amongst themselves. "We are, your Honor," Stephano's father announced.

"All those in favor of this union, say 'yay'."

"*Yay*," called a strong majority, if not a consensus.

"All those in opposition, say 'nay'."

There was no response.

"The 'yay's have it," Beatrice proclaimed. "The defendants, Stephano and Victoria, are hereby sentenced to marriage, forthwith." She gave the sound block a healthy whack. "The reception will be convened promptly at 14-hundred hours in dance hall number three. Court is adjourned."

Horus sighed, letting his own relief wash over him as he looked back at his table one last time. Deborah had a smile and an affirming nod for him. Stephano and Victoria were, by this time, oblivious to anything and everything but each other. He saw them exchange their first licks as man and wife. Perhaps it was only his imagination, but in that moment, reality itself seemed to take on a soft-focus quality, and the edges of Horus' vision were inexplicably rimmed in a pale halo. Even the noise of the crowd gradually diminished as sweet music suggested itself ex-nihilo. Actually, the whole scene quickly became so hackneyed by picturesque overtures that it was almost a bit of a nuisance. But on the whole, Horus was happy for them. They'd been granted this cheesy moment... and the promise of a lifetime together... in the face of long odds. Perhaps it was just as well they had no idea *how* long...

* * *

Almost before they knew it, everyone found themselves immersed in the festive atmosphere of the wedding reception. The hall was filled to overflowing with smooth jazz, clear laughter, classy dance moves, and only the finest grape juice. Horus didn't mind being helped to a healthy glass by a passing garçon. After a rich lap, he nearly had to take a step back as a whole string of line dancers whizzed right by him. He chuckled as he watched them wind almost recklessly around the floor. But after another steep arc that led them back toward the north end of the hall, their dashing away happened to reveal Deborah, standing in place, facing right at him ...

Horus could only hope he didn't look too obviously stunned. Deborah always dressed well, but she managed to pull out some extra stops for the occasion. She had on a necklace of ivory rings that went perfectly over her brightly patterned shawl. Complementing these intricate pieces, she wore a long, seamless gown of dark beige and a pair of slight, simple gold bracelets. And in her delicate hands were a pair of stemmed glasses...

"Well, well," she said, further arresting Horus' vital functions with her sarcastic smile. "So much for my little errand. They sent me straight from the head table to bring you a glass of their best vintage, compliments of the happy couple. But it looks like you already helped yourself."

"Not to worry," Horus replied, as the two of them closed to a more sociable distance. "I've every confidence that extra glass will come in handy soon enough."

"Planning to cut a little loose, are we?"

"You know, I really needed a case like this. Something to break up the thankless monotony of trying to save people's lives."

"Don't forget the even greater monotony of having no cases to work at all."

"Well, we'll have that to face down in the morning. But I'd say we worked pretty hard to make this party happen. Let's enjoy it."

Deborah grinned and raised one of the glasses. "Here's to us, then."

Though he knew what she meant, Horus couldn't help a special fondness for her word choice. He raised his own glass. "To us."

No sooner than they tinked and took a lap, they were suddenly aware of a big, tough, hard-boiled presence in their midst. "Say," Art said. "Is that other drink for me?"

They both looked over at him, pretending not to be too startled. "Why, Art Mallard... as I live and breathe!" Horus greeted him. "What a pleasant surprise. I had no idea you were invited to this."

"I could've told you that," Deborah chimed. "Cousin Victoria's known Art since she was small. But I *am* surprised to see you actually showed."

"Probably against my better judgment," Art admitted, gesturing at the full glass. "But really: Mind if I wet my whistle?"

Deborah seemed a bit hesitant. The juice *had* been meant for Horus... who soon realized he would have to be the one to give permission. "Not at all," Horus replied. "We didn't know we were saving it for you, but it's yours if you want it."

"Thanks." Art accepted the glass from Deborah and downed about half of it with a single swig. "*Ahhh*... that's the good stuff. Anyway, sorry to drink and run, but I've got time for one, maybe two down the hatch before I gotta put the smokescreen back up."

Horus noted the program rolled up in Art's other hand. "Ah, that old nose-in-the-paper trick of yours... no wonder you caught us off guard. But why so discreet? It couldn't be that you're hoping to avoid the happily wedded hostess?"

"Nah, not Victoria herself," Art replied. "She's all grown up and puttin' down roots now. It's her pack of chuckle-headed sisters I'm not crazy about running into. Trust me: It's better if I just stay invisible."

Deborah put a hand on her hip. "Well you know, Art, if you really wanted them to leave you alone, all you had to do was bring Blucille."

"Goodness, yes," Horus went along, suddenly realizing how unusual it was to see Art socially, without the company of the young Assistant District Attorney. "Where on earth are you hiding Ms. Cordon? Have you taught her your disappearing act?"

Art's expression went blank as an abrupt beat of silence cast a shadow over the whole conversation. "Heh..." he began at length. "I, uh, don't actually know where she is. All I could get out of her was she was busy and couldn't make it."

Horus and Deborah found this a bit of an impasse. Nothing Art had just said foreboded anything, really... but the *way* he said it sounded ominous...

"Well, we all know what a hard worker she is," Deborah managed. "Cases at Civil Headquarters must be stacking up."

"Yeah..." Art agreed weakly. "I hope that's all it is."

"Of course it is," Horus assured him, clapping a hand on his shoulder. "What reason would you have to think it was anything else?"

Immediately, Horus felt like putting his foot in his mouth. The tendency to ask too many questions came with his trade, and he could tell by looking at Art that he'd asked one too many just now...

"Well... mostly a lotta little things, I guess," Art replied. "Maybe it was just my imagination, but I could swear the moment I invited her to the wedding, all the air just kinda flew out of the room."

"We know the feeling," Deborah commiserated. Horus nodded his agreement.

"I mean, she didn't *officially* back out until this morning," Art went on. "But the way the question stopped her up, I think she was bound and determined from the get-go not to be here. I only worked up the nerve to remind her about it once... and when I did, I had the same sinking feeling." He took Horus' half-drank glass and downed it morosely. "It's been eating me up, I tell ya. We've been going steady for a long time now, and I mean, I've got no complaints... it's been swell. But lately I've been worried, ya know? Just kinda worried that maybe I've been waiting too long to get serious. Like she'll start to think I'm stringing her along. But then, I got the invite to Little Vicky's wedding. And I thought, 'Man, this is just the thing!' I thought inviting Blucille to this would send just the right message. That I really *do* have something more in mind for us than just the next big night on the town. Except that now, I can't help thinking it all completely backfired. And I can't figure out where I went wrong. What if I jumped the gun a bit and scared her off? What if... what if she's been stringing *me* along? Man, if *that's* it, then... then I don't even know where to go from here." He studied the blank expressions of his captive audience. "Or... well... I don't know. Do you think maybe it's all just in my head?"

Horus and Deborah exchanged a look. They returned their eyes to Art, feeling incalculable pressure to offer an answer. *Any* answer...

"Oh, yes... definitely!" Horus nodded exaggeratedly. "Textbook mid-relationship jitters, if ever I've heard them. Don't worry, Art. You and Ms. Cordon will be back on track before you know it."

Deborah was obliged to share another look with Horus. A look in which her face read, 'Are you kidding me? How could you just write everything off like that?' To which Horus' face, accompanied by a slight shrug, replied, 'Well what was I *supposed* to say, him suddenly going to pieces on us?'

"*Whew*, that's a relief," Art sighed, apparently none the wiser of their faces' private chat, and quite ready to take Horus' word for it. "I'm glad I got that off my chest." He looked at his empty glasses of grape juice. "You guys got any more of this stuff?"

Suddenly, a shrill call of, "*ART MALLARD*!" pierced their ears from across the dance hall. Their hackles all stood on end as they were rather instantly surrounded by an encroaching assault of girly laughter...

"Oh, great..." Art boded. "Here comes the Giggle Squad."

Within moments, Art was indeed swept up in a tidal wave of Victoria's immature little sisters, who vaguely but inexorably herded him to the center of the dance floor with a flurry of shoves, heaves, and a continuous droning of excitable chatter. Horus, and even Deborah, were again left a bit incredulous.

"Poor Art," Deborah finally said. "Things were going so good with him and Blucille. I can't imagine why she'd be having second thoughts now."

"You know, it really *might* be nothing," Horus replied, hoping to believe it himself. "They're at a stressful juncture in their relationship. It sounds to me like Art's ready to commit; it's only natural he'd be afraid to get his timing off. Now he's reading into every little thing. But even if it *is* something more than that, they've handled rough patches before." He grinned down at her. "You'll remember the rocky start they got off to. If they can overcome *that*, I'd like to think they can work just about anything out."

Deborah sighed, absently watching Art as he was mobbed into dancing by doting adolescents. "You're probably right." She looked up, meeting Horus' gaze with a grin of her own. "I better go see if I can save him from my cousins."

Horus nodded. "Best of luck to you both."

"It might take a while," she warned, as she began to amble off to Art's rescue. But before she got too far away, she stopped. "You'll save me a dance, won't you?"

Horus blanched. Though he'd been looking at her the whole time, the question hit him squarely in the back of the head. "I, uh, well yes," he answered at length. "I mean, I suppose that would be appropriate for two coworkers in a social engagement such as this." He strained to smile, wishing he could bite his own big, stupid mouth off.

"Alright," Deborah laughed. "I'll put it on your itinerary, Boss."

He nodded dumbly as she waved and steeled herself to the task at hand. Looking on, Horus felt his light mood return through the hail of butterflies. Today was a day where love had triumphed. Why should any of them doubt for a moment that Art's story would turn out any different? Yes, as he watched Deborah practically beat her juvenile cousins off him with a stick, he was filled with nothing but hope for his friend... and for the future in general...

"Mr. Templar!" he heard, quickly pivoting to meet the familiar voice of Stephano. "Mr. Templar! I'm so glad we found you," Stephano said, coming up to Horus with Victoria on his arm.

"Ah, Stephano, and *Mrs.* Victoria," Horus answered them, feeling all the more validated to see their smiling faces up close. "I didn't expect to see you this side of the head table for some time. What can I do for you?"

"Why, nothing at all!" Stephano laughed.

"We were hoping to find out if there was anything more we could do for *you*," Victoria explained.

"You mean *besides* the toast you sent, in care of Deborah?" Horus asked. "I'm sure that's thanks enough. And more than a Public Defender is accustomed to getting."

"Well, it certainly doesn't *feel* like enough," Stephano replied. "Not to us. We're very much in your debt, Mr. Templar. I don't know how we'll ever repay you. You literally did the impossible for us."

Horus' brow furrowed. "The *impossible*? I'm afraid I don't know what you mean."

"The letter from my mother," Victoria said. "I still don't understand it."

"How did you ever get through to her?" Stephano asked. "Let alone in time for the trial?"

Horus chuckled, shaking his head. "Ah, yes, I see now. Perhaps an apology is in order. It seems I lured the two of you into the same trap as your brother. Suffice it to say, it wasn't for lack of personal experience that I suggested an honest man might resort to misdirection in times of great need."

"So... there wasn't a letter?" Victoria asked.

"I never said there was," Horus stated. "Clearly, your mother the attorney never passed on to her children the wonderous powers of the word '*suppose*'. All I did was walk up to your brother with a sheet of paper and bid him '*suppose*' I'd been in correspondence with Mrs. Donovan. For while it *is* true that some countries allow censored mail to pass in and out of closed court, I'm afraid Maenea isn't among them. The only thing I had left was to call his bluff with one of my own. It's really just about the oldest trick in the defense attorney's playbook."

After a moment of looking flabbergasted, the couple soon appeared almost more pleased with him than before. "Well, one way or another, you're still a miracle-worker to us," Stephano said. "We really can't thank you enough."

"Well, that's very kind," Horus replied, feeling genuinely embarrassed by all their appreciation. "But just to know the work I've done is valued is more reward than you realize. We defense attorneys tend to be frowned upon by politer society at large."

"Eh, that kind of thing doesn't bother us," Stephano waved it off.

"You're among your own kind here, Mr. Templar," Victoria added, gesturing out to the room. "Most of us have at least one lawyer in the family. We get it."

Horus nodded with a smile. "Then I suppose it's true what they say: An attorney has no honor, except in his own country."

Just then, a younger fellow came running up to them, looking aghast, even as he called out, "Mr. Stephano!" Horus quickly noted the frilly shirt under his jacket, indicating he was part of the band. And it suddenly dawned on him... they'd been playing without the most important instrument, these last few minutes...

"Excuse me, Mr. Stephano!" the young musician went on appealing.

"Barnabee?" Stephano questioned. "Aren't you guys right in the middle of a waltz? Why aren't you playing?"

"I'm sorry, Sir, it's..." Barnabee began rather frantically. "That is, I would be playing, but..."

"It's alright, Barnabee; get a hold of yourself," Stephano encouraged him. "What's going on?"

"It was a guest, or somebody," Barnabee panted. "He came right up to me in the middle of the song and stopped me. Said the piano was out of tune, but he'd fix it. Frankly, Sir, I don't know what he's talking about. We tuned everything up just before the reception, and I told him so. But he was insistent. He just started reaching right under the lid and making crazy demands. He wanted the whole band to stop for him!"

Horus exchanged looks of incredulity with Stephano and Victoria. Something sinister was afoot, but he couldn't begin to guess what...

"Well, thank you for coming and getting me, Barnabee," Stephano said at length. "Whatever it is, I'll handle it."

Barnabee shook his head. "But I didn't come to get *you*, Sir. I mean, when I saw you were here, I knew I had to stop and explain myself. But it was *him*. He sent me to get help..."

"What do you mean?"

"Well, I watched him work for a while, and he didn't even look like he knew what he was doing. I asked if he could use a hand and he said he could. But he refused *my* help." Barnabee stopped there, turning his bewildered eyes on Horus. "He suggested I should go get *Mr. Templar* to help him."

Horus froze. In an instant, he had the answer to all the riddles. But even the dreadful certainty of what was going on begged new questions. Why *now*? Why would they come to call on him so suddenly, after *all this time*? And what did they plan to do with him, now that they had?

"This is ridiculous," Stephano concluded, starting to roll up his sleeves. "I won't stand for it – some bozo spouting nonsense and harassing the band! I'm going to throw this guy out on his ear!"

"No," Horus said, gently but firmly stopping Stephano right at the onset of his stomping march on the band. "The man would like a word with *me*; I say we give it to him."

"But...!"

Horus took Stephano by both shoulders. "Listen: I want the two of you to go open the banquet. That'll excuse the band for a bit. There doesn't have to be a scene. There doesn't have to be any trouble. Not for you."

Stephano gradually simmered down as he began to realize just how deadly serious Horus was. There was a knowing intensity in his gaze, and Stephano wondered at it. But in the end, Horus' stone face was enough to convince him there was no wisdom in any recourse. He would have to do as Horus told him. "Alright," he said.

Horus watched as Stephano and Victoria withdrew to the banquet table, casting a few anxious glances back at him as they went. He kept up his impassive expression. He watched them until they started calling out for everyone's attention. Then he turned, setting a hand on speechless Barnabee's shoulder as he marched past him to the orchestra pit...

Coming up on the scene, he found things very much as Barnabee described. There was a fellow fiddling around under the shadow of the piano lid, facing away from him. Who it was, Horus couldn't yet say. The rest of the band sat by and watched him with frightened expressions. As Horus drew close, their eyes snapped to him, and he made a quick gesture toward the banquet table. They all quietly took their cue to go...

Finally, Horus reached the piano. He didn't go unnoticed. The man under the lid paused, his ears snapping back. In the moment before he turned, Horus recognized his hopelessly tattered pelt. It was honestly a bit surreal... just like stepping decades back in time. But it was nothing next to seeing the old fellow face-to-face, as Ducard finally stood up straight, meeting Horus with a smug grin...

"Well hello, Horus," Ducard said casually. He pointed vaguely at the piano with his thumb. "You still know how these things tick? I'm afraid I may've done more harm than good."

"That would be usual," Horus replied, his face turning downright surly.

"Oh, come on now Horus, don't be like that. There's too much water under the bridge for you to still be sour. Can't bygones be bygones?"

"Why are we even talking right now, Ducard? Surely not for the sake of this piano. Don't stand there and lecture me about bygones when all you had to do was leave me be. I'd like to think we've all been better off trying to forget the old days."

"Ah, but you know as well as anyone that we never forget." Ducard remained smiling, even as he lowered his voice. "Don't mistake our silence, Horus. Don't imagine you've been given anything on your own terms. We just haven't needed you. Now we do."

Horus shook his head. "Sorry, Ducard, but whatever you have in mind, it's out of the question. There's nothing you can compel me to do for you."

"Well, I think you could at least hear us out." He fiddled with the tuning key in his hand. "Might help the wedding go smoother."

"Alright," Horus agreed, crossing his arms. "I'm listening. But you shouldn't expect anything beyond that. I work *for* the law now, not outside of it."

"Oh, we know. Trust me, we know. In fact, you may be pleasantly surprised to learn: It's your attorney alter-ego I was sent to enlist."

Horus blinked. "What do you mean?"

"Well, let's just say we know of a fellow who came into some legal trouble this morning. And we thought the charitable thing to do would be to seek you out on his behalf. He could use a good lawyer right now."

"No doubt. What sort of atrocity was he caught in the middle of committing?"

"*Atrocity*?" Ducard challenged. "That's a hard accusation to make of a man that had to be fished out of the Harbor and sewn back up. It's the ultimate hard luck case, actually. Absolutely circumstantial. He just happened to be in the wrong place at the wrong time."

"Perpetrators usually are," Horus said with a shrug.

Ducard laughed, exposing his chipped canine. "You certainly haven't lost any of that self-righteous wit that made you so popular. I wish you'd drop it for just a second and consider your good fortune in this. You get to do your lawyer bit and advance our purposes at the same time. It's the perfect chance for you to redeem yourself."

"Your brand of redemption I can do without," Horus replied. "At any rate, the District Attorney will have *his* say in who defends this fellow with the hard luck you're so concerned about. If I *am* to defend him – and I deem it unlikely – it'll be at Mr. Blackforest's urging... not yours."

Ducard let a rather lengthy silence build between them, as he made a systematic study of Horus' resolve. "You'll understand..." he began finally, "...we have a lot of vested interest in this case. Quite a lot. So, if you really intend to leave this in Blackforest's court, you'd better hope he picks someone with real panache. I'd *pity* the attorney who delivers anything less than a sterling defense." He cocked his head. "Is that clear enough?"

Horus paused, working the bile out of his mouth. "Yes, I believe it is. In fact, I should've expected as much from the start." He shook his head. "Same old Vigil. You wouldn't know what to do with something like integrity if you couldn't exploit it."

"Well, I guess none of us have changed very much over the years," Ducard sighed, adjusting his jacket and sleeves as he took a few steps away from the piano. "Great ends justify hard means, Horus. You've never really understood that. I always hoped we'd overcome your way of thinking one day. But at the very least, we'll outlast it." He handed the tuning key off to Horus as he readied to depart. "The Eighth Vigil is forever." As he walked away, he called back over his shoulder. "We'll be seeing you around, Horus. Sooner rather than later."

Horus made no effort to reply. He simply rode out the parting threat, knowing full well what had to come next, and resigning himself to it. But hardly had he wound himself up to leave, when Deborah suddenly cut in from the side, jarring him out of his intense train of thought...

"Well, it took some elbow grease, but I finally got Art free," she explained. "Between the break in the music and the open banquet, I think they..." She stopped herself, eyeing him questioningly. "What's the matter, Boss? You look like you've just seen a ghost."

"I would've preferred a ghost," Horus replied rather absently. He looked down at her, at a sudden loss to explain the situation... let alone himself. "Some, uh, business has come up, Deborah," he settled on. "We have to go."

She watched, temporarily speechless, as he abruptly began marching for the exit. "But...?" she started weakly. Her appeal never reached his ears. Horus was halfway to the door...

Chapter 3

"No – we need to set up patrols as well," Miloje explained sternly. "Five men strong... more, if we have them. Once around the building every fifteen minutes."

"But Sir, we've already set a guard at every access point," Lieutenant Osmund reminded him. "And you've doubled the guard since then. I don't know how many men we can spare for all this added security."

"Too few, in any event," Miloje quipped. "But posting a troop at the door isn't going to be enough. If those rogues out there can't find an open access point, they'll make one. Do you understand?"

"Yes, Sir."

"Then see to it! We can reexamine our options when reinforcements arrive from the garrison. I have every confidence the High Constable will recognize our need."

"Aye, Sir; of course, Sir."

Miloje waved the lieutenant off, but he was already springing away. The old Deputy Constable removed his bobby and commenced dabbing his brow with a handkerchief as he sighed. It was just then that he spied Horus Templar approaching in a gale, with Deborah Boulevard rushing to keep up. He grumbled incoherently to himself, seeing he was squarely in Horus' sights...

"Oh, capital!" Miloje called out, oozing sarcasm. "No sooner do we set a double guard to deter any unwanted canine folk, and the old reprobate Horus Templar himself immediately slips our nets." He replaced his hat, if only to tip it at Deborah. "Miss Boulevard, of course, is quite welcome."

"I've no time or patience for verbal jousting today, Milo," Horus replied shortly. "I understand you're holding a Mesomela man you apprehended this morning in the Harbor. I need to see him immediately."

"Hmph, do you, now?" Miloje asked, unimpressed. "I'm afraid that's out of the question. Mr. Blackforest anticipated some bit of melodrama or other from you. He was quite explicit: This case is none of your concern."

"Very well. In that case, I demand to see the District Attorney immediately."

"Impossible. He's been recalled to the Palace, there to receive a complete briefing on the matter from the Joint Chiefs of Staff. I expect he'll have appointed counsel for the suspect by the time of his return."

Horus shook his head. "If he hasn't yet appointed counsel then I'm still at liberty to volunteer my services. I do so now. And I ask again: Take me to the man. Or at the very least, don't bar my way..."

Miloje stepped in front of Horus, even as he was being asked not to. "Not so fast. For all we know, Blackforest may have already made his decision. And in any event he made it very clear that you didn't rate high on his list of candidates. Frankly, I'm inclined to suspect there's wisdom in that. Your insistence on this thing is curious. Borderline insubordinate."

"You haven't seen me insistent yet," Horus boded. "Now I'm going to ask you again, Miloje... once, twice... a hundred times, if necessary. Let me see my client."

Miloje scowled under his thick mustache. "There's no client of yours here, Templar."

"If not mine, then whose?" Horus demanded.

The question hung in the air a goodly while. Miloje, of course, had no real answer... only a reflex to keep firing back that he couldn't seem to articulate anymore. But even as he fumed, he happened to look over at Deborah, finding her so astonished that he himself was more than a little taken aback. She appeared even more surprised at Horus' ill temper than he was. His resolve to further escalate the scene quickly diminished. "Alright," he finally assented. "Have it your way, Templar, if it's really so important to you."

Horus at last began to soften. "It *is* important, Milo – trust me, it is. I wouldn't be so stubborn otherwise. I don't want to make trouble for you."

Miloje sighed, staring off into space. "A crime syndicate scuttles a heavily guarded barge on a top-classified mission in broad daylight – in the middle of the Harbor, no less. Those of us who knew nothing are scrambling just to comprehend the scope of this catastrophe. But those of us who *did* know something... well, we may yet have it worst of all. Trouble, you say? Yes, Templar, I already have more of it than you could hope to take credit for. I fear this case of the vengeful Vigilant is going to mean a great deal of trouble for all of us."

Horus wasn't quite sure what he meant, but as he watched the Deputy Constable turn away, he quickly dismissed his questions and rushed on ahead, fearing to lose his resolve if he slowed down for long...

* * *

Hastening down the halls to the detention area, Horus' eyes searched the floor, still straining to tease out any way to represent a Vigilant that wouldn't demand a fundamental betrayal of conscience. He tried reminding himself that he was jumping to conclusions. He was *assuming* that his client was guilty, when he didn't know anything beyond the haziest details of the crime yet. Even to assume he was dealing with a proper Vigilant and not merely a liaison or sympathizer was nothing but presumption on his part. But of course, given the fact that the Vigil itself had forced him into this job, there seemed no conceivable way the man was innocent. That, of course, was the real problem. Representing guilty clients, though an unavoidable part of his profession, had always been an ugly prospect. But it was times like this when he couldn't even glimpse a good reason to apply himself... except that throwing the case would mean the private shame of knowing he'd willfully done less than his best. Perhaps that was a black mark he could live with. After all, what if he really *did* apply himself, and in the end, his client went free? What would a Vigilant do with that kind of cheap exoneration? Horus felt quite sure he knew exactly what...

Finally, in the midst of his endless back-and-forth, he was suddenly aware of Deborah. She'd been right there through all his silent musing, being none the wiser to anything. He had admitted once to her that there was bad blood between his family and Berlie Beirels... but the story he gave her was so doctored... so watered-down and censored... that she would certainly have no present way of connecting the dots. Horus was rather amazed at her longsuffering, knowing that by now she must've had a million questions. But he also sensed that that tension had just reached its breaking point...

"So, Boss..." she began. "Would it be too much to ask what's going on?"

Horus sighed. "I'm not even sure where to begin. There's a lot I don't know yet myself." He looked over at her, an apprehensive question on his face. "What do you know about the Eighth Vigil of Aridos?"

She shrugged. "Just the old children's story, really."

"Tell it to me," he replied. "It'd help if I knew what version you were told."

"Well, okay," she went along a bit doubtfully. "It was about a little village in ancient Bakhanu where pirates used to run rampant – a whole town full of helpless widows and orphans. Then one day, a man named Aridos was appointed district judge over the town. When he got there and found out about the pirate problem, he took matters into his own hands and drove them off. Not once, not twice... but all of seven different times... his seven vigils. But eventually, the pirates caught up with him... and killed him. They assumed they'd have free reign over the town again just like they used to. But by then, some of the orphans were grown, and they took up Aridos' name and set their own watch over the village. That was the 'Eighth Vigil'. Beyond that, I don't know anything for sure. The orphans supposedly went on to be folk-heroes... or bandits, or something. It always seemed to depend a lot on who was telling the story. I heard it a few times where they basically became off-brand Indigo Knights."

Horus nodded. "For a time, I'd say they measured up to that. Their original tenets were protection and deliverance for the powerless. But somewhere in the course of the 770 Years War, they reformed around the one basic obsession of avenging the fall of our homelands to Aedeloma's armies. They've been stuck in that rut ever since."

Deborah shook her head in disbelief. "All this time, I never thought they were anything more than another urban legend."

"I only wish it could've stayed that way," Horus lamented.

She turned a searching look on him. "This has a special kind of reality to you, doesn't it? Something personal."

They came to the final bend in the hall; Horus stopped them as they caught sight of the guards barring the door to the maximum-security cell. "There's no time to explain all that now," he said. Then he set a hand on Deborah's shoulder. "When we get in there..." he began, weighing what to say next. "...I don't know what my client's liable to say. There will be... *words.*"

"I would think so," Deborah quipped with a half-hearted grin.

"I just need you to promise me... that you won't draw too many conclusions. That you'll take anything he says about me with a grain of salt. I'm... only sorry we didn't have this discussion years ago. Certainly not the way we *should* have had it."

"Horus..."

"Just... promise me. Promise you'll give me a chance to explain everything... in my own time."

Deborah swallowed. Every appeal he made to her understanding only deepened her anxiety. But she rallied, and nodded. "I promise."

Horus grinned. "Alright." He turned a determined look down the hall. "Let's see what's waiting for us on the other side of the door."

* * *

Immediately upon entering the cement bunker – before he even had a chance to look in from the doorway – Horus palpitated at the sound of an all-too-familiar voice. Not a voice from days of yore, but one that he'd learned to dread in more recent times. He could hear her droning on about something distantly. He finally set his eyes through the glass barrier, finding her plying her instruments at a newly-installed operating table, which had been angled at a steep grade. Interestingly, she was surrounded by a whole contingent of other Doctors...

"For a patient of this size, a competitive inhibitor dosage of .02 grains is sufficient," Nokkaeru explained, withdrawing from the table as guards proceeded to unhook the patient and replace him on the cot. "He should begin to regain consciousness in no more than ten minutes. Are there any questions?"

"What of the bald patches?" another Doctor asked. "Will the fur grow back?"

"Most of it will, up to the scar tissue around the surgical areas," Nokkaeru answered. "The immediate submersion of this subject protected him from extensive damage to the dermis." She glanced over her posse. "Is there anything more before we go?"

"I have a question," said a Doctor with a deep and dashing voice. "Supposing the subject *had* suffered permanent, disfiguring hair loss. May I assume you've read about Gehrbrite and Randetti pioneering a procedure whereby viable, hair-baring dermis is transplanted in strips from other areas of the body, less conspicuous? And if so, what is your professional assessment of such a process?"

Nokkaeru's goggles reflected an icy luster at him. "Only that it is pure vanity, unfit even for discussion among self-respecting surgeons," she replied, sounding very much as if she'd forced the answer through teeth, rather than a beak. "Your question disgusts me, as you do. Now come along. We were instructed to depart while the subject remained under sedation, and that window is..."

"Oh, look!" the suave Doctor interjected, looking right at Horus – the lenses of his own mask surprisingly warm and bright. "Your timing is impeccable, my dear! The patient's first visitors arrive just as you countermand the sedative. Hallo there, countrymen of Jast-Madiir! Could this be the party of the esteemed District Attorney, Mr. Hamilton Blackforest?"

"For goodness' sake, you buffoon, do *not* engage unnecessarily with the local peasantry!" Nokkaeru scolded him. "However are we to maintain the poise of aloof condescension with your constant inverse-hobnobber…?" She cut herself off as she finally turned her own eyes beyond the glass barrier. "Counselor Templar?! What in the depths of infamy are you doing here… *now*?!"

Horus was rather mystified by the question. He shrugged. "I'm lawyering… naturally."

"Oh…" Nokkaeru replied weakly.

"What about you, Doctor?" he asked, feeling the gravity of the moment alleviate somewhat, seeing that he'd apparently caught his old foil in an uncharacteristically frazzled state. "Is this… some sort of apprenticeship?"

"Uh… yes," she answered. "Essentially. I've been selected quite against my will to mentor these three promising students and one insufferable nuisance in surgical and pharmacological practice on exotic species. Now, if you'll excuse me…"

"*Templar*?" the 'insufferable nuisance' chimed. "Could this in fact be *Horus* Templar, whose recent work at the Annex Tribunal made for such regaling reading material? What an unexpected privilege to encounter you in person, Sir!"

"Why, thank you," Horus said, mentally reeling. This was about the last time or place he would've expected any positive recognition. "May I ask whose acquaintance I have the pleasure of making?"

The Heron bowed his head. "Doctor Forasius, at your service." He turned to regard Deborah. "And this must be the redoubtable Miss Deborah Boulevard! I have tried your cereal, ma'am. It is not good, but rest assured that is no reflection on your great secretarial acclaim, most duly owed."

"That's very kind," Deborah said with a smile.

"*Forasius*!" Nokkaeru steamed, sounding suspiciously practiced at the vehement use of his name. "The authorities were quite clear: We have to *go*!"

Doctor Forasius looked back at her. "I understand. My apologies." He nodded at Horus and Deborah. "Excuse me. Duty calls." He chuckled. "Or maybe something yet more demanding. It was nice to have met you. Perhaps our paths will cross again."

"No, they will not," Nokkaeru insisted. "Away now! Or I'll have you ejected from this internship for insubordinate behavior!"

"Well we mustn't have that," Forasius said, leaping into action. "Again, I say: goodbye!"

"Goodbye, Forasius." Horus grinned and nodded at Nokkaeru. "Doctor."

"Don't look so pleased at my adversity, Horus Templar," she warned in a low voice. "You'll remember I have somewhat of a sense for these things... and I've more than an inkling that a great tormentor of yours is equally close at hand."

Horus frowned, looking over at the motionless form on the cot. "Yes, I think you're right."

* * *

Horus stood by, scratching under his chin until the skin was raw, watching and waiting for his client to awaken, feeling minutes pass like hours. The long wall of glass didn't afford him the best view. Naturally, his client's face was turned away, making him impossible to identify positively. Still, after a close study of his lean build and lustrous fur, Horus took some comfort in a strong suspicion that he'd never met this man before. He simply looked too young to be anyone familiar. It seemed like a stroke of incredibly good fortune. Horus had to hope this would all go much easier, if his client had no idea who he was. Who he *had* been...

"How about a seat while you wait, Boss?" Deborah threw out there. She was already sitting at a nearby desk, lightly tapping the quill of her pen against her notepad.

"Thanks just the same," he replied gently. "But it only seems right to stay on my feet."

"Suit yourself," she sighed. "I just thought it might be a while."

He shook his head. "Doctor Nokkaeru all but guaranteed ten minutes. I trust her expertise."

"She seemed a bit high-strung to me. People don't always work their best under added pressure."

"Not *all* people. But some do."

"Are you one of those people, Horus?"

He grinned slightly. "I guess we'll find out soon enough."

True to Nokkaeru's estimate, as Horus turned back to his watch over the cell, he saw that his wait was coming to an end. It began with a slight twitch of the ear, followed by a full-body convulsion. Then, the young fellow lay motionless again for a while. But it was a different kind of motionlessness,

Horus could tell... a defensive, thoughtful sort. He was awake now. He was calculating...

Finally, when the sight of the cement wall could serve no more, his head moved. Horus at last had a clear view of his face, and final confirmation that the two of them were perfect strangers. He watched the young man's bleary eyes blink until they were surprisingly clear and alert. At once, the fellow knew where he was. The disgusted look on his face made that clear enough...

"Well, this is a fine mess..." he sighed, reaching up and rubbing the flanks of his face. "You won't get anything out of me until I speak with my attorney."

"I *am* your attorney," Horus replied, stone-faced.

The man laughed. "Oh... better yet. Today must really be my lucky day."

Horus wasn't at all sure what he meant by that, but he quickly decided to simply move on. "What's your name, son?"

The young man sat up, looking cross. "Khonshu. My name is Khonshu. Don't call me 'son'."

"Take it easy, Khonshu," Horus advised him. "I wouldn't advise sitting up all at once like that. You've been under sedation..."

Khonshu stood. He took a few steps toward the glass. He folded his arms. "So that's how you want to go about it, huh? You're going to feign some kind of motherly instincts right up 'til they lead me to the firing squad? You're even more of a coward than I imagined you'd be."

Horus' brows knit. "What are you talking about?"

"Don't play stupid, Horus," Khonshu warned him. "I know exactly what this is. The State put you on my case to stack the deck!"

Horus was incredulous. "How... how do you know my name?"

Khonshu grinned sarcastically. "How could I not? I'd have to be blind to miss the family resemblance." He chuckled, pointing to Horus' left hand. "The tuning key was an especially cute touch. Believe me, I've heard plenty about the wayward son in my day, but they never told me you were so sentimental."

Horus looked down at his own hand – finding with no small astonishment that it indeed remained filled with a tuning key. He turned questioning eyes at Deborah...

"You've had a death-grip on it ever since we were leaving the party," she explained.

"You didn't see fit to ask why?"

She turned up her palms. "There were a lot of things going on I didn't ask about."

Horus slowly pivoted back to the cell with a frown. "Alright," he said, tossing the tuning key aside. "So you know who I am. But in identifying me, you've also given a fair bit of yourself away, Khonshu. You've already removed any possible doubt of your membership in the Eighth Vigil of Aridos."

"Have I, now?" Khonshu scoffed. "How's that? Because I may have had a conversation or two with Eighth Vigil members in my lifetime? Because it's plainly obvious that the State intends to railroad me, operating under the *assumption* that I'm a Vigilant myself? I know a bit about your trade, Horus. Enough to know when my own attorney's trying to build a circumstantial case against me."

"We've yet to even address the *case*," Horus replied. "Perhaps it's time we started. What precisely have you been accused of?"

Khonshu pointed reprovingly at him. "You see... that's exactly what I'm talking about. You're the first person I've talked to, and you ask me a question like that? I haven't been accused of *anything*. What you're really asking is, what have I *done*?"

"If you know as much as you claim about my trade, you'd know that's not an unreasonable question. What *have* you done?"

Khonshu frowned. "Nothing. I haven't done a thing. I don't even understand why I'm being detained."

"Really?" Horus demanded. "A young Mesomela – let's say – with *connections* to the Eighth Vigil of Aridos just happens to wash up next to a newly-sunken cargo ship, purely by chance? Your circumstantial case isn't of my building, Khonshu... the facts speak for themselves. And your plan is to cling to some pretense of total ignorance?"

"That's right," Khonshu said with a nod. "I'm just a babe in the woods."

"Well," Horus laughed mirthlessly, "that's going to be exceptionally difficult to prove."

"I'm sure you'll find a way. You know how upset our mutual friends will be if you don't."

Horus shook his head. "That kind of talk isn't going to get you anywhere. I've already had my belly full of the Vigil's insipid threats. I believe a man should always do the best job he can... and I hold myself to that. But so help me, if all this coercion keeps up, I might be tempted to make an exception just to spite you all."

"Well that would be an incredibly stupid move on your part." Khonshu turned his look to Deborah. "Pardon me, ma'am, but do you think you could remind your boss just how irresponsible he's being?"

She blanched. "I… I'm not sure I…"

"Don't drag her into this," Horus insisted. "This is between you and me."

"Wait a minute…" Khonshu intoned, once again looking deviously amused as he studied her blank expression. "Wait just a minute, now. She doesn't know… does she? About the old days? About the life you abandoned? You've been working together how long now, and it's never come up?" He furrowed his brow. "Is that your policy, Horus? Oh, that's good. Are you too afraid to share? Too *ashamed* to own up to backing out – to running away?"

Horus knew he should've been incensed. But instead, he *was* ashamed. "I admit, I've told fewer people than I should have…"

"I'll bet," Khonshu quipped, sitting back down on his cot. "Wow," he marveled. "You've built a whole new life for yourself on nothing but pure disinformation. I must have a pretty good lawyer after all."

"Enough!" Horus fired back. "You're the one on trial here, Khonshu, not me. I came here to learn the facts of the case and find out how you intend to plea. But seeing you're unable – or in any event unwilling – to relate anything about the crime itself, I have only one question left for you. If you weren't on any kind of clandestine sabotage mission, then why *were* you there?"

Khonshu's face went blank. He frowned. "I don't remember."

"Well then, I'd advise you to think long and hard on it. I can guarantee the police are going to ask the same question. And they'll be even less impressed with your answer than I am." He turned to storm off, but Khonshu stopped him by calling out…

"Horus," he called. "What did you mean… about Vigil threats? Do you mean… do you mean they've been in contact with you… about my case?"

"Yes," Horus answered. "They chose me for it."

"*They* did?" Khonshu asked, astonished. "They entrusted me… to *you*? A coward and a deserter? Why would they do that?"

Horus turned back to face him. "There were reasons to desert that had nothing to do with cowardice," he said in a gentler tone. "Reasons you obviously haven't begun to fathom." He managed a small grin, feeling the faintest glimmer of hope about the mess he was in for the first time. "Not yet, at any rate. But who knows? All this trouble you're in may yet be good for you, Khonshu. Perhaps the best thing for you."

"I wish I could know what you meant by that," Khonshu replied dubiously. "Be honest, Horus: Can I really count on you to try? To do your best? Tell me. Do you want to win this case, or not?"

Horus gave his chin a final, thoughtful stroke. "Those are two profoundly different questions. Do I hope to win or lose? I honestly don't know. But can you trust me to represent you to the very best of my ability? The answer is: yes. Absolutely."

Chapter 4

Blucille Cordon let her eyes stray back to the dismal grey of the world just beyond her window, caught in the drear of a moment that demanded nothing of her... the very worst kind of moment. It had threatened to rain all day, and she knew instinctually it would go right on threatening, no matter how much she wished the brooding sky would simply get it over with. She sighed. There were so many things going on. Big, daunting, ominous things. How could she presently have nothing to do?!

Finally, she just couldn't take it. She reached deep into her handbag and snatched out the soap. She took down the little box from the top of the shelf rack and retrieved her pipe from it. She fitted the holder, poured the soap, gave a quick stir, and sent a stream of bubbles flying. The prep time to first blow couldn't have been more than seven seconds. She'd lost nothing of her veteran efficiency...

Just then, there was a knock at her office door. *Brilliant timing*, she thought, dratting herself. "Come in."

She turned to her door with a business air, expecting any old department functionary. What she got was Deborah Boulevard. She blanched, setting aside her pipe too late...

"Ms. Boulevard..." she said. "What a surprise. Please, have a seat."

"Thank you," Deborah replied. Blucille couldn't help noticing a flash of judgment in Deborah's eyes as they traced the pipe, however she might politely grin afterwards.

They sat opposite each other at Blucille's desk in relative synchronous. "So, how can I help you?" Blucille asked.

"I need information... some of which you might not be willing or able to give me."

"Well, as long as it pertains directly to the Vigilant case, I can probably tell you anything you want to know."

Deborah nodded absently. "Okay, good. That sounds hopeful."

Blucille leaned in with a questioning look. "Really? You don't seem very hopeful."

Deborah sighed, rubbing the side of her head. "Honestly, Ms. Cordon, this case's been nothing but vague drama from the start. I was sent here to talk business... but no matter which way I turn, I can't seem to get very far away from personal concerns. To tell the truth, I was hoping to meet with

Blackforest. But they tell me he's still out. Even that concerns me. I just... don't know what to make of everything that's going on."

"Well, I guess it's a fine time for rumination all around," Blucille admitted morosely. "I'm not without a few personal concerns myself. Perhaps we can be some help to each other there. But let's start with the business. What do you need to know?"

"Alright," Deborah said dubiously as she got out her pen and notepad. "Now mind you, I know this is a big ask," she qualified. "But what I really *need* is the scoop on the cargo barge. Its mission... its cargo. They say all that's classified. But Horus is insistent to be in the know. He doesn't feel he can mount a proper defense if he's being shielded from the particulars of the crime. Besides that, he's afraid Blackforest might pull a fast one on him and get the details declassified in the middle of the trial, if he decides he can turn them to his advantage. He doesn't want to be blindsided."

"Say no more," Blucille said with an upraised hand. "I can put all those worries to rest here and now. There aren't going to be any red tape issues. As of this morning, the ship's manifest and itinerary have already been declassified."

Deborah's ears perked. "Wow. I certainly didn't expect that much cooperation."

"You won't feel like we've done you any favors when you hear the what and why. You see, it was an arms deal with the Twin Queens. The barge was tasked to deliver four cases of Fire Magic elixir to Tophthaeran brokers in the north or south – I don't honestly remember which. Supposedly we were planning to fill orders for both in the long run. I'll get you the precise details before you go. But at any rate, I'm sure you begin to see the negative implications for your client."

Deborah shook her head. "I'm not sure I do."

Blucille puzzled at this for a moment. "The buyers tell the whole story. The Eighth Vigil's whole MO is basically to get back at the Berlie Beirels any way they can. Somehow, they found out this shipment of cutting-edge magical armament was bound for Tophthaera, despite everything we could do to keep it a secret from them."

"Hold on a minute," Deborah interjected, looking bewildered. "To keep it a secret from *them*? Are you saying the Eighth Vigil is the whole reason the shipment was classified in the first place?"

Blucille nodded. "It was a well-deserved precaution. Did you know the State's also started hiring out mercenaries to fight in the Queens' War?"

"Yes... I've heard about that much, at least," Deborah quipped.

"That's where this whole mess really started. It's been kept out of the press, but the Vigil already sank two other ships that were going to be transporting state mercenaries. Given the high price-point of magic, the Czarina was adamant to ensure we delivered this time around. But seeing as we've already failed, there's really no sense in keeping a lid on the deal anymore."

Deborah's eyes searched the desk as she worked it all out in her head. She sank back in her chair. "I feel like I've been living under a rock or something. Imagine finding out the State's been in a private game of cat-and-mouse with characters from an old bedtime story. But your explanation clears up more than you would know. Horus has always had this thing about Berlie Beirels. I thought I knew why. He told me once that his family had a black mark on it from the days of the 770 Years War. That his ancestors cut and run before Aedeloma's hoards ever reached as far as Bakhanu and Manaanu." She went on remembering the whole conversation silently for a moment, feeling more sorely misled the longer she reflected on it. "He, uh... he had kind of a breakdown about it, actually. He talked about his uncle and his father getting roped into some... well, fringe organization or other. He didn't get into specifics. Honestly, he made it sound like they were just protesters, leading a misbegotten call for the Berile Beirels to be ostracized from the Archipelago. But evidently, it goes much deeper than that. Evidently it goes right back..." She caught herself, but decided to complete the thought anyway. "Back to his *own* time with this Vigil..."

Blucille frowned. "What has he told you about that?"

Deborah laughed mirthlessly. "Nothing yet. I gather from his chat with Khonshu there must've been a pretty ugly parting of ways. I... I'm afraid he must still have family in the Vigil. I only *hope* that's the reason he did such a poor job of characterizing all this before. That there's just too much grief left over from being put at odds with his father. Khonshu even called Horus 'the wayward son'. I don't think that was purely hyperbolic."

Blucille nodded. "That's as good a guess as any, I'm sure. I'm sorry to hear that Templar's been keeping so much from you, but I think you should try to be patient with him. Everyone has their baggage... things too personal to share. Family betrayal is a big one. Maybe the biggest. Small wonder he's been retentive."

"Well, I can see how any connection at all with some kind of *insurgency* would be hard to talk about. He said he'd get around to explaining everything – an ominous statement in itself. A part of me wishes he'd just spill it. But, well..." She hesitated. "He's been so guarded... I'm not entirely sure I want to know." Suddenly, her eyes narrowed at Blucille. "What do *you* know about it? Must be something, if you asked what *I* know."

"Only inference," she replied with a shrug. "I made a trip to the Palace yesterday. I reported to the boss how Templar was insistent to represent Khonshu. He almost went through the roof. I could tell from his reaction there was history... that Templar was too close to the subject for his own good."

"Well, it's a relief just to hear that Blackforest seems to have some idea what's going on," Deborah mused. "Maybe Horus managed to be honest with *him* at some point. I don't suppose he vowed to fight tooth and nail to get Horus off the case?" she asked hopefully.

"Worse than that. He resolved right away to wash his hands of it all. He said he's had enough of trying to stop Templar from torturing himself. He said if this is what he really wants, he's welcome to it."

Deborah sighed. "That's a shame. I was kind of depending on him to talk Horus out of this."

Blucille grinned weakly. "Has he ever been able to talk him out of anything before?"

"Well, no," Deborah chuckled. "But they say there's a first time for everything. This would've been a really good time for a truism like that to pay off."

"How's Templar holding up?" Blucille asked with concern. "Not well, obviously. Has he been hitting the lard again?"

"Worse than that," Deborah replied. "He's been incredibly focused and composed."

"That's terrible," Blucille commiserated.

Deborah reached up and rubbed her own head. "It all seems so senseless... his taking the case in the first place, I mean. It could've gone to anyone else. It *would've* gone to anyone else. All this bad blood could've easily been avoided. But this wouldn't be the first time Horus let his sense of duty and honor tie him in knots."

"Maybe I can convince the boss to have a heart-to-heart with Horus when he gets back... for what it's worth," Blucille offered. "But of course, don't get your hopes up. He's in quite a mood himself right now."

"What exactly is it that's keeping Blackforest away?" Deborah puzzled. "Granted, this is a very serious crime... the most serious we've seen in quite a while. But I think he knows that. Does he really need two days of browbeating at the Palace?"

"You have to consider the broader implications of the attack. The Czarina's on the warpath alright, but she has more than just the Eighth Vigil in her crosshairs. The barge's mission was *classified*. Which means we're looking at an intelligence leak."

Deborah's eyes bugged. "Good grief. I didn't even think about that." She quickly reached an even more alarming conclusion. "Does... does that mean Blackforest is under suspicion?"

"No, nothing like that," Blucille was quick to assuage. "He had no knowledge of the mission until after it failed... which is just another thing he's hopping mad about. Almost as mad as if he *had* known." She briefly paused as she reached a crucial point. "But there apparently *were* some in the police department who were advised ahead of time. And in the military too. That's the real substance of the Palace summit. Mr. Blackforest and the High Constable are formulating a plan for pinpointing the leak."

"Wow," Deborah marveled. "Nothing like internal affairs to cast a shadow on an already bleak situation."

"It never rains but it pours," Blucille said with a shrug. "But personally, I'd be willing to bet good money the mole turns up in the military camp. Miloje and Mr. Blackforest run a tight ship here. I can't imagine any honest inquest that doesn't end up vindicating their leadership."

"I'm sure you're right," Deborah agreed confidently.

"We have some heavy lifting to do now, but it should come out right in the end," Blucille said, standing from her desk. "My advice: Don't worry about our problems. You've got enough on your own plate. Unless by some miracle Templar can be made to see reason... and drop this trial before it even starts."

"We're doing the best we can to encourage it," Deborah sighed, checking her pocket watch. "As of right now, Horus should be on his way to a lunch we quietly arranged with an old friend. Someone whose experience puts him in a better position to give advice Horus will have to take seriously. We *hope*, anyway."

Blucille squinted. "*We*?"

"Yes. I've already brought Art in on the conspiracy."

"*Art...*" Blucille repeated, feeling a redoubled flash of anxiety. "Yes, I suppose he would have to be involved." She managed to fix questioning eyes on Deborah. "How has he been, lately? We... we haven't found much time together in the last few weeks."

Deborah took a moment, obviously weighing her words. "Honestly, he's not his best. When you backed out of going to the wedding with him, I think it shook him up a bit."

Blucille couldn't breathe, at first. But under the ever-mounting pressure, her fight reflex eventually kicked in. "Why that's... that's absurd," she laughed. "Surely he's mature enough that the world doesn't hinge on my ability to follow through on *every* date! We've had to cancel or reschedule dozens of times in the past! He knows... my job just gets in the way, sometimes."

"He's also bright enough to sense when the job's just a convenient excuse," Deborah replied. "Anyway, that's what he suspects. Seeing you now, I have to admit: I have more than a hunch he's right."

Blucille's eyes fell. The trap had fallen on her much too fast; there was no way to maneuver out of it now. She couldn't even decide where to go from here. Should she try to justify herself? Should she simply turn Deborah out? She couldn't make up her mind...

"What is it, Blucille?" Deborah ventured to ask. "Obviously *something's* wrong. Couldn't we just talk about it? Maybe I could help."

Blucille whirled violently around, throwing one of her hands back. "I *did* just tell you to worry about your own problems, didn't I? Maybe all I need is some time... some space. But I certainly don't need any unsolicited advice from *you*. This is none of your business."

Deborah stood up. She walked quietly to the office door. But just before she would've pushed through it, she stopped. "I'm sorry, Blucille. Sorry I asked. I guess I jumped out of bounds. But Art *is* my friend. Protecting him *is* my business. So whatever's going on with you – whatever you have to work through – please, don't hurt him."

Blucille turned back, clutching her pipe. "I'm... I'm trying not to. Believe me: That's the very last thing I want to do."

Deborah angled a frown at her. "But everyone has their baggage."

Silence gripped the room. Deborah shot a few uncertain looks over her shoulder, appearing conflicted. But ultimately, she elected to let her accusation stand. She pushed through the door and was gone.

Blucille looked down at the pipe in her hand, then chucked it across the room. She plopped back down in her seat, cradling her head on the desk, utterly beside herself...

Chapter 5

News travels fast in a gigantic city. A mere day had passed since he stepped forward to Khonshu's defense, and already Horus could hear the *whisperings*...

"Hey, look," a random citizen quietly remarked to another. "I think that's the guy working the Harbor bombing case."

"Good," the other man replied. "I hope he sticks it to those lawless maniacs."

"No, dummy!" the first man bit. "He's the *defense* lawyer."

The other man made a horrific face. "*Ulgh*..."

Here we go again, Horus thought, knowing at once the whole commute would be typified by ugly scuttlebutt. And of course, he was right. His strong, swiveling ears caught another exchange at the corner of Chanson and Tobias...

"Check it out; over there! The creepo representing the bomber!"

"Nah... are you crazy? That can't be him. He wouldn't dare show his face in broad daylight."

...And another one on the outskirts of the Ransom Produce Market...

"Get a load of this. Horus Templar at 16-o-clock..."

"You mean the degenerate from that Mantid case a year or two back?"

"Come on, man, get with the times. He's going to bat for other top-tier fiends and menaces now."

"Like who? Surely not the ones who burned down half the Harbor yesterday?"

"The very same."

"*Good night!* He oughta be branded a menace to society himself."

...But the one that took the cake was yet to come. Just about the time Horus passed the last alleyway leading back to the market, he was struck suddenly in the face from parts unknown. After a moment of reeling and seeing nothing but stars, he steadied himself. His flurry to identify the source of the attack quickly turned up a kumquat rolling on the ground at his feet...

"Hey, you!" a heckler called out. "Why don't you go crawl in a hole somewhere?! We don't abide lawyers of ship blower-uppers in *this* town!"

"*Ship blower-uppers*?" an accomplice repeated doubtfully. "Is that the best you could do?"

"Well, it's accurate, isn't it? You try to come up with something better! At least I nailed him right in the gourd."

Horus probed the bruised flank of his snout, standing deliberately in place. He said nothing, hoping a sustained gaze and a slow withdrawal would at least prove he wasn't afraid – knowing that to engage further would almost certainly be a mistake. Finally, he turned and moved on...

"That's right, get outta here!" the heckler called after him. Horus forced himself not to care...

* * *

The place was a bit on the smokey side... dim, and poorly ventilated. A sign to match the one over the front door was going up inside: *So This Is Food*. New restaurants were always in vogue among Mesomelae, who held out unspoken hopes that between the administrative challenges of starting a business, and the foibles of greenhorn chefs, the food stood a much better chance of being "undercooked". Judging by the smell and the ambiance though, Horus could safely assume this restaurant's troubles went the other way. Unfortunate. Regardless, he had an appointment of sorts to keep...

He passed up the benches by the gloomy windows, choosing something more like a card table under a sconce, sitting in murky desolation, trying to force some measure of attention at the menu in his claws while he waited for his friend to appear. He had a hunch it might be a while...

"Horus Templar," he heard suddenly. It wasn't the voice he'd expected. But after all, it'd been his day for being spotted everywhere he went. His reflex was to continue staring impassively at his menu, as if he hadn't heard his name called. Setting the menu down – seeing who was calling – he knew at once that his reflex was a good one. His eyes quickly flashed between two colleagues of his as he plastered on a hospitable smile...

"Ah: Rosencrantz; Guildenstern!" Horus greeted them. "What a surprise!"

"Shouldn't be any surprise at all... if you were *thinking*," Guildenstern said with a grin, a clawed finger tapping the side of his narrow head. Or, was this one Rosencrantz? Horus strained to remember. "We come here all the time now!" Rosencrantz – or Guildenstern – went on.

"My mistake. Though I'm not entirely sure how I would've known that." Horus shrugged. "But it's a relief that men of discerning tastes stop here. Must be the food is better than advertised?"

"Ha, no way!" the other Guildenstern or Rosencrantz laughed. "It's terrible! But that's what keeps us coming back. We enjoy getting to warn all our legal cronies that they're about to have a miserable lunch!"

"A thoughtful gesture, to be sure," Horus replied.

One of them pointed to an empty seat at Horus' table. "You're not busy, are you? We'd be glad to hang around and talk shop for a while."

Horus leapt at the opportunity to politely excuse them. "Well actually, I was just about to meet with..."

"...Great, don't mind if we do," one said, as they each pulled a chair out and sat down. "So... we heard you got the big case. Our hats off to you, Horus. We can't help a green streak of envy."

"Well, that's kind," Horus said, "but it's not the glamorous thing you suppose." He pointed at his bruised spot. "You probably can't see it, but I took a bit of bad press to the side of the nose, on my way here."

"That's just because you go about your job all wrong... and the people know it," Rosencrantz waved it off. Horus was becoming pretty confident this one was Rosencrantz, anyway, because it seemed to him he'd heard once that Rosencrantz was the really tall one. But then again, it could've been that Rosencrantz was the really *short* one. "Would you like a little friendly advice, Horus?" the fellow went on, whichever one he was. "Obviously, you could use it."

Horus nodded, seeing no way around the friendly advice anyway. "I'm all ears."

"Just do like we do. Get up there, put on your best dumbfounded expression, and stammer for all you're worth! Don't raise any objections... and for Heck's sake, don't prepare a *case*! That's the biggest sign there is of an amateur defense lawyer."

"We built our entire practice around one simple idea," the other Rosencrantz explained. "Everyone's happier when the defense loses. The State is happier. The people are happier. Even the defendant is usually happier! And the surest way to lose is to do nothing. It's easy! And believe me, it works. You don't have to plan; you don't have to apply yourself. You don't even have to pay attention! What could possibly be more simple? More amicable?"

"We really do have the best job in the world, once you cut through all the mustard and see how it's meant to be done."

Horus furrowed his brow. "Well, that's certainly one way of looking at it," he said. "I admit, the notion of throwing this case has been on my mind. It *is* tempting..."

They watched him hopefully.

"...Unfortunately, I'm afraid I'm going to have to insist on trying, just the same," he resolved finally. "I already promised my client I would... to say nothing of the promises I made myself, when I began this career. I'm sorry."

Their disappointment was immediately apparent. "Well, how do you like people these days?" maybe-Guildenstern asked. He shook his head. "So ungrateful."

"We give him the best advice he ever got, and he throws it out over silly promises," also-maybe-Guildenstern concurred. They turned determined eyes back on him. "Look, Horus, if you ever want to reach our level, one of these days you're going to have to..."

"Hey, naw," another voice interjected, as a tall figure in a white suit loomed over the table, crossing his arms. "What's this here all 'bout?"

"Mr. Thalymus, Sir..." one of them said, as they both looked up timidly. "We were just... sharing a few trade secrets with Horus here."

"Is thet right?" Eb Thalymus asked skeptically. "Looks ta me more like you fellers is badgerin' a friend I aims ta have lunch with."

"Oh. He's meeting *you* for lunch? We didn't realize."

"We don't mean to impose. We can be moving on now, if you'd like."

Eb nodded. "I'd appreciate thet."

Unable to contain a grateful smile, Horus watched as Rosencrantz and Guildenstern, P.C, cleared out with gale force.

Eb sighed. "I'm mighty sorry ta see ya run afoul o' them 'Bungle Brothers', Horus," he said, slowly and methodically seating himself at the table. "Specially on ma account. If I hadn'ta been so late..."

Horus checked his pocket watch. "On the contrary, Eb... looks like you're right on time. I simply had the misfortune of being early."

"Welp, yer fault er mine, at least they's gone." He clapped his hands together. "Naw... let's git us some grub."

* * *

Horus retired his napkin to the empty plate. Fortunately, despite the misery he was promised, the entrée had turned out to be no worse than immediately forgettable. Eb let out a contented sigh as he leaned back in his chair, resting one arm on the back of an adjacent one. He busied the other hand picking his teeth with his old, broken wishbone. "Wahl, thet wasn't s'bad," he said. "Beats havin' the same ol' caferteria slop day in an' day out."

"How *are* things on campus, Eb?" Horus asked. "Last I heard, it sounded like you were getting along quite well."

Eb nodded. "It's been nice, Horus. Real nice." He pocketed his wishbone, by way of coming to a major segue in the conversation. "How-ever..." he intoned, "...I gotta admit: There's been times I get thet old itch – thet fahr in ma belly. Sometimes it jist don't seem right that I's *teachin'* law, when I could still be out there *practicin'* it. I ain't quite warshed up yet, Horus. An' lately, I's had a mind ta prove it."

Horus chuckled. "I see. No beating around the bush, then? We're going to lean right into the inevitable proposition."

Eb looked at him quizzically. "Whaddaya mean by thet?"

"Now, don't mistake me, Eb," Horus said with a dismissive wave of his hand. "I consider your part in this conspiracy quite blameless. But that doesn't stop me knowing the real reason we're here. No doubt, a pair of concerned citizens by the name of Art Mallard and Deborah Boulevard reached out in the hopes you could dissuade me from my present course. But rather than merely try talk me out of it, you came up with a more elegant solution: to play the part of the retired litigator itching to get back in the ring. You'd get around to asking if you could handle my case... and I could let you have it, feeling like we'd both done each other a favor." He raised a brow. "Am I hitting pretty close to the mark?"

There was no immediate answer. "...Could be."

"Hm," Horus replied, grinning sarcastically. "Well, it's always a pleasure to be reminded how much confidence my friends have in my judgment."

Eb's face was impassive in the low, smokey light. "They jist want what's best for ya, Horus. Ain't no blame in thet."

Horus grew somber. His eyes fell. "I know."

Eb made a quick survey of the room before leaning forward, elbows on the table. "An' furthermore, it ain't stretchin' things too far ta say I been missin' ma glory days. I been known ta reminisce now an' agin. An' I'm sure I got at least *one* big case left in me." He shrewdly donned that vulnerable look that all old people make good and sure to master. "You believe thet... don't ya, Horus? Don't ya think ya'd be leavin' yer client in good hands?"

Horus laughed despite himself. "I don't yet know whether even the best hands could succeed at a case like this." He returned to a very serious expression. "I do, however, have more than an inkling what the consequences of failure could be. Our defendant has some very powerful, very dangerous friends. Friends who won't think twice about coming after their pound of flesh."

"Wahl, I say bring 'em on!" Eb said, balling up a pair of fists. "I's an ornery ol' cuss when I needs ta be."

"I'm sure you are," Horus replied, again unable to contain momentary amusement. "But you have to understand, Eb: I can't pass a case like this onto a friend. Even to pass it onto an enemy would be a gross betrayal of conscience. I understood the responsibility I was taking on... and now, I need to see it through. There's just no other way."

"I und'rstand," Eb granted reluctantly. "I might not like it much, but I respects it. A man's gotta stand on his principles." He got up from the table, extending his hand. Horus returned the gesture, and they shook. "Look out fer yerself, Horus... thet's all I ask. Sounds ta me like yer expectin' a whole heap o' trouble."

Horus grinned as he shook his head. "Well, all I can say is, whatever's in store for me, it's been a long time coming."

* * *

Thankfully, the return trip was only a sulky shadow of his harrowing journey to the restaurant. Horus couldn't escape the undertow of gossip and slander, but at least he managed to avoid getting decked by another vegetable. The only time he really felt violated was the moment he returned to his own door. The door with the fine monograms, and the ham-fisted graffiti...

...Horus Templar – Public ~~Defender~~ Enemy

Whirling inside, Horus almost ran into Deborah, who appeared in a hurry to get out. She regarded his sudden arrival with wide eyes. "Sorry about the door, Boss," she said. "I meant to fix it before you got back, but I just can't seem to wash it off with anything."

"No matter," he sighed tiredly. "Cleaning it now would only inspire a follow-up act at this point. I can ignore it for a while, if you can." He gave her an inquisitive look. "How was your meeting?"

"Informative," she replied. "More so than we expected." She put on a weak grin. "How did lunch go?"

"Not quite as well as you hoped, I'm afraid," Horus quipped, reaching for the top button of his overcoat.

"It was that transparent, huh?" Deborah asked. "You're not angry, are you?"

"Perhaps a bit stymied," he admitted. "But ultimately undeterred."

She stopped his unbuttoning arm. "Well, if the case is still on, you might as well leave your coat on, too."

He looked at her with furrowed brow. "Something's come up?"

She nodded. "Blackforest is back from the Palace."

"Well, that does seem to call for our presence." He reaffixed his top button and turned back to the door, holding it open for Deborah. "Things are really going to pick up from here."

Chapter 6

For a while, all Deputy Constable Miloje could do was scowl at the mountainous ogre in a soldier's costume from across the room. Crossing his arms as he watched the stranger absently fiddle with some misbegotten hybrid of brass knuckles and a switchblade, Miloje assured himself that his own present silence was entirely the product of trying to work through outraged incredulity, and certainly had nothing to do with feeling even the slightest bit intimidated. And for the most part, that was true. Always a man of sarcastic wit, such was the abundance of red herrings at play here that he couldn't seem to decide which one was best to start with...

Fortunately, the stranger eventually broke the silence for him. "What are we waiting for, Pops?" he asked, never looking up from his contraption.

"Oh, I don't know. Why don't you tell me?" Miloje riposted, all his pent-up feisty sarcasm finally breaking loose. "I was advised the High Constable's military Chief of Staff would be coming. Where is Lieutenant Thermidor? Should we be expecting him any time this century?"

"No, you shouldn't," the big man said, before finally meeting his gaze. "Thermidor's been replaced. You've got me now."

"*Replaced*, eh?" Miloje shifted from one skeptical pose to another, placing balled-up fists on his hips. "That's big news to me... especially in the midst of an internal affairs investigation. Any reason I should know about, Mister...?"

"Carbine," he answered, standing up straight and tall as he approached Miloje from where he'd slouched against the wall, so that the long string of pistols down the front of his uniform jangled. "And before you go and get your hopes up, Thermidor's not your mole. It was simply decided that I was better suited to his job."

Miloje huffed. "A likely story. I didn't know Thermidor well, but I can say this much in his favor: He would never have been *late*. *You* were, Mr. Carbine. By almost twenty minutes. There's no excuse for that."

Carbine hardly bothered to shrug it off. "Then I make no excuse."

Once again, Miloje found himself at a temporary impasse, unable to do more than search up at Carbine with prickly eyes. "Well, I suppose there's no sense holding the meeting up any further," he said at length. "We can discuss the gravity of capital tardiness some other time."

"Any time you like, Little Man."

Miloje only grinned, opening the door and gesturing through. "After you, Big Boy."

Carbine flicked his knuckle-knife one more time before striding into the next room on heavy feet. Miloje followed through, closing the door quietly behind them...

* * *

Art Mallard checked his watch again as he avoided looking at Blucille, while she avoided looking at him. Their awkwardness alone would've been enough to banish all cheer from any conference room. But after a careful survey, Art quickly realized that everyone else was pretty much lost in brooding of their own. The police Captains, Alexei and Brocksmith, were moody and dejected. The newly promoted Huxley looked terrified. Blackforest was on the verge of tremors in his fierce, raging impatience. And there, hunkering in the farthest, darkest corner, was some other Human that Art didn't recognize. Arms folded and head down, the shadows and contour of the man's hat hid all but his narrow jawline and squeezed-out looking lips from view, so that Art was hopeless to deduce either his identity or his disposition. On the one hand, his shadowy, downcast gaze gave him perhaps the most hardboiled appearance of them all. But then again, he might've only been dozing off...

Finally, a good twenty minutes past the time the meeting was slated to start, the door opened, and in walked a big scary military guy and Deputy Constable Miloje. Blackforest immediately rose from the table...

"Well... now that we're all finally here..." he said, politely confining himself to only a mild seethe, "...there's no time left to waste on ceremony or sentiment. We each have a heavy load in front of us and nothing for it but to soldier through. Now, for those in the private sector who might not be up to speed, a classified asset was violently attacked yesterday and is currently resting in pieces at the bottom of the Harbor. We have strong reason to believe that this was carried out by a subversive group of criminals known as the Eighth Vigil of Aridos, but that is not our primary concern *here*. Rather, you've all been called upon in regard to an even more compromising matter: the question of how the attackers were able to obtain classified intelligence in the first place. Someone within the chains of command – whether by coercion or willful culpability – has passed that information along to those we most meant to keep it from. It is absolutely imperative that we identify the source of the leak at once... and our starting point is clear. We must investigate those who had knowledge of the asset." Blackforest, already in full speech-giving mode by now, gestured at the army man in the room without further sign of annoyance. "Now, High Constable Amadeus is ultimately overseeing investigations into both the police force *and* the military... hence, the presence of our esteemed observer, Lieutenant Carbine. The combined list of potential informants is long... but for our purposes here at the department, there are only three names of consequence." He held up a sheet of paper, as if he would need it. "The officers in the civil sector who were briefed on the classified mission are as follows: Deputy Constable Miloje, Captain Alexei, and Captain Brocksmith. They will be the subjects of our investigation."

Blucille was mortified at once. *"Stenya..."* she gasped at the Deputy Constable. "Surely, you didn't. You didn't pass along your classified knowledge to both your right *and* left hand!"

Miloje turned up his palms. "Perhaps it was rash, in retrospect. At the time, it only seemed prudent to bring in my most trusted subordinates. So they were then... and so they remain. And not without good reason."

"I wouldn't be so sure of their loyalties, if I were you," the man Carbine insinuated. "The military's initial investigation already strongly implicates the leak came from your department."

"Oh, yes?" Miloje fired back. "Pray tell what investigations the military has had time to initiate!? Let alone what evidence of any pedigree would point so lazily in our direction."

Carbine grimaced. "That's fine talk, coming from someone who's on the blacklist himself."

Miloje struck the table. "If you think your little promotion gives you free license to..."

"Enough!" Blackforest cut in. "I can appreciate the desire to exonerate yourself and your men, Stenya. I share it. But as I said, we have to put in the work. And it's going to take all of us." He quickly searched the eyes of everyone in the room in turn. "First thing's first. The investigation into the attack itself is ongoing. I'm hoping that – with a bit of due diligence – we can keep our entire staff on the case. That includes the Deputy Constable and both his Captains. However, while the three of you are under observation, you can't be permitted to function in your high offices. Therefore, I'm putting Lieutenant Huxley in temporary command of the SAPD."

Huxley stood and saluted, eyes bulging like grapefruits. "Aye, aye, Sir."

"Of course..." Blackforest went on, "...the compound irony is, with all his direct superiors out of commission, we have no actual policemen to instruct the Lieutenant in the rigors of his command. And, as my concentration will be demanded by the case against the suspect we have in custody, I'm leaving it to my own right hand – Blucille Cordon – to assist Lt. Huxley wherever possible."

"I won't let you down, Sir," Blucille put in. Art gave her a pained look, which she momentarily returned. She was going to be busy again...

"That leaves only one order of business," Blackforest explained. "The internal investigation itself. Naturally, to assign anyone on the force to audit their own bosses would create a gross conflict of interest. That's why I've reached out to the private sector. We need someone objective to run this inquest. Someone with brains, guts, and an impeccable track record of getting the job done."

Now, Art stood solemnly. "Say no more, Chief," he said, by way of acceptance speech. "I'll do it."

"Not *you*," Blackforest groaned. "Considering your trouble with the media during the Tweed case, you're lucky to even be shortlisted for this assignment. Our point man is going to have to be someone we can trust to watch the watchers too, if need be." He nodded across the room. "I'm appointing Mr. Steward Jamison as head of this private task force."

For the first time, the man sitting in the shadows under the dark hat looked up. His tall face and round, buggy eyes surveyed his surroundings just as if he had no idea where he was or how he got there. Slowly, he rested his wrists on the table in front of him, turning an ear to the district attorney. "How's that?"

"I said, you're in charge, Mr. Jamison," Blackforest reiterated.

"Oh, I see... I see..." Jamison intoned – his voice an enchanting sort of croak – a slight whistle on each of his 's's. He stood, stroking his long chin as he began to pace. Such was his thoughtful intensity that no one could seem to bring themselves to move on with the meeting, until he at last volunteered his profound thoughts. "Of course, we can't go about this... the *wrong* way. We... we've gotta do it *riiight*..."

Blackforest nodded. "Preferably."

Jamison looked down, waving a finger in the air. "Now, it seems to me, a situation like this calls for continual surveillance of each subject." He took the finger down and worked out advanced mathematics on his other hand. "I'll need a team of one... two... three investigators."

"That matches our calculations, yes," Blackforest obliged. "Name your third man; we'll see that he's assigned to your team. Only, we do hope you'll accept the assistance of Mr. Mallard."

"Oh sure... sure-sure." Jamison nodded with pursed lips. "I hear he's one of the best. Get him, if you can find him."

Blackforest froze, before slowly pointing over at Art. "He's right here."

"Well, how do ya like that?" Jamison marveled anew. He walked over and extended his hand. "Good to meet you, Mr. Mallard."

"Backatya," Art replied, shaking hands with a nervous grin. He'd never heard of any 'Steward Jamison'. And from what he'd seen so far, he could only surmise he was meeting some kind of a wackadoodle.

"Now, let's see..." Jamison went on, replacing his hand to his chin, so that his various profundities might continue to flow more freely. "I'm also going to need... a room. Not a big one. But not too small, either..."

"...Whatever you need..." Blackforest interjected a bit forcefully, his pocket watch in a sheering grip. "Just... get the list to Ms. Cordon by 21:00. Alright?"

Jamison grinned. "Alright."

"So now, if there are no more questions..." Blackforest said, daring anyone to have a question with fiery eyes. No one was quite so bold. "...Then let's snap to it." He crisply clasped his briefcase shut and whirled out the door, leaving a silent void behind him.

The meeting ended so quickly that everyone still in the room found themselves at a momentary loss. The scary lieutenant was the first to move on. Investigator Jamison left next, still absorbed in his deep thoughts – perhaps weighing his options for a third PI... perhaps trying to remember which way to the front door. The rest of them remained motionless.

"Wow..." Mallard said eventually, turning to Miloje. "I guess Blackforest really *didn't* have time for sentiment." He shook his head. "All those years you've worked together. He just threw you under the bus and stepped out."

Miloje only grinned. "If he believed me capable of any duplicity, perhaps it would've been otherwise. Blackforest detests a scandal... and this has all been a sublime headache for him. But he knows it is nothing more. We'll be cleared, inevitably."

Art's face bunched up. "You're sure this Jamison guy can handle that? He seems kinda..." He reached up and drew circles beside his head.

The Deputy Constable shrugged it off. “Steward Jamison is a rather inscrutable character, I grant. His methods are his own… which is just as well. They would never work for anyone else.”

Finally, Lieutenant Huxley stood up. “I… I think I’d better be moving on as well.” He gestured weakly at the door. “Let me show you back to the processing room, Sirs.”

“Yes, once more unto the nursery,” Miloje quipped. “What strange chance that I should so eagerly await the custody of a babysitter.” He tipped his bobby to Art as he withdrew with his two Captains in tow…

Then, the door closed again. And whether by chance or other intention, the only people left in the room were Art and Blucille. Their eyes met. Hers diverted. But it wasn’t long before she fixed a sheepish grin on her face…

“…So, it’s been a little while,” Blucille said.

“Yeah,” Art eloquently agreed.

“I’m sorry I missed… well.. the last date,” she went on.

He shrugged. “Things get busy.” He worked to remember the excuse she gave him. “How did things turn out with that jaywalking investigation? You mentioned some shoeprint they found outside a couple crosswalks?”

“Right, yes,” she nodded quickly. “We’re quite sure the prints match… which strongly suggests we have a serial jaywalker on our hands. We’re already looking at drastically expanding the search, if another matching print turns up someplace else. It’s early to say, but we might be dealing with a bonified crime spree.”

“That’s terrifying,” Art empathized.

“Yeah… it is…” Blucille said.

Their conversation ground to a miserable halt. Just a few weeks ago, they would’ve been chewing the fat and laughing as thoughtlessly as breathing. Now, it was this. Art hadn’t the foggiest clue what to do or say. But then, unexpectedly, she gave the conversation another jumpstart herself…

“So, obviously we’re going to have a full plate for a bit here,” she said. “But maybe we should start planning our next outing, when we get the time for it.”

Art’s ears snapped into place. In one moment, his heart went from ashes to soaring the heights. “W… I mean, sure, *sure*!” he elated. “Like, I’m sure we’ve got a few minutes to spare before we start all this heavy police junk. Let’s plan something! What did ya have in mind?”

She smiled, shifting and facing him directly. “Well, I heard there’s a really good production at the Talberk Theatre going on for the rest of the month.”

"I like the sounda that," Art said with an eager grin. "What's the show?"

"A Goodbye to Arms," she answered. "Have you ever seen it?"

Art laughed nervously. "Nah; can't say I have. Double amputation stories aren't really my flavor."

She shook her head with a glint in her eye. "You're adorable sometimes. But alright. What would you suggest instead?"

"Well, hey, if it's gonna be my turn, I've got something special in mind..."

Blucille hesitated. "Alright. Let's hear it."

Art held out a demonstrative microcosm in his hands. "Okay, so you know the Carlisle District?"

"Of course. It's a suburb, but it's still in St. Argonsburg jurisdiction. What about it?"

"Well, I've got five brothers and three sisters that all live right in that area!" Art revealed. "I've been thinking maybe we could set up some kinda meet-and-greet."

She looked at him aghast. "You... you want me to meet some of your *family*?"

"Well... yeah," Art replied. "Of course I do."

Blucille went on acting like she was at a loss. "That's... that's very thoughtful but... I'm... I'm not sure..."

"...But I mean, we don't have to go that route if you're feeling shy or something," Art interjected, seeing he was rapidly losing her. "I'd be tickled pink to meet some of *your* family! Do you have any living around the city?"

It was immediately obvious that his counterproposal only made it worse. "No!" She replied breathlessly. "I mean... no... I don't. Not really."

"Blucille...?" Art practically whispered, hopeless to decipher her behavior. He took one of her hands gently in his. "Blucille, is there something wrong? I... I just can't seem to say the right thing lately. It's like we're out of sync or something. For the life of me, I don't understand why."

"Well it's just..." she tried, a flash like anger in her eyes. "I... I don't see why you're suddenly so interested in sharing *our* time with all these other people. First it was the wedding you wanted to go to... milling around with friends and acquaintances on every side. Now you're talking about spending time with... *siblings*, and whatnot. Don't you have fun anymore, when it's just the two of us?"

"Oh, Blucille... I do. You *have* to know, I do. We've had the best times of my life! I wouldn't trade them for a thing. Not a thing in this world. But..." His throat got all tied up. His heart was pounding; he was getting light-headed. "I'm... I'm just getting to the point where I need you to know that I'm looking for the whole package. I'm looking for... for a *wife*. Maybe some pups. The whole nine yards. I'm not trying to push you away, Blucille. I'm trying to invite you in. To take it to the next step. I... I was hoping that's what you would want, too." With effort, he swallowed. "But now, I... I can't seem to shake the fear that it's not."

"Oh, Art..." she gasped, pulling away. "If... if only it was as simple as what we wanted. But it isn't. It never has been. That's the part of it no one sees coming. Not until it's too late."

He searched her blankly. "What does that mean? What are you trying to say?"

Her mouth moved, but nothing came out at first. Her eyes fluttered and moistened. "I'm... I'm saying that – whatever we might want – that next step might be a bridge we just can't cross."

Art was absolutely dumbstruck. "Well... if we can't move forward... then where do we go?"

She started to back away slowly. "I don't know. I don't know..."

In a flurried action, she was gone. Art reflexively started after her, but stopped dead in his tracks after only a step or two. Through all the raging emotion, the desperate need to rationalize suddenly leapt in and took over. She was more than just upset by his proposition. She was terrified. *Mortified*. But why? What could be at the root of a pain and fear so powerful that she couldn't even seem to articulate it?

In the end, Art didn't need to reason it out very long before an answer to all the riddles presented itself. And the more he thought about it, the more he felt sure. He could hang the whole tragic turn of events on one short, melodious word...

Bob...

* * *

It was times like these that Horus found a confident stride most helpful. Something in the cadence of it just seemed to keep excessive doubt from latching on and piling up. He needed that right now, in the face of meeting Blackforest for the first time since making his fateful choice. For while his friends could be remarkably subtle and resourceful in their attempts to talk him out of things, he knew Blackforest had the audacity to employ a much more devastating approach – the direct one. Worse yet, he knew he couldn't hide behind any benefits of doubts with Blackforest. That made this both the conversation he most needed to have right now, and the one he most dreaded...

"Oh, Mr. Templar!" one of the secretaries of the District Attorney's Office called out, arresting his advance on Blackforest's door. "I'm... I'm afraid you won't find him in there. He's currently in conference with..."

"Never mind, Merida," Blackforest's voice cut in, just as he stormed into the room behind Horus, on a beeline straight for his own door, looking twice as confident and infinitely more aggressive in his stride than Horus could hope to project. "I'll see Mr. Templar in my office now." About the time he reached for the handle, though, he did a double-take. "Hello, Ms. Boulevard," he said, with notable uncertainty.

"Hamilton," she replied with a nod.

"Horus..." Blackforest intoned, low and venomous. "With all due respect to your esteemed Secretary, do you suppose you could see your way clear to have this chat in *private*? Words may very well be exchanged that aren't suitable for polite company."

Horus looked over at Deborah apologetically. "Sorry to drag you all the way here only to leave you out. But Hamilton may have a point. Perhaps it's for the best."

She folded her arms, but made no other protest. "Alright."

Horus and Blackforest both nodded at her as they withdrew into the office. Deborah found a seat by the door and plopped down with a sigh.

* * *

Horus sat staring thoughtfully into space while Blackforest paced the floor in front of him. The long minutes stretched on as Horus waited for the browbeating to commence. Eventually, though, he recognized the familiar routine. Blackforest was baiting him into being the first to speak. Horus let out a slow breath. There was no counter for such a technique. Better to simply start the talking now...

"I had no other choice, Hamilton," he explained.

"Phlhh..." Blackforest replied, interjecting a brief glare into his pace.

"You know deep down it's true," Horus countered. "However you might want to protect me from..."

"...Oh, get over yourself for a moment, would you, Horus?" Blackforest growled, finally arresting himself. "This isn't about *you*. Think about what you're doing to *me*!"

Horus blinked. "I... I guess I don't know what you mean."

Blackforest leaned against his desk. He folded his arms, searching Horus with intensity. "When you first told me about your time with the Vigil, that was one thing. That was just two law students sharing a dark secret in confidence. But all that changed the moment I was put in charge of this district. *Your* district. All of a sudden, the secret I was keeping had *implications*... whether I realized it at the time or not."

"I begin to see..." Horus said, scratching under his chin. "You're afraid what it would mean, if my old ties to the Vigil came out in the course of the case."

"Wouldn't *you* be, in my place? At best, I'd have something *else* to make me look oblivious – incompetent. At worst, they'd find out I've known all along! Just imagine how *that* would go over. Especially now."

"It does paint a grim picture," Horus mused. "Fortunately though, perhaps I should remind you: I'm not the one on trial."

Blackforest stuck his tight little beard out. "Well it does encourage me to hear that coming from *you*. I've got enough good people in hot water right now. The last thing I need is you getting one of your funny ideas and implicating yourself on purpose."

Horus grimaced. "You really think I would do that? Take someone else's trial and turn it into a referendum on my own past sins?"

"I couldn't exactly rule it out. You're just self-righteous enough sometimes to be capable of anything."

"Well then, let me lay your fears to rest. That's not why I took this case."

"Then *why*, Horus?" Blackforest insisted, balling up his claws. "Help me understand that much. Could it be that, deep down, you still feel some sort of loyalty to their cause? To your family ties, at least?"

Horus frowned. "No."

"Okay, then... maybe the opposite extreme? Are you going to hand the State a victory just to get revenge for what they did?"

"Absolutely not," Horus announced.

"Oh, you're impossible!" Blackforest resigned, throwing up his hands.

"I'm sorry, Hamilton," Horus said with a shrug. "All I can say is: It's my past. And now that it's finally come calling, I've chosen to face it. I'm not sure I could explain it any better than that."

"Horus-Templar-logic, if ever I heard it," Blackforest quipped. He eyed Horus with a gentler expression. "How is Deborah handling all this? I hope it didn't come as too much of a shock. But perhaps you'd already found occasion to tell her everything you told me, all those years ago?"

Horus cast his gaze down. "I regret, I never did. Some hints and half-truths, but nothing like the whole picture. I still have yet to truly explain myself."

Blackforest's eyes narrowed with a new kind of indignation... a quieter one, if no less intense. "*Still*? And you were just going to let her into this meeting?"

Horus shrunk back. He turned up his palms. "I didn't see that it could do any more harm than the meeting I already had with my client. Certain details have already escaped. And after all, Deborah's exceptionally clever. I imagine she's worked out most of the puzzle for herself by now."

Blackforest walked right up and stood over him. He pointed a deadly-sharp claw in his face. "Now you listen to me, Horus. You are going to sit your Secretary down and you are going to give her the *exact* same confession you gave me back in law school... word for word, if necessary. That is not a request. It's an *order*."

Horus surprised himself, feeling more than a little cowed into obedience. But he consulted his pocket watch. "The trial begins tomorrow morning. I'm not sure I could adequately broach the topic before then."

"Well, you'd better find the time soon. Or else *make* it."

Horus nodded. "You're right, of course. I know it would help to get it off my chest."

"Don't you even start to make this about *you* again," Blackforest cautioned. "She deserves to know what the whole truth is, and only *just* the truth. Don't give her imagination a chance to make your past a darker thing than it really was. That's the cruelest thing you could do."

Horus sighed as the magnitude of his error finally began to dawn on him. "What a fool I've been. Keeping her in the dark... begging her understanding. Expecting it. Taking it for granted. And yet, she's treated me with unwavering respect. I don't deserve it."

"I couldn't agree more." Blackforest rounded his desk, sitting behind it, casting a supremely focused gaze at all the papers thereon. "Now get out of here. I have my own preparations to make. And I'll need all the time I can get, if I'm going to do the merciful thing tomorrow and disembowel you."

"That's certainly true," Horus assented, rising from his seat. "The crime is indeed sensational... and my client's sheer proximity to it highly suspect. But your case still hinges entirely on prejudicial presumptions... a fact I intend to make abundantly clear to the jury tomorrow."

Blackforest looked up with a sneer. "You really *are* going to fight this thing out to the bitter end, aren't you?"

"That's my job," Horus answered. "Duty demands nothing less."

Chapter 7

Now in the closing moments of zero hour, the stage being set was appropriately bleak. In place of the usual paneled mahogany, there was only concrete and cast iron. The damp, musty, windowless chamber was much more a bunker than a courtroom. But then, that was the point. Nestled greedy depths beneath the already deep and secure holding cells of Civil HQ, the room was tailor-suited to a case like this, where the mere act of transporting a suspect from detention center to courthouse would be to invite disaster...

Horus watched the slow trickle of people coming through the doorway, each one being checked-in by a team of sturdy policemen. The court was gradually filling up with its regular assortment of experts, witnesses, jurors... and, indispensably, excitable spectators. Whatever security might demand, the trial was simply too sensational not to pack the house with an audience to gasp, murmur, and be called to order at the appropriate times, even if every one of them had to be carefully curated. Horus didn't have to wonder if the department's caution was adequate... he knew the answer soon enough. He was obliged to raise his one good eyebrow as a couple old faces filtered into the room...

But finally, the one face he was really watching for arrived. He stood, pulling out her seat at the defense table...

"Thank you," Deborah said, hurriedly sitting and unpacking. "For what it's worth, I really *meant* to be here sooner. There's quite a lot yet we could go over. And not to beat a dead horse, but if you hadn't insisted we come here separately, we might've..." She stopped and gawked as she finally took her first good look at him. "Horus... what happened?" she asked, aghast at the sight of his face.

Horus reached up and gently found the bump over his eye. "It looks as bad as it feels, I take it?" he replied with a dismissive grin. "A bit of carelessness on my part. I walked into the path of a flying celery on my way here."

"Celery?" she demanded, her face settling into another pattern of sheer disbelief. "Whatever happened to good old-fashioned tomatoes?"

He shrugged. "I've been wondering the same thing the last few days. For no reason I'm conscious of, the citizens of St. Argonsburg seem to have adopted their own ideas about ballistic produce."

She shook her head. "Well it looks insufferable." She suddenly leapt back to her feet. "I'll go get you a wet washcloth..."

Horus reached out for her wrist just in time. "No, please," he insisted. "It'll keep until court is adjourned. I need you here right now."

She slowly sat back down. "Alright."

"Deborah..." he began gently. "There's so much I should've told you by now. These last few days, I've been hiding behind duty and obligation, all the while avoiding what should've come first. How could I have been so arrogant? I can't do it anymore. I can't go on keeping you in the dark..."

Her brow contorted. She looked around nervously. "You really want to discuss this *now*? In *sidebar*?"

"Perhaps this isn't the ideal time for the full account," he admitted. "But before we go any further, I need you to know this much: I *was* with the Vigil, for a time. They taught me the art of combat, and of stealth. I did things for them I'm deeply ashamed of now. I played the saboteur for them. The infiltrator. The petty thug." He leaned in... close, and serious. "But I was never the butcher. I never killed for them. You have to believe that."

"Of course I do," Deborah quickly assured him. "Horus, I admit the last few days have been... difficult. Even a little disorienting. But give me some credit. I know the man you are *now*. And I may've already pieced together more than you think about your past. I gather – for instance – that joining the Vigil probably wasn't so much your own idea, as it was a family affair. Anyway, there must've been *someone* in your family that wound up deeper in their business than you did." She searched him, hesitant to continue. "Your father, I suppose?"

Horus hung his head. "I guess I can't entirely deny that he was... *involved*. Not that I lay the blame on him... for his own associations, or for mine. Actually, I consider him far more innocent than myself. He was about the last person in the world that should've had anything to do with them. But you're right about one thing: They did get to me through him. He *was* my closest tie to the Vigil."

Deborah frowned sympathetically. "*Was*?"

He nodded, eyes still downcast. "Yes. I'm afraid that tie is broken forever now."

She shook her head. Horus watched her eyes dance as she studied his. There was earnest sympathy in them, he knew. But he couldn't help detecting a bit of exasperation as well. *He was –* ***involved****. That tie is broken forever now*. He recounted his own phraseology to himself, wondering at its obscurity. He was still mincing his words… clarifying without being clear. He'd finally admitted to his own past involvement with the Eighth Vigil of Aridos… the travesty that would have alarmed her the most. Why be the least bit oblique about what had ultimately become of his father? Was the full truth still too painful to share? Apparently, it was…

"I'm sorry…" she said, snapping him out of his private train of thought.

"It's alright," he replied. "Well… to be completely honest, it's *not* alright. But I've had many years' experience learning to live with it."

She patted his hands with her free hand. "Any time you want to talk about it, I'll be there for you." She grinned. "Except, maybe not right now. We're on the clock, after all."

Horus cleared his throat. "Yes, of course. We'd better get our heads back in the game."

"How about a review of Blackforest's star witnesses?" she suggested.

"I can't think of a better place to start."

Deborah scanned the room, eyes and ears trained smartly. "You see that man with the navy jacket and matching hat?"

Horus homed-in on a Human matching that description, watching him nervously scratch his stubble. He took his hat off just long enough to run his fingers through grey-streaked hair before hurriedly replacing it. "I see him," Horus confirmed. "He certainly appears… agitated."

"That's Harbormaster Fitzgerald," she explained. "He was as close to the action as anyone Blackforest could get his hands on. He spoke with the three phony lawyers himself. They've had him put up in the high security block ever since."

"As well they should," Horus quipped. "A witness of his caliber wouldn't be safe walking the streets."

She shifted her gaze, pointing. "And then we have the lady in the fur coat… Mrs. Nora Van Snoot."

Horus nodded. "The one with her nose in the clouds? Yes, I see her. What a windfall for Hamilton, to land a professional busybody as a witness."

"And what a witness at that. She claims to have seen Khonshu and two others entering the barge."

Horus sighed. "Her cross examination should be fun. Nothing like casting doubt on positive identification to really make a day in court."

"Better yet, you're going to have to fight that battle twice over."

"The diving bell witness, I suppose you mean." Horus made his own survey of the crowd. "Which one is he?"

"The one in the beret and the ruffled shirt," Deborah answered with a leading nod. "And he's as sure of the bell itself as the one he says rented it."

Horus rested his chin on his hand, puzzling. "This is going to be a tough one."

"Don't tell me you're having doubts already," they heard, amidst a rattling of chains and the approach of many feet. As they turned to look into the aisle, there was Khonshu, wrapped in a veritable cocoon of iron, being led to the table by a squadron of big and exceptionally ill-humored policemen. And though Khonshu himself was grinning, it was far too sardonic a grin to consider him in a much better humor.

"Well, here comes the public spectacle now," Horus riposted. "Evidently, they don't teach cat burglary like they used to. I should say we'd have a lot more room for confidence right now, if you hadn't been spotted by half of Jast-Madiir."

Khonshu's eyes were a fire, fixed steadily on Horus as his handlers locked him to the table. "There you go again. My own lawyer, trying to make it sound like I had something to do with this... oh, what was it, exactly? Some sort of boating accident?" He shook his head, the policemen tethering the final set of manacles before withdrawing to a post by the doorway. "You know that kind of attitude won't win you many points with our friends. And if you need any more incentive to do your best work today, you'd best believe you have eyes on you, yourself."

"So I noticed," Horus replied, turning back to the gallery again. "Now, let's see. I spy old Arthur Cromwell, posing as a journalist with his pen and pad in the middle rows. Definitely his most classic ruse. He always did have the look of a doomsday poet about him... especially with the phony spectacles. But then, he's no spring chicken anymore... perhaps the spectacles aren't merely a prop any longer." He swiveled further in his seat. "And could that be Robert Sutherland in the back? I suppose he doesn't even need a disguise anymore, at his age. But at any rate, I'm not surprised to see some things haven't changed at all since I left. It's the same old lineup of Human charlatans and snitches."

The wind was noticeably taken from Khonshu's sails. "Fantastic. I suppose you mean to hand all three of us over to the firing squad? Go ahead; see what good it does you."

Horus shook his head. "Their secret's safe with me. But we'll have to see what we can do about yours."

Khonshu appeared ready to fire back with something, but at that very moment, a voice called out over the court...

"Hear ye, hear ye! All rise for the right honorable judge, Vice-Vizier Lionel Ramesses!"

Everyone stood as ordered, a cymbal crash kicking off a lively drum and saxophone ensemble, heralding the approach of Ramesses, the right honorable fashion plate himself. He hurled out of his chambers in a flowing judge's robe and cool shades, holding up two forked fingers on each hand to his large gallery, and even larger imaginary fanbase. Whether the callsign had any particular meaning or not, Horus couldn't say for sure... nor bring himself to really care. Under all the flashy pizzazz, what was important to know about Ramesses was his track record. He got the death penalty every time. A younger judge who'd grown up idealizing Senahktenre as the undisputed model of success, Ramesses labored under the rather conspicuous delusion that he could improve on the formula with just a heaping helping of showmanship. Horus could only frown... though his spirits lifted somewhat when he looked over and saw an even more disgusted look on Blackforest's face. They both understood intrinsically that a bit of theatricality now and then was a hallmark in the wheelhouse of a skilled *attorney*. But on a *judge*, it was nothing more than gaudy shades and blaring horns. And confetti poppers...

"What is this?" Khonshu hissed.

"Exactly what it looks like," Horus replied.

Ramesses slowly sat down, giving his band time for a smooth fade-out. He gestured for the crowd to sit, smiling a smile that couldn't be controverted by the sea of glum and nervous faces in front of him. "Good morning, ladies and germs. Thanks for coming. I *am* Lionel Ramesses – **the** hot-button name in crime and punishment – and I'll be judging this here shindig. Big ticket mayhem on the docket for today... a mystery man and alleged member of the Eighth Vigil of Aridos known only as 'Khonshu' facing indictment for Grand Demolition of State Property – a top-classified cargo barge that went up in a fire ball on Monday, the last. As earth-shaking as anything we've seen go down in the Harbor since the Ebenezer incident, and kicking off a whole wave of high-profile internal affairs investigations, this one's really captured the imagination of the capitol, *and* the country at large. Serious questions of national security remain unanswered. The stakes are high... and tensions even higher. But that doesn't mean we can't all enjoy a nice, relaxing day in court. I believe in keeping things cas'. So, without further ado, I'm gonna turn things over to our beloved District Attorney – the judicious, jubilicious, and always nutritious, Hamilton Blackforest." He shifted his gaze and gave Blackforest a thumbs-up. "You're on, Hamster."

Blackforest stood again, wrestling his clenched fangs into the best semblance of a grin he could manage with a slight snap of his neck. "Thank you, your Honor," he said, fairly dratting his whole existence. "I'd like to begin with an opening statement... if that's not too formal."

Ramesses shrugged. "Sure. Go for it."

Blackforest nodded as he whirled around, his steely look instantly commanding the bleak mood that all gathered were more inclined to be in anyway. "Citizens and patriots of Jast-Madiir: We have – all of us – come under attack. A group of militant criminals has seen fit to brand us as acceptable losses – targets of opportunity in a misbegotten war of attrition. This is an injustice which we can't – and won't – take sitting down." He pointed a menacing finger squarely at the defendant. "The State will prove that this man – Khonshu – perpetrated a devious, premeditated act of destruction against a highly prized and carefully guarded asset of Jast-Madiiran commerce. We will prove his participation in a conspiracy that ultimately led to the sinking of this classified cargo barge – a most heinous affront to the crown, carried out in broad daylight, in the sight of countless witnesses. Finally, we will demand justice be done upon him, both in answer to his own crimes, and as a solemn warning to all his compatriots, lest they should ever again presume to act in defiance of the Czarina's designs."

Blackforest returned to his seat, leaving the courtroom in the grip of silence, until Judge Ramesses volunteered a little clap. "Mad props, Hamilton... very nicely done. Next up is Horus Templar, currently known and reviled far and wide as 'The Lawyer to the Ship Blower-Upper'. Has he got anything to say at this time?"

"Yes, your Honor," Horus replied, rising... brushing away some private disbelief that such a name had caught on. "The defense strenuously calls for a forestallment of this case, in light of the aforementioned ongoing internal affairs investigations. It is our contention that the entirety of the State's case currently hinges on numerous assumptions which are, as yet, unproven... from my client's participation in an alleged conspiracy, to his very agency. The prosecution may very well save itself effort – and possible embarrassment – if we wait."

Judge Ramesses shifted thoughtfully in his seat, slumping into an even more relaxed position. "Hm..." he mulled, giving a beat or two of apparent consideration. "Nah," he arbitrated. "I think we'll just stick to the script and go ahead with things now."

"Just as well," Horus said. "Perhaps there'll be occasion to call for a mistrial later."

"Hey, now... no need for nasty asides like that, Mr. Templar," Ramesses cautioned. He turned back to Blackforest. "Let's bring up that first witness."

Blackforest reassumed command, fixing his eyes into the gallery. "I call Harbormaster Fitzgerald to the stand."

* * *

"And that's when the shot went off," Fitzgerald said, kneading his maritime cap, as he'd done all throughout his lengthy account of the classified mission and the morning of the crime. "It all happened so fast I didn't even see which one of them drew the gun. They bolted; they knocked down everyone in their path. Oregano was left on the ground. He'd taken the shot in the leg." The Harbormaster hesitated, but managed to carry on before Blackforest could introduce any further questions. "He... he ordered me to sound the alarm. I made for the bell tower, quick as I could. I was still ringing it when the explosion took the barge." The tension in his twisting cap could be heard from across the court. "I suppose I stayed too long in the tower. Honestly, Mr. Blackforest, I didn't know what else to do. I followed orders... I did everything just as the Sergeant told me. I... I just didn't know what else to do..."

"It's alright, Mr. Fitzgerald," Blackforest coached him. "As I've assured you before, the State doesn't intend to hold you liable for any miscarriage of duty. We're depending on your full cooperation to catch the real culprits. Now, is there anything else you can tell us?"

Fitzgerald shook his head. "No, I don't think so. I'm afraid I was too far away to be any more help. I suppose Oregano could've given you the rest of the story... if only he'd lived to tell it."

"Objection," Horus called. "Assuming facts not in evidence. We've heard nothing thus far of Sergeant Oregano's supposed demise."

"Well he wasn't where I left him when I got back," Fitzgerald was quick to explain. "He was in no shape to chase down the imposters. He must've realized they were only a diversion and doubled back to the barge... been on board when it blew..."

"Objection," Horus repeated. "The witness is now volunteering conclusions."

Judge Ramesses pursed his jowls. "Pretty good conclusions, though."

"Nevertheless," Horus persisted, "I'm going to have to stand by my objection."

Ramesses sighed, looking down at the stand. "You're not supposed to testify to anything you don't *know*, Fitzgerald," he explained. "Even when it's super obvious." He struck the bench with his gavel. "Objection sustained."

Fitzgerald turned his nervous eyes back to the DA. "Sorry, Mr. Blackforest. I didn't mean to overstep my bounds."

"Well, no matter. Let's see if we can get things back on track. When you returned to the dock, did you find that Sergeant Oregano had gone?"

Fitzgerald nodded. "Yes."

"But he was hobbled by the gunshot?"

"Yes."

"Was there anything to suggest where he went?"

"Well, not that I..." Fitzgerald mulled, before he cut himself off, eyes suddenly bulging. "Wait, yes! I remember now! There was a blood trail! It led toward the barge's ramp."

Blackforest grinned. "Thank you, Mr. Fitzgerald. I have no more questions."

Horus stood. "Defense has no questions at this time."

"Good deal," Ramesses replied drumming on his bench. "Moving right along, then. Let's have witness number two."

* * *

"So, on the morning of the crime, you happened to be patrolling that stretch of the Harbor?" Blackforest asked.

"Oh, yes," Mrs. Van Snoot answered, her beady little eyes turned down to meet him. "The Harbor lends itself exceptionally well to professional disapproval." She frowned, even more than she'd already been frowning. "All that water they sail through," she began to explain with a dismissive little wave. "It's all so very excessive."

"But you had more to disapprove of than usual that morning."

"Indeed. There was, a gunshot – a whole commotion. I approached the scene at once. It was clear that my presence was called for. But before I could arrive, there was an even more insufferable racket: Mr. Fitzgerald, and his *raucous* bell." The way she rolled her 'r' on the word 'raucous' was truly impressive.

"But when you reached the source of the gunshot, you found something else out of the ordinary, didn't you?"

"*Hmph,* I certainly did. I noticed a trio of Mesomelae scurrying down a flight of stairs on one of the barges – all crouched down and mischievous. And I daresay they noticed me, too. The leader froze in his tracks, staring back at me with wide eyes – the eyes of a naughty child, caught with his hand in the cookie jar."

"I see. Can you describe these suspicious characters to the court?"

She nodded. "The one in front had silver-blue irises. That much was clear even from such a distance, so great was his look of astonishment. He had a smallish nose on the end of a long, narrow snout, and tall ears with a wide flair that did much to complement his comic expression. His fur appeared matted, and his clothes clung to him in such a way that he must've been sopping wet."

"And what of the others?" Blackforest encouraged her.

"In the back there was an obnoxiously big, brutish fellow. His look I disdained the most. Perhaps sheer bulk serves some function in the criminal enterprises, but he might've shown at least an ounce of moderation."

Blackforest leaned over the stand. "And, the one in the middle? Can you identify him?"

"Yes," she answered, pointing the accusing finger, even as she turned her face away in contempt. "It was *him*! The defendant!"

The crowd muttered that special mutter... the one reserved for moments of dramatic accusation such as this. Ramesses appeared most pleased, making no effort to silence the crowd. Blackforest himself had to signal them to quiet down...

"Now, now, let's hear the rest of it," he implored, turning back to his witness. "Mrs. Van Snoot, is there anything more you can share with us about that morning?"

She crossed her arms in a huff. "I don't suppose I know what you mean, Mr. Blackforest. I spied the defendant in his skulking. I turned my nose up at his whole lot and moved on. I fulfilled my civic function. There would seem nothing more to say."

"Very well. Thank you, Mrs. Van Snoot." Blackforest spun around, returning to his table. "Cross examine."

Horus quietly and thoughtfully took his time replacing Blackforest in front of the witness stand. "Now, Mrs. Van Snoot, I do hope you can help me put some of your testimony in perspective."

"Only under strenuous protest," she answered, vaguely attempting to ward him off with a handkerchief. "I do not fondly exchange words with the likes of a defense lawyer. Even one so battered as yourself. Doubtless, that ghastly shiner was well-earned."

Horus blinked a slow, painful blink. No stranger to contempt, he'd nonetheless had his belly full by now...

"Yes, well... your protest is duly noted. At least you seem to have some idea that the court demands your response to my questions. Perhaps it would interest you to learn that the court *also* expects that you refrain from personal remarks."

Van Snoot huffed. "I am a busybody by trade, Mr. Templar. My remarks – be they disparaging – are not merely *personal*, so much as they are *professional*. And you have no right to criticize me for my profession."

"I could say the same," Horus rejoined.

She shook her head. "On the contrary. Criticizing your profession *is* my profession."

Horus looked up at Ramesses. "Your Honor, would you please ensure the cooperation of this witness?"

"*Oooo*, I don't know..." Ramesses deliberated. "I hate to spoil all the savory animosity going on here."

"*This witness* is still awaiting a question to cooperate with, Mr. Templar," Van Snoot put in. "Perhaps you ought to try one."

"Very well," Horus agreed, pivoting back. "Mostly, I couldn't help noticing how *remarkable* it was supposed to be that you saw three Mesomelae on a barge in the Harbor. Tell me, Mrs. Van Snoot, were there many barges moored where you patrolled? A dozen or so? Perhaps even two dozen?"

She chuckled mirthlessly. "You have a talent for understatement. They are numerous beyond reckoning, of course."

"And none of the others had any Mesomela hands aboard?"

"Perhaps they did. But none who so stood out for their subterfuge."

Horus gripped the stand with both hands. "Mrs. Van Snoot, let me be more direct. Assuming the verity of your positive identification – an assumption I fully intend to challenge in due time, if need be – what makes you so sure you've placed my client on ***the*** barge, and not merely ***a*** barge?

You testified that you were not present for the skirmish that Harbormaster Fitzgerald witnessed. You also admitted being absent by the time of the explosion. Are we expected to accept that you could tell *exactly* where the gunshot rang out from? That your ears were equally precise at pinpointing the explosion you heard later?"

"Hm..." she mused, while the rest of the court waited breathlessly. "You make a fair point, Sir, I must grant you that."

Horus couldn't help grinning – out of all the happy times he'd put one over on a witness, this had to be one of the most satisfying. "Thank you, Mrs. Van Snoot," he said, before getting in just one good step toward his seat...

"However..." she intoned.

Horus locked up. He hesitantly returned to meet her. "Yes?"

"I feel it merits mentioning that I also noticed a man scrambling on the ground at the foot of the ramp by the barge in question. He wore a long, grubby coat, though it appeared he had a soldier's uniform underneath it. And though I couldn't be entirely sure what in the world he was doing, he seemed to be engaged in tying a length of wooden planking to his bloody leg."

Horus could think of nothing to say. He merely swallowed.

"It seems to me, this connects up rather well with the ballad of Sergeant Oregano, don't you think? Or, would you have the simple, unassuming jury believe that this is nothing more than another commonplace sight down at the Harbor's edge?" she went on, twisting the knife.

"I..." he stammered. "No, I would have to admit that's rather unusual."

She smiled haughtily. "It is well for you that you would. I would only have gone on to explain that I returned to the scene after the explosion, finding nothing but splinters and a horrible, stinking reek where the barge had been. There was then no doubt that what I had seen would be of interest to the authorities. I waited there for them to arrive, so that I could give my statement. And I should say it took them long enough."

"Yes, well, how *professional* of you to notice," Horus sighed, rubbing his one good eye. "One more line of questioning, then, if you don't mind. You said you saw three Mesomelae onboard the barge?"

"Yes."

"How far would you say it was, from your vantage point to them? Fifty feet? One hundred?"

She shrugged. "A good distance, admittedly. I'd be hopeless to assign a precise measurement to it."

"A good distance, you say? And what characteristics of the defendant did you recognize from that encounter? What defining traits leapt out at you from across such a distance?"

"Ah, yes... you would have to question *that* now, wouldn't you?"

"I would," he replied with a nod. "And you would have to answer that question now."

She seemed to consider it for a spell. "General things, mostly, I suppose. His height... his build. They match."

"His height and build?" Horus repeated dubiously. "I call that rather vague, Mrs. Van Snoot. You described the other two much more vividly."

"Only because they happened to be much more clownish in appearance. It's not my fault that your client is so plain."

Horus had another thought just then... a small tangent he might chase. "As you say. Though I do believe we'll have to examine your sureness further at a more opportune time. Right now, I find myself intrigued by the fact that you saw *three* Mesomelae on the deck."

She rolled her eyes tiredly. "Why, pray tell?"

"No special reason... except that the Harbormaster was approached by a team of the same number. Tell me this, Mrs. Van Snoot: Of your own knowledge, is there any way to be sure the three Mesomelae posing as lawyers didn't simply manage to double back and infiltrate the barge on their own?"

"Of that, I know nothing certainly," she replied, maintaining her tired air. "What possible difference could it make if they were the same three?"

"Perhaps none," Horus admitted. "Though in that case, it would be quite strange that the Harbormaster managed not to identify the defendant. After all, he got a much closer look than you did... no matter how imprecisely you measure the distance."

Her prominently displayed nostrils flared at Horus' remark. He returned to his seat, relieved to have put even a very small one over on her after all. "I have no further questions at this time."

"Hm... I don't much care for that," Judge Ramesses said. "What do ya think, Hamilton? Should we get Fitzgerald back up here to point the finger at the defendant too?"

"No, your Honor," Blackforest replied in a low voice as he stood. "The State does not in the least subscribe to Mr. Templar's double-back theory.

There *were* two distinct teams of three, as evidence will soon reveal. The testimony of our third witness should put all doubt to rest."

Ramesses rubbed his hands together with anticipation. "Better yet. Let's get the next guy up here, then."

Blackforest nodded, turning to his third witness. "I call Andrew Campbell to the stand."

Horus watched the man in the beret be sworn in. Always a close study of witnesses in those disarming moments before testimony, he managed to turn up a nugget every so often... an odd tick or tell... an eccentricity that revealed something of the man behind the message. Often, these idiosyncrasies were simply that... artifacts of personality. Just recently, he'd seen a witness with a bad tremor in his left hand that turned out to be the result of nerve damage from a childhood injury. And not long before that, there was a lady who kept adjusting her stockings. Another textbook nervous habit, all it really indicated was that she was in masonry and more accustomed to thick pants than the formal dress she wore to court. But even so – once in a while – these little things would turn out to be huge. Horus couldn't know it at the time, but this was to be one such occasion...

"Please take the stand," the court officer instructed as the whole swearing-in process came to a close.

Campbell nodded, turning and rounding the iron panels that surrounded the witness stand, just like anyone else would do. Only, when he got back there, he merely stood awkwardly *beside* the seat. Horus was quickly joined by the entire rest of the court in feeling a bit put off. For long seconds, everyone waited breathlessly for the man to finally sit down. When he didn't, the Vice-Vizier took it upon himself to remedy the situation...

"Hey, Buddy," he said. "Do us a solid and take that seat, would you? You're supposed to sit down."

Campbell audibly scoffed. "Some joke, then... calling this thing 'the stand'. What's a man with my condition supposed to think?" He cautiously probed around for the seat before he planted himself in it at last.

Blackforest stalked up to his witness, apparently unphased. "Now, Mr. Campbell, would you tell us where you were the evening of Sunday, Septembruary 41st?"

"Yes. It was low-tide, and I was out at the coast, tracing my normal route from the 6th to 7th meridian. I'm a border painter, you see."

"I understand," Blackforest replied. Border painters, of course, were an old phenomenon of the Continent, where sovereigns of neighbouring countries had long ago determined that staking out their claims with lines on mere maps was not nearly vivid enough to suit them. Rather, the intuitive thing to do was obviously to impose those borderlines on the very world itself. But when the Czarina of Jast-Madiir – not to be outdone in any expression of her authority – heard about this mainland fashion, she was quick to appropriate the idea for her own, island country. After all, to merely accept the ocean as a de facto border just seemed too lazy... and too dated...

"And what did you witness while you were painting?" Blackforest continued.

"Well, I passed a vendor booth that was renting out diving equipment. There were two Mesomelae there... one was running the booth, and the other was renting a diving bell. I mean, I admit: I couldn't hear what they were saying from all the way out at the water's edge. But they both kept gesturing at the bell, so it was clear what they were haggling over."

"Alright. Can you explain the significance of this action to the court?"

"I think so. You see, I heard the police retrieved a diving bell from the scene of that explosion the very next morning, not too far from where I'd been. The rental booth would've been required to close its wares only minutes after I passed by, so I realized the bell I saw must've been rented out for the next day. It seemed like enough of a coincidence that I should explain what I witnessed to the authorities, and get a look at the bell they fished from the crime scene. See if it was the same one."

"And, was it the same bell you saw being rented?"

Campbell nodded emphatically. "Yes, it was the same."

"Very good," Blackforest replied. "And now, can you tell us who you saw renting the bell?"

"Yes I can," Campbell said. He turned and bobbed his head at Horus' side of the room. "It was that one there! The one standing at the defense table!"

Though similar to Nora Van Snoot's initial identification in many respects, this rehash didn't quite fetch the same crowd effects. There was *some* excitement in the room... but the normal, spirited murmuring was notably muddled by an element of confusion...

"Mr. Campbell... I'm afraid no one is standing at the table," Blackforest gently explained. "Could you please clarify your statement, for the record?"

"Oh, for goodness' sake!" Campbell exclaimed, extending his finger repeatedly. "I mean *him*! The defendant!"

Finally, the gasps and strained whispers reached the satisfying crescendo they were meant to.

"Thank you, Mr. Campbell," Blackforest said. "I believe that will be all."

Horus didn't wait for Blackforest to return to his place before he rose and addressed the court. "Your Honor, I call this entire line of questioning improper," he asserted. "The prosecution laid no foundation for the introduction of this diving bell. If the police regard it's rental and usage as part of the *res gestae*, then we should've had an officer on the stand to explain its part in the commission of the crime."

Blackforest turned a bristly look at Horus. "With respect, the prosecution had *hoped* the defense would be willing to stipulate the admission of the bell as an accessory. Certainly, the State *can* produce Lt. Huxley to testify to the body of forensic evidence. To the diving bell's discovery mere feet behind the site of the wreck. To the claw marks found imbedded on pieces of the aft hull of the barge. If Mr. Templar is really *that* intent to further inconvenience our embattled police force – to momentarily obstruct what he can't ultimately refute – then by all means, I'll go forthwith and get the Lieutenant myself. Is that what you want, Counselor?"

Horus set his jaw, immediately feeling lousy. He *was* sympathetic to the plight of the police... to Milo, Alexei, Brocksmith... and those currently scrambling to fill their shoes. Blackforest was right. To add to their troubles for nothing more than a short stall in the case would be unconscionable. "No. Defense is willing to stipulate the introduction of the bell."

"Good," Blackforest replied. "Cross-examine."

Slowly, Horus arced toward the stand. "Mr. Campbell," he began. "Again, we find ourselves accepting positive identification from a witness who admits to being quite a distance from the subject. You said you were out of earshot from the rental booth?"

"I did," Campbell admitted.

"Then I put to you the same question as Mrs. Van Snoot: How can you be sure that the defendant is the one you saw at the booth?"

Campbell squinted, tapping his chin as he stared up into space. "Well, let's see. There was that distinctive downward curl to one of the whiskers on his right jowl... and those tiny white spots at the ends of his forearms."

Horus blanched. He looked back at his own client, straining just to notice both features for the first time. "Well. Your eyesight is... *impressive*, Mr. Campbell."

"It serves me well in most ways," Campbell said with a smirk.

"I suppose there's not much point in asking how surely you recognize the bell?"

"Probably not."

Horus fed his own brain through the wringer, grasping for something... *anything* to ask that could cast so much as a shadow of a doubt on Campbell's testimony. "I..." he began. But all he could do was stare blankly at the man in the beret, smugly basking in his own confidence. "...I have no more questions at this time."

Ramesses offered a single clap. "Alrighty! Feels like we're moving right along here." He checked his watch. "Where would you say we're at, Ham-hock? Close to a good stopping point for the day?"

"Yes, your Honor," Blackforest answered. "In fact, the State is ready to rest its case. We have learned from Harbormaster Fitzgerald that the illegally sunken barge was originally classified top-secret in order to avoid the attention of the Eighth Vigil of Aridos – a criminal organization that had by that time already scuttled two other commercial ships set aside for trade with the Queens of the Berile Beirels, who are the Vigil's sworn enemies. We have shown that – despite the extreme measures taken to prevent it – the Czarina's barge was sunk by the efforts of just such a Mesomela conspiracy. We have subsequently placed the defendant both on the barge just prior to its destruction, and also at the scene where equipment was procured to commit that very crime. We therefore motion that the defendant be bound over for sentencing."

"Radical," Ramesses replied. "But how about the defense? Does he intend to put on a case?"

"Yes, your Honor," Horus answered with a nod, presently wondering what sort of case he could even scrape together.

"Oh-kay!" Ramesses said, still eager. "It'd be a shame for the fun to end so soon anyway. Court is adjourned. We'll reconvene in two days' time. Until then, stay cool."

Horus watched the judge finger-gun away from the bench, feeling his guts congeal. He looked over to Khonshu, and into his incendiary eyes...

"So that was your best, huh?" Khonshu spat as the police returned, unbolting him from the table. "What a joke. I'll see you in Heck, Horus... before the week's out!" Fortunately, the cops whisked him away before he could hurl any more threats and obscenities. Seeing him disappear behind all the people collecting themselves to go, Horus sank into his chair, carefully cradling the busted-up side of his face. But before he could really begin to untangle his own malaise, he felt Deborah's hand on his shoulder...

"Alright, so it didn't go so well today," she said.

"Khonshu would seem to agree," Horus quipped.

"Where do we go from here?" she asked.

Horus revived somewhat at the question. In anyone else's mouth, it would've sounded hopeless. But coming from Deborah, he took it for what it was... a call to forge ahead. And it didn't take him long to chart a path...

"Go dig up everything you can on Andrew Campbell. There's something off about him. Maybe if we find out what it is, we can use it. Meanwhile, I'll have to work out an angle on Van Snoot. Her ID wasn't the strongest, but it could stand to be a lot weaker."

"Meet you in the morning, then?" she asked.

"Yes. We'll debrief then."

"Alright, Boss," she said with a pat. "Maybe find time for some sleep. And an ice pack."

Chapter 8

Art looked up into the cheerless sky, wishing it would hurry up and rain already. The city was on something like day three or four of this damp, still, earthy-smelling weather. Once in a while, there was a vague, half-hearted rumble of thunder, or maybe a knee-jerk gust of wind. But no rain. Not a drop. It was annoying.

Of course, if he was at all cheerless himself, then it wasn't really about the weather. Somehow, in the few blocks left between him and Civil HQ, he was supposed to wind himself up for the start of the big new case. He was supposed to have his thinking cap on… to don the persona of the brilliant gumshoe, for which he was so well known. But he just couldn't seem to give a darn. He already had everyone's assurances that the cops he'd be investigating were straight shooters, and he knew two of the three of them well enough to be sure it was true. But even allowing for the off chance that that third guy could actually *be* the mole, Art's head just wasn't in the game. Sure, this was a national security case. Maybe the biggest case of the decade. But all that stuff didn't grab him. There was a totally different mystery holding him captive, and he couldn't get loose. It was a caper without so much as the sketchiest clue as to what crime had even been committed. All he knew was the principal victim… and the alias of the perpetrator. And in his total ignorance, all he could seem to do was brood endlessly on that hideous name…

Bob…

Bob…

Bob…

Nothing so stuck in the craw of a sleuth as an unresolved mystery… let alone one that was currently bulldozing his whole entire personal life. And maybe the worst of it was, Art *knew* he could solve it. He knew he could at least figure out what happened – assign a shape to Blucille's past, which had apparently left much deeper scars than he ever imagined. He'd scarcely forgotten what she once told him herself: That her life was an open book to someone in his line of work. But that was precisely the problem. He'd resolved from the start to not go poking into such matters. That night – that nightmarish first date that ended in so many venomous accusations – his simple courtesy turned out to be the one saving grace that made their eventual reconciliation even possible. How could he go back on it now? How could he go digging up the truth about Bob, and not betray the trust he'd so narrowly built? But at the same time, how could he *not*? How could he hope to be any help to her when he had no idea what she was dealing with? How could he totter on the edge of losing everything and not even know *why*?

Just then, Civil Headquarters came into view.

Art sighed...

* * *

Following the directions from Muriel at the front desk, Art slowly shouldered his way into a dark little interrogation room. His eyes traced straight to the small pool of light on the table, under the lamp that hung from the ceiling, and there he was met by the bright gaze of Detective Jamison.

"Well hello, there, Mr. Mallard," Jamison said, standing and nodding. "You're just in tiiime. Everyone else should be arriving momentarily."

Sure enough, at very that moment, the door that had only just closed behind Art hit him in the back side...

"Step aside, plebians!" a familiar voice squawked into the room. "Heavy-duty, bleeding-edge medical equipment coming through! Those who bar the way will be run down!" Nokkaeru turned a dumbfounded pair of goggles up at Art. "Oh... Friend Mallard... I beg your pardon."

"Hey, Doc," Art replied. "Fancy meeting you here." His gaze wandered to the big, inscrutable black box she was toting on a cart. "What's the gizmo?"

"That, my lad, is what is known as an electrocardiogram!" a deep male voice chimed in, even as the head of another Heron craned into the room, from just behind the machine in the doorway. "It is a highly refined new instrument that records the impulses of the heart. Typically, the inputs are configured to monitor the P wave, QRS complex, and T wave, respectively, which are each magnified and etched along a paper feed by corresponding needles. However, we have been hard to work refitting this particular unit to monitor and graph three separate QRS readings, per the demands of this experiment." This mysterious, chipper Plague Doctor turned a questioning look at Nokkaeru. "Did I indeed hear you call him 'friend', my dear? How delightful! I would never have imagined you made any friends here!"

"It was only one!" Nokkaeru protested. "And only quite recently, under extreme duress. Do not attempt to turn this around on me! I don't recall giving you permission to speak in the first place."

"Of course; how thoughtless of me. I'm afraid I allowed the excitement of the occasion to carry me away. All the more so, in such company! To think I should chance to meet a friend of the fa..."

"...*Faculty*, yes," Nokkaeru cut him off. "This is Artimus Mallard, a detective who holds great distinction and acclaim here at the department. You are to shut your incontinent mouth whenever he is near."

"Understood," the doctor replied with a slight bow. "It is for me a most somber gaffe that I should fail to exchange proper introductions with this most highly esteemed Mr. Mallard, but if holding my peace will better serve our dear detective, then I shall say no more."

Nokkaeru shook her head. "Even your compliance is a torment. Never before has anyone vowed their silence with so many words."

"Well now, hang on a minute," Art stopped them up, scratching quizzically behind his ear. "Are you guys sure you're even in the right place? We've got this room for an investigation, not some kind of high-tech checkup."

"That was more or less my sentiment," Steward Jamison interjected. "We're about to employ a method that's tried and true in its own riight. I'm still not sure what all this scientific mumbo-jumbo adds to it."

"I suppose our mere presence here is yet another symptom of Forasius' foolhardy gregariousness," Nokkaeru admitted. "Even so, Mr. Jamison, if you wish for this song and dance of yours to carry any weight, you would do well to accept the tangible aspect we can provide it."

"Now... now..." Jamison replied, turning up defensive palms. "I'm not turning you away, y'know. But you might be surprised at the success this technique's enjoyed... even before anything like an 'electrocardiogram' ever came along."

"*Hey-hey-hey*," Art reasserted. "This really isn't the best day for a lotta double-talk. What's this 'special technique' we're all hinting around at?"

Before anyone could answer, the door bumped Art from behind again. He shuffled huffily out of the way, watching the surly, anxious, and neutral faces of Miloje, Alexei and Brocksmith usher into the room, respectively. And coming in behind them was a fellow Mesomela, jotting a raging stream of consciousness down on a tiny notepad with his great clawed fingers.

"Weeell! Here's the rest of our party now," Jamison commented. "Thanks for rounding 'em up, Elmer."

"Eh," the big fellow grunted at his notepad.

Jamison turned back to Art. "Art, perhaps you'll know Elmer Ehmstein? He's gonna be our point man for this investigation."

Art nodded. "We've met. Nice to see you again, Elmer."

"Eh," Elmer replied absently.

Art managed a slight grin. *Same ol' Elmer...*

"As for the rest of you, have a seat," Jamison said, waving over the interrogation table. "A...and don't mind the doctors running a bunch of wires down your shirts, now."

Captain Alexei's brow rose as he sat at the table. He looked just beside himself into Nokkaeru's ghastly visage...

"Please expose your midriff," she explained.

Shaking his head, Alexei nonetheless pulled up on the tails of his uniform with pursed lips, wincing as the first ice-cold sensor was glued to his abdomen. "Whatever this is, it strikes me as quite odd... even by urban standards."

"Hear, hear," Miloje concurred. "I don't know what it is you're playing at, Jamison. To be summoned to an interrogation room did not at first raise any alarms. Learning that we'd been summoned *collectively* rang a bit off-key. But to endure the prodding of these – ehm – *medical professionals*... it leaves me with a few pointed questions."

"Well, never mind about any of that," Jamison replied, as he began to orbit the men in the chairs. "Right now, there's only three acceptable questions I need each of you to consider..."

He leaned over the table, looking deep into the eyes of each policeman gathered roundabout. He studied, and stared... prickling impatient nerves, filling the room with the particularly noisome silence of a list left unlisted. The tension continued, until finally, Miloje could stand it no more...

"Well?" he demanded. "Out with it, man! What are the three questions?"

Jamison pointed first at his own eyes, before waving the same two fingers vaguely around the table. "Each of you," he intoned, "look at the man on your left. Ask yourself: Did he do it?" He allowed another brief interval to pass before continuing. "Now, turn to the man on your riight. Did *he* do it?" Again, he paused. "Last, and most important... look deep, deep down inside. And then, ask yourself: Did *I* do it?"

"Oh, this is silly," Miloje scoffed.

"N-now, you've gotta trust me on this," Jamison encouraged. "Just keep at it for a while. Search each other's expressions. Search yourselves. You're all seasoned investigators. You know what frayed nerves look like. Sweaty brow. Clenched jaw. Wide, shifty eyes. The face tells all. All we've gotta do is keep the pressure on. Whichever one of you has something to hide, he'll show it."

"And what's more, it will be recorded here!" Doctor Forasius added exuberantly. "Elevated heartrate is another sure sign of distress. One which we can reliably chart, review, and perhaps even be permitted to submit as evidence!"

"*Forasius*!" Nokkaeru crowed, low but forcefully. "You have spoken again in the presence of Mallard! I warn you... do not test his patience a third time. He is not so longsuffering as I am."

Forasius got no more than halfway through another syllable, caught himself, and fluttered all over before mustering a tremoring zipper motion around his beak. The herculean effort it took to restrain an audible apology nearly caused an implosion.

"Wait a second," Brocksmith interjected. "Are you really suggesting that we're going to sit here and stare each other down, and whoever's the first to get a little jumpy must've been the one who did it?"

"Well, it fits, doesn't it?" Jamison replied. "The way I see it, there's only *one* thing any of you should be concerned about hiding right now. And if you really mean to hide it, the mere attempt will be self-evident. So, I ask you: isn't that an unnerving thought in itself?"

"It certainly is..." Alexei breathed, staring off vacantly.

The other two turned an accusatory gaze on him.

"...That is... I mean... the reductive logic of it all," he was quick to explain. "Is it really fair to assume that criminal conspiracy is the only *possible* thing we would be concerned with keeping secret?"

Jamison stroked his long face. "I guess that depends. Do you *have* some other burning secret, Cap?"

"Well... no. I only meant that..." Alexei stammered, before grinding to a wide-eyed halt. "Oh, for goodness' sake, what *did* I mean?" he groaned.

"I think I understand," Brocksmith covered for him. "There's just too much room for false positives, when all it would take to incriminate one of us is if we get a little nervous... or even just *look* like we're nervous. What if we crack for no real reason at all?"

"Well, I don't know, Brocksmith," Jamison retorted. "Do people really do that? Crack up for no reason? Or, do you just want me to believe that could happen?"

Brocksmith's face drew back, and he dared say no more.

"Pulses are spiking," Nokkaeru reported. "Alexei and Brocksmith's readings both show promising elevation. The Deputy Constable's vitals remain..." she paused, leaning over the chart. "Wait. Now this is curious. Forasius? Take a close look at these R crests. What do you make of that? You are hereby granted momentary permission to speak."

"...I... I don't know," Forasius admitted, incredulous. "It is an abnormality beyond my reckoning."

Now, all eyes were trained on Miloje.

"Well, Mr. Deputy Constable?" Jamison spoke up. "No one's put you on the spot yet. But even so, it sounds like your heartbeat is the most extraordinary of them all. *You*... the fella that called this whole thing silly. Why do you suppose that is?"

Miloje returned each of their gazes in turn. His face was stone, but his eyes danced ever faster from one of them to the other. Finally, he cleared his throat. "I have a heart condition."

"...*Had*!" Nokkaeru corrected. "I still live in ire of your 'miraculous' recovery. How convenient that you would forget it now, when ordinarily, you are so quick to remind us."

"Many thanks for reminding *me*," Miloje quipped with a furrow of his mustache.

"Hm..." Jamison mused, continuing to pace around them as he gently rapped his chin with curled fingers. "Well... it seems we've all got off to a rocky start here. What say we start again... now that we know what we're up against? Would you like thaat?"

They all exchanged looks before slowly nodding their compliance.

Jamison grinned just before checking his watch. "Alright. We're on the clock, starting... *now*. Just remember: the three questions. Stare it out. Back and forth... forth and back. And *whatever you do*... don't get nervous."

"But of course..." Alexei half-snickered.

"No problem..." Brocksmith shrugged it off curtly.

"Simplicity itself..." Miloje added, straightening his tie.

The first few seconds oozed glacially along to the sound of needles scratching paper. Pointed looks were turned from left to right... from right to left. And three questions spun around in as many disquieted heads...

A minute stretched by. Two minutes. Brocksmith shifted in his seat. Alexei wiped the condensation out of his glasses. Miloje ran a handkerchief across his brow. And before long, every kind of fidgeting had been used up, twice over. Jamison, after checking his watch again, settled into a seat along the room's outer edge... pulling his hat down over his eyes... folding his arms. And though it was lost on the three policemen – locked in their mortal struggle not to show even the slightest trace of nervousness – it seemed to Art that Jamison might've dozed off, then... lulled away to pleasant dreams by the steadily intensifying rhythm of the electrocardiogram...

* * *

Scarcely more than a twenty-minute nap, two full hours of meticulous observation, and ten reams of graphing paper later, Steward Jamison finally took one more look at his watch before calling the whole experiment off...

"Say, Elmer?" he called over his shoulder very gently, startling all three of his subjects half out of their wits.

"Eh?" Elmer inquired attentively.

"I think these boys've had enough. Why don't you take 'em back out to the lobby, while Art and I confer?"

"Eh," Elmer agreed, nodding his compliance.

The three men all seemed to require a moment to sink into their chairs, audibly decompressing, before they could entertain any idea of martialing out. But at last, they drew themselves up on quaking limbs, seeming not to notice as the Herons ripped the sensors from their skin. Their huge, unblinking eyes were trained so deep into space that they could only have shuffled to the door by pure reflex...

"I'm... going to need a glass of water," Miloje muttered as they filed out. "Or perhaps a whole pitcher..."

When the door had finally closed behind them, Art found Jamison's searching glance on him. "Well? Whatdaya think, Art?"

Art shrugged. "This is your dog and pony show. If something was supposed ta stick out, I must've missed it. Seems like you turned all three of them to jelly."

Jamison nodded thoughtfully. "That was my thinking, too. Maybe it's too soon to tell, but... I'd almost have to say that any one of them could've done it."

Art couldn't hold back an eye roll. "We knew *that* much before we started."

"Hm... yes," Jamison reflected profoundly.

"Forgive me, O greatly revered Master Mallard," Doctor Forasius ventured, unable to contain himself. "In no wise do I mean to intrude upon your muse. But perhaps our data might prove revealing."

Art snapped his fingers. "Right! The heartbeat thingy! Maybe we've got something to go on yet. Thanks, Doc."

"You are so very welcome, Sir!"

Nokkaeru sighed her annoyance, but drew into the huddle just the same, as they all surrounded the enormous pile of chart paper.

"Alright," Jamison said a bit dubiously. "What're we looking at?"

Forasius looked to Nokkaeru, seeming to plead with his masked face. "I know I have already been quite bold, my dear. Shall I go on to explain? Or would you prefer to step in?"

"With regret, I admit your familiarity with this mechanism is the more extensive. You may continue. But in the name of all that is melancholy, you *will* constrain your excitable tendencies."

"Most assuredly!" he laughed. "Now, we have here the parallel readings of each man's QRS complex – the ventricular contraction cycle. As one might expect, increased frequency and amplitude are the earmarks of stress being put on the heart. So, we would be looking for exaggerated spikes, close together. Higher frequency; taller waveforms."

Art sifted through a long stretch of the chart. "All I see is page after page of the same huge zigzags," he deduced.

"Yes... our sample size was rather extensive," Forasius admitted.

"I'm sorry, but I still don't see how this helps us," Art went on. "They all look just as nervous on paper as they did sitting around the table."

"Ah, but you have yet to look as close as we have." Forasius held up a fold in the chart. "You see here? The topmost chart – the man Alexei's – recorded forty-two beats on this page. But the other two men recorded only forty apiece. That is a five-percent margin... and that holds across the majority of this chart."

Art cradled his chin. "So, Alexei was five percent more nervouser than the other two? Is that significant?"

Forasius seemed to shrug with one of his talons turned up. "That is a matter of some subjectivity. But I'm afraid it is the most significant anomaly we can demonstrate."

"I disrespectfully disagree," Nokkaeru challenged, pointing insistently at the bottom graph. "What of *that*, Forasius? What of Miloje's blunted R-spikes?!"

Forasius sighed. "I still don't know what to make of it. I can only think it must be a malfunction."

"No," she flatly stated. "We reconfigured this machine ourselves. We verified its proper functioning. It is *not* equipment failure. It must be something else."

"But what else could it be, my dear?"

"What else could what be?" Art questioned, squinting at the graph. The only difference he could find between Miloje's heartbeat and that of the other two was that, at the very height of each of the tallest spikes, the chart leveled off instead of continuing to a fine point. "You mean those little flat spots at the top?"

"Yes! Keenly observed, O Mallard!" Forasius confirmed.

"Evidently it's not supposed to do that?" he reasoned further.

"No. Suffice it to say, it is *decidedly* not supposed to do that. It is..." Forasius paused mid-muse. "It is almost as if a force of electrical inhibition is preventing Mr. Miloje's heart from overexerting itself."

"*Yes*..." Nokkaeru agreed darkly. "How very interesting..."

"Okay," Art interjected. "So Alexei has the fastest heartbeat, and Miloje has the freakiest heartbeat. Does that at least mean we can rule out Captain Brocksmith? He's apparently the only one who didn't stand out at all in Mr. Jamison's little triangle of nervousness."

"Now, now... there's two sides to every triangle," Jamison argued. "Just because Brocksmith had the most *normal* heartbeat, doesn't make him any less of an outlier. They all had *some* defining characteristic."

Art facepalmed. "I feel a whopper of a headache coming on."

Jamison patted him on the back. "I'm right there with you, Aart." He withdrew his hand, scratching his chin as his gaze wandered into the vast distance. "There's... there's just something about this case. Something screwy. I can't quite put my finger on it..."

"Maybe because we haven't learned a single thing yet," Art suggested.

"Hm, I suppose. Either way, I get the feeling this one's gonna stick with us both for years to come..."

"Well, brooding about it isn't going to get us anyplace. We tried it this way. It didn't work out. We need a new game plan."

Jamison cut his deep ruminations short to regard Art with a raised brow. "Any suggestions?"

"I say we follow the money. The Vigil must've done *something* to buy off their inside man. There's no better place to start than looking for giant piles of dough where they don't belong. We can audit their bank accounts; search their properties. Elementary investigation stuff."

"An interesting approach," Jamison replied, though he sounded rather ambivalent. "I never would've thought of it."

Art failed to restrain a sigh. "No, I suppose not."

Jamison checked his watch again. "Well, you're free to pursue the matter for the next hour and a haalf. After that, we'll turn our suspects loose to go about their business. You'll shadow Alexei; I'll shadow Brocksmith. But I'm gonna make a point to turn Miloje over to Elmer. After all, he's the craftiest. But Elmer never misses a thing."

"Works for me," Art acknowledged.

"We'll meet up again, same time tomorrow. And when we do, you and I are gonna hit the streets."

Art gave him a quizzical look. "The streets?"

"W'll sure, sure," Jamison assured him. "Never had a case once where I didn't learn something by hitting the streets. I promise, we won't come up empty handed again."

"If you say so."

Jamison grinned, crossing his arms. "Do I detect a hint of doubt, Mr. Mallard?"

Art turned up his palms. "Honestly, Mr. Jamison, I think we're just spinning our wheels here. I don't believe any of these guys did it. Do what we may, it's only going to be found out in the end that the mole was in the army all along."

Jamison nodded. "There may well be some truth to that. But at the same tiime, I think this thing's hitting closer to home than you're inclined to accept, Art."

"What makes you think so?"

"Well, I've got a nose, don't I?"

Art chuckled, immediately amused despite himself. "If you call that a nose. What about it?"

"Well, now... it's faint, and infrequent. And I'm used to something more like old stegosaur eggs. But mark my words... there's something rotten in the department." Jamison tapped one nostril. "You get your snout on straight, Art, and I'm convinced you'll smell it, too."

With that, the slim Human detective turned on his scarecrow legs and strode out of the interrogation room. Art could only shake his head as he was left alone with the doctors. Jamison was right about one thing... Art was still off his game. If there was any scent of duplicity or subterfuge on this case at all, he couldn't smell it. Ultimately, he was in the exact same fix as he was to start the day. How could he make himself *care*? Guys like Miloje, Alexei and even Brocksmith simply didn't do the sorts of things they were accused of doing. Art knew without question the truth of that would see itself through. So, what was the point? How was he ever going to wind himself up to the task ahead, when the threat he was supposed to help unmask felt so impossibly far away?

Chapter 9

What's that smell?

It started off as something less than a thought, but when his subconscious failed to explain the scent, Horus began to come around. His long, slow climb back to the waking world inspired more questions than it did answers. Inhaling, he couldn't place that toxically sweet aroma any further out than the rim of his nostrils. It was like a residue left behind from something even more potent that he'd smelled earlier. But *what*?

He convulsed violently at the thought, awakening a landslide of other alien sensations. Had he fallen asleep at home, or in his office? Nothing felt or smelled like either place. The very weight of his body seemed drawn in all the wrong directions. His eyes rushed into the fight to get his bearings... but no matter how he blinked, everything remained a dim and inscrutable haze. A more conscious attempt to bolt upright met with unyielding resistance. A second and third try – each more powerful than the last – utterly failed.

But it was on the third try that he heard a clear sound... a sharp, staccato, wood-on-wood scraping noise. And somehow, all the pieces started falling into place. There was no use bolting upright because he *was* upright... bound hand, foot, and torso to a wooden chair. He was conscious now of the tight rope, the hard seat, and the cloth fabric draped over his head. And the smell? It was just as his instincts suggested... a thin film left on the damp end of his snout, from when he must've been chloroformed...

Yes. That was it. There could be no question what was going on.

Fighting his reflex to further test the security of his restraints, Horus simply drew himself up as straight as they would allow. The mere act of raising his head sent him swimming for a few seconds, but he forced himself not to waver...

Time went on without a sound. Even so, Horus had no doubt he was being watched. Their silence was deliberate. He was supposed to wonder what would come next. And, honestly, he did. But rather than be frightened, he determined to be annoyed. Every time the Vigil made him the subject of their familiar repertoire of mind games, it felt like some sort of insult to his memory...

"Alright," Horus began, speaking as if to sigh. "Obviously you want me for something; looks like you got me. What is it now?"

There was no answer.

Horus rolled his eyes dramatically under the cloth bag, trying to ignore the way his tongue was drying up...

"Well? Do I have to play the guessing game? Don't give yourselves too much credit for being mysterious. I know you had eyes and ears in the courtroom. I'm sure by now you've had a lengthy account of my supposed mishandling of things. So, if you've already given up on me, then fine. Take me off the case, if that's what you want. Take me off to whatever extent you see fit. I'm not afraid."

"This is not about your performance in court, Horus."

There it was. The same old *voice*. And no matter how much Horus might've believed himself prepared to hear it again, it struck him dumb. It transfigured him across time and space, so that in an instant he was reduced once more to a mere boy, chafing under the tired wisdom of a man who wielded unchallengeable authority over him. And how he *hated* to feel that way again. How he despised to be weak and unsure at the merest utterance of the one man in all the world he truly reviled. *Why did it have to be him? Why should it* **still** *be him who spoke on their behalf?* With all the old Stentor's mastery of inspiring dark zeal in even the most unlikely of vessels, he should've – by this time – brought about the poetic justice of creating the monster that could've unseated him. But of course, that wouldn't be Horus' luck. They would *have* to still be one, and inseparable. The Vigil, and its *Voice*...

"Then... what?" Horus managed at length.

"We have devised a contingency plan," the Voice replied. "We recognize that little can be done for Brother Khonshu through due process, and our solution has been adjusted accordingly. His acquittal will no longer be required of you. Instead, the matter must be settled *out* of court."

"Out of court?" Horus repeated dubiously. "How?"

"It will be for you to broker a simple plea deal with District Attorney Blackforest. You will explain that we are in possession of something he greatly covets. Something of greater worth to him and his Czarina than the life of one of our agents. Tell him that we are willing to barter... one offender for another. He will deliver us Khonshu. And in return, we will give him the name of the traitor in his midst."

Horus needed a moment or two to process this. As with so many things the Voice had said over the years, the 'solution' being put forth sounded wise enough in the telling... but was ultimately founded on hollow presumptions. Horus rallied a bit. The old façade was already beginning to crack...

"You'll forgive me saying so, but that's ridiculous," he said. "The St. Argonsburg Police Department is stalwart to the last man. That goes double... *triple* for its Captains, and its Constable. Hamilton Blackforest would never go along with a deal like you propose. The traitor who sold you state secrets is in the *army*. He knows that... even if his duty dictates an internal investigation. You can't hope to deceive him."

Another long silence followed, this one reeking of judgment. Horus registered the faint sound of a long, labored breath...

"If you could only hear the folly bound up in your eternal obstinance. Do we not *know* who it is we bought secrets from? The traitor did not conceal his identity from us. We were quite sure of him and his intentions before we acted on his intelligence. We left no room for uncertainty. And we offer no lie of convenience." There was a rustling sound, so that Horus could see without seeing as the Voice leaned into his next point. "Would it surprise you, Horus, to learn that this denizen of your most virtuous police department reached out to *us*, seeing something of the marketability of his classified information? The bargain we struck was of *his* initiation... and I daresay it was indeed a bargain. Had he asked, we would have been prepared to pay much more for his abject duplicity."

As verbal boxing matches go, this was a swift punch in the gut. Even though he couldn't rationalize it, Horus knew at once that the Voice spoke the truth. "Who?" he asked, utterly dumbfounded. "Which... which one of them could've done this?"

He heard the Voice scoff. "Do you really expect us to trust you with the *whole* truth, Horus? Not before the release of Khonshu has been thoroughly negotiated."

"But I'm telling you, it *won't* be," Horus challenged. "Even if all you say is true... even if Hamilton were to *accept* it as true... he won't bargain with you. Not under any circumstances. He'll simply continue his investigation until he finds the answer for himself."

"Then he would surely fail!" the Voice answered, his frustration resonating throughout the apparently expansive room. "It is not within the scope of his vision to uncover the truth on his own. It is too well hidden. You know this man, Blackforest. You are well acquainted. You will find a way to explain his situation to him. That is your new mission."

Horus shook his bagged head. "My 'mission' hasn't changed at all. You appointed me to represent Khonshu... to redeem his life, if I could. I tell you, it can't be done this way. Like it or not, the only real hope remains to demonstrate reasonable doubt in court. I believe I can still do that. But if you want my help at all, then you're going to have to trust me... and let me do it my own way."

"Unacceptable! The Eighth Vigil has spoken its piece on the matter. You *will* strike our bargain with the District Attorney. Then you will signal us his consent by placing a single orchid on the mantle of the sitting room in the old Greyson Estate. We expect to find your callsign within the next 21 hours. Is that very clear?"

"I understand perfectly," Horus replied. "But what *you* fail to understand is that there will be no consent from the DA's office, whatever I tell him. Furthermore, it would be a mistake for me to even venture the proposition. Blackforest would only turn around and introduce our conversation as evidence in Khonshu's trial. I'm sorry... but you won't be finding any flowers on the Greyson mantle anytime soon."

Suddenly, Horus' restraints were cut. He was hoisted to his feet by the steely grip of two incredibly large and robust Vigilants. They issued him a few paces forward... roughly, so that he lost his balance, belayed entirely by their crushing grasp...

"I'm warning you, Horus," the Voice cautioned him. "Failure to comply with our demands will have consequences. You know this better than most."

"I do," he admitted. "And yet, I'm prepared to do my very best for Khonshu, despite all you can do to hinder me."

Horus heard a final huff. "Behold Horus Templar... ever willful, and defiant. But we will see who is the first to yield."

With an unspoken command, Horus' muzzle was wrapped tightly in a damp cloth over the sack, so that he nearly suffocated. What little air he got was saturated in that same odor from earlier, now intensely more potent. And before he could long debate whether he might asphyxiate first, he blacked out...

* * *

"Horus...?" he vaguely registered. "Horus...?" More distinctly the second time – or perhaps the third or fourth – he realized it was Deborah waking him. He wasted no more time rousing himself, sitting up bleary-eyed behind his desk. Blinking and scanning the office car in the dreary morning light, he was quickly assured that all was well. Even Deborah herself appeared unaccountably upbeat. But of course, she didn't know what had happened the night before. Horus cleared his throat before pasting on a grin, deciding at once that it was better if she didn't find out...

"Good morning," he said.

"Well, at least I won't have to wonder if you slept at all," she quipped. "I'm sorry to even wake you, but I knew you'd be more upset if I let you snooze the whole day away."

He checked his watch. "Goodness, yes. Time's a-wasting."

"First thing's first," Deborah interjected, producing a handful of envelopes before Horus could even attempt to bolt up. She set them on the desk in front of him. "Your morning mail."

Horus raised a brow, slowly reaching for the stack. "If you insist. Something interesting in here, I take it?" he asked as he paged through piece after piece of invisible junk mail. "Looks like just a lot of Dronehood surveys to me."

"Not *just* surveys. You have a hand-written letter in there from a particular Clerk you might remember. A one... *Mobipetroluck*."

Horus paused his search to give her a wide-eyed look. "*Lucky*? Well... that's wonderful! Poetic, even." Finally, he found the letter. He took just a few moments to cherish it... before setting it back on his desk. "Still, perhaps this isn't the best time for personal correspondence. But I'll be sure to read it soon... and let you know what he had to say."

She shrugged. "No need for that. I've already read it."

Horus only smiled. A pass had to be given to Secretaries who feloniously read their boss' mail... particularly if the Secretary in question happened to be the world's *best* Secretary. "Really? Well then, how is he?"

"He's doing very well," she assured him. "He's already returned from the Queens' War. It's back to business as usual."

Without a thought, Horus sank back in his chair, heaving a contented sigh. "It's times like this, that kind of news goes a long way," he said.

"Well, so long as you don't just take my word for it," she replied. "Do be sure to read that letter soon, Boss. My best summary wouldn't do it justice."

He nodded. "I will."

She frowned, just then, looking down at the floor. "I... also found a *parcel* waiting for you this morning. I hate to even bring it up, but you're bound to notice it sooner or later."

He winced. "What sort of parcel?"

She took a step back from the desk, leaned over, and retrieved a huge, heavy instrument from the ground at her feet, before carefully setting it on his desk. Horus' mouth left agape, his eyes swept over the familiar contours of the old hickory warhammer, carved in the magnified likeness of a judge's gavel...

"A gift from the Eighth Vigil, I take it?" she asked.

"Gift...?" he repeated absently. "More like another warning. About the most tasteless... the most irreverent..." He trailed off, not finding the words.

"What is it? A ceremonial weapon?"

"Ceremonial? Hardly," Horus laughed mirthlessly, taking the hammer in his hands. "This has been the Vigil's weapon of choice for generations. It may look like just a heavy-handed metaphor, but believe me, it's effective."

She stood in place for a beat, holding back another question. "Was this yours?"

"No. Mine's currently collecting barnacles somewhere at the bottom of the Farjean Sea. This was..." He stopped himself too late. "This was my father's."

Sympathy led her to take another brief moment of silence. "So he *was* a Vigilant, then? Not just an accessory... or a sympathizer?"

Horus winced, looking away both from her, and the hammer. "My father was a concert pianist. He was absolutely brilliant in his craft... even if he proved a bit timid and weak-willed in other areas of life. And he was the gentlest... the most unassuming soul I ever knew. But the Vigil had no use for a man like that. Or anyway, only *one* use. They simply couldn't rest until they ruined him." There was a dull, low thud as he let the hammer drop to the tabletop... hardly more than a half inch.

Deborah could only look on, uncomprehending. Of course, why would she understand? Horus was well aware of his own artful dodging. Apparently, it remained easier to talk about his personal sins than it was to be completely transparent about his father. But then again, what was the point of discussing it, anyway? The morning was fast escaping. Hadn't he wasted enough time already?

"Well, no matter," he sighed, standing up. "The Vigil's sent it's little message, and I've received it loud and clear. It doesn't change at all what we have to do today."

"Something might," she said. "Looks like we have a visitor."

Before Horus could reach over to take a proper look through his blinds, or long wonder what tipped Deborah off, there was a knock at his door. He went and opened it himself...

"Oh, hello, Art," he said, seeing who it was darkening his doorway. He could tell at once that Art's mood was a good match for the weather, which continued to brood, just as it had for the last few days. Horus didn't really have the time to offer personal counseling, and wasn't in the best of spirits for it himself at present. Nevertheless, his sympathy won over as they both stood silently at the threshold. "You nearly missed us, but why don't you come in for a moment?"

Art took his hat off, stepping in. "Thanks, Horus. A moment's about all I've got, too. I've still gotta make a stop at the bank before I meet back up with Detective Jamison."

"Steward Jamison?" Horus asked. "He's a bit of an odd duck, isn't he?"

"The word 'quack' has come to mind a time or two since I've met him," Art admitted, plopping down in a seat by the window. "Just as well he has the lead on this though. I haven't really been feeling it."

"No good news on the Blucille front, I take it?" Deborah asked.

"Decidedly not. She's upset, alright. But just try to get her to talk about it."

"*It's endemic,*" Deborah replied absently with a shake of her head. She looked aghast at Horus, covering her mouth too late. "Sorry."

"No, I'm sure I deserved that," Horus assured her. "Art," he went on, looking seriously at his friend. "Coming from a guilty-as-charged retentive personality, just remember that as frustrating as this is for you, Ms. Cordon is likely even more frustrated. I say, give her time. Don't force the confrontation... let her come to you when she's ready to explain herself. And if nothing else, trust that she'll eventually see the foolishness in the distance she's created between you. We're never more tempted to hold things back than in the hopes of protecting those we care about most."

The office car was filled with flabbergasted silence.

"...Wow..." Deborah breathed at length.

"What?" Horus said. His eyes darted nervously between the two of them. "Did I say something horribly wrong?"

"No..." Deborah replied, still in deep disbelief. "Actually... that was kind of incredible."

Art nodded slowly, unblinking. "Yeah. Borderline spooky-good."

Horus wasted no time smiling broadly. "Well, in that case, it seems I've outdone myself."

Art stood back up, sighing. "Yeah, but even the best pep-talks wear off quick. Yours was a gem, don't get me wrong. But I give it twenty minutes tops before I'm down in the dumps again." He flung out his arms, adjusting the fit of his suit jacket. "Anyway, this is more than a friendly visit. I brought a message from the department. Apparently Khonshu is adamant to speak with you as soon as possible. I guess he has his own ideas about how to move ahead with the case."

Reflexively, Horus scoffed. "Him, too?" Furtively, he read the questioning look on Deborah's face. "...I mean... we already have so much planning of our own to do for the next court day," he covered. "The last thing we need right now is to waste more time arguing with him."

Art shrugged. "He's *your* client. I guess you can ignore his request if you want to."

Horus ran a hand down the length of his head, hardly avoiding his sore eye. "No, I suppose that won't do. I'll see him right away."

"Alright," Art replied. "I'd tell them you're coming, only you'll probably get there before I..." He paused, blinking as he looked over Horus' shoulder. He extended a finger toward the back of the car. "What's that on your desk?"

Horus turned, having been diverted just enough to forget for a moment himself. "Oh..." he practically groaned, remembering. "It's a memento, courtesy of the Eighth Vigil of Aridos."

Art walked right past him, picking up the warhammer and admiring it like a boy who'd just been handed a giant lollipop. "Far out and nifty," he marveled. "Man, I've got like three or four weapon cabinets that this would look awesome in."

"By all means, take it," Horus said with a shrug. "It's no use to me. Just be careful who sees you with it."

"Sure will," Art replied, taking off his jacket, wrapping the business end of the hammer with it. "I'll just stow it in the back of the carriage for the day."

Deborah put her hands on her hips. "Three or four cabinets just lying around, waiting for a trophy warhammer to come along? Where in the world do you stash all this stuff, Art?"

"I'll never tell," he said, reaching for the door. "Good luck to you guys. Duty calls."

Horus got a grim feeling, suddenly connecting Art's duty with everything he'd just learned about the mole, and not really knowing what to do with the knowledge in the moment, besides offer a friendly word of caution. "Best of luck to *you*, Art. Keep your eyes peeled. Watch your back out there."

"Okeedoke," Art replied, taking one step out. "Wait a sec..." He froze and pivoted. "One more order of business before I go." He slowly walked up to Horus, before seizing him in a powerful bear-hug. "Thanks, Horus ol' buddy. And not just for the slick loot, if you catch my drift."

"Glad I could help," Horus grunted through the constriction.

Art withdrew, giving Horus a last slap on the shoulder before waving his last goodbye to Deborah and grinning his way out of the car. Deborah turned to Horus, wearing a grin of her own.

"Was all that really true, Boss? About you retentive people?"

He nodded. "Absolutely."

"Well then, I'd say you earned that thank-you."

"Don't you get any ideas about crushing me, too," he quipped, ushering them both to the door.

"I don't suppose you had any breakthroughs on the Nora Van Snoot front?" she inquired as Horus reached for the handle. "Maybe a muse while you slept?"

"If there was any muse then, it wasn't any real help," Horus replied, holding the door. "How about you? Any luck with Andrew Campbell?"

She coolly turned up a palm. "I may've found something."

Horus' eyes bugged. "Really?"

She nodded. "I'll tell you about it on the way."

* * *

"Well, Well. Look who actually decided to show his face," Khonshu sneered, standing and crossing his arms at the first sight of Horus.

"You asked for me, didn't you?" Horus fired back. "Couldn't we suspend the hostilities until after you've told me what your ludicrous plan is? There should be plenty of time for it then."

"I want to testify on my own behalf!" Khonshu came right out and explained. "But they say I need your permission to actually do that. I can't imagine why, unless they're just trying to hinder my one good chance."

"*Ha*! Well, fortunately for you, you *do* need my permission to testify. Which you certainly won't be getting. That's far and away the worst idea I've heard yet."

"Oh, really? Worse than letting all the witnesses make a fool of you? Worse than stipulating anything and everything the District Attorney asks?"

"Yes. Worse than all of that. You have no idea how deep a hole you'd dig yourself if you got up there and told a pack of lies."

"What lies!?" Khonshu balked. "I'm not even guilty of the crime they've accused me with!"

"Is that really the best you can do, Khonshu? Do you honestly believe that if you deny everything in a whiny enough voice, that'll clear you?"

"But it's true!" he insisted. "They can't stick me with sinking that stupid barge! I *didn't do it*!"

Horus actually took a moment to silently ponder this. Khonshu seemed... sincere. Not that that would help on the stand, of course. But maybe he was finally prepared to tell Horus the truth about what happened. Maybe...

"Alright."

Khonshu went blank. "*Alright*? What does *that* mean?"

"It means: alright. You didn't sink the ship. So why don't you tell me what you *were* doing?"

Khonshu's face remained inscrutable. "I was immigrating. I used to have a little law practice on the island of Magna Koepna. Then one day, some gang of revolutionaries came along and sacked my village." He stared off vacantly. "All that senseless death and mayhem. I... I couldn't bear to see it all again, knowing the Countess' army would be coming some day to reclaim the town. I fled for my life."

Horus could only shake his head. "You know, for a second, I thought we were getting somewhere. I thought you might entrust me with the truth. But instead, you lazily reached for the international gossip mill. I don't have time for you to try your phony stories out on me. And neither will Hamilton Blackforest."

"But the jury might," Khonshu argued with a shrug. "The point is: I've had enough of doing this your way, Horus. I've got a better shot with my worst lie than I do with you."

"And what do you think you'll do, when the District Attorney is the one directing the conversation – asking the questions? You had a law practice, did you? What if he asks the name of the village? Or the cases you've worked?"

"I'll make it up. Improv isn't hard. Who's going to know enough about rural Maenea to call my bluff?"

"Even supposing you don't *immediately* make a fool of yourself, his interrogation won't end there. He'll ask leading questions. Questions of allegiance."

"Like what? Why not give me some examples, so I'll be ready?"

Horus got an odd feeling, just then... a rogue hair that wanted to pick a whole new fight. To get right at the heart of the matter. To argue the crux of everything rotten about the Vigil, even in the likely case he'd be better off lecturing a wall. "How do you feel about Berlie Beirels, Khonshu?"

Khonshu's whole face convulsed. He took a moment to silently calm down before answering with a hollow grin. "Well, that's kind of a loaded question, isn't it? How do people *usually* feel about vainglorious monsters that stole and murdered for almost eight centuries?"

"Some people get over it," Horus replied. "Some people have noticed that the real architects of all those atrocities have been dead for thousands of years now. Some people see they only hurt themselves by holding onto ancient baggage."

"Or maybe some people are so chicken-livered that they'd forgive *anything* just to stay out of the fight."

"What fight do you mean? There's no formal war with the Berlie Beirels at present, excepting their own civil war. Are you a Tophthaeran national?"

"Ha! Not in a million years."

"Then I can't imagine what fight you're referring to. You belong to no country in any conflict with the Berile Beirels."

"And just whose fault is that!?"

"Why don't you tell me?"

"It's *theirs*!" Khonshu exclaimed. "Those heartless, spineless hellions took our homes – everything we ever built – and wasted it! Tore it all down, never to be remade! Splendors and wonders of an enlightened civilization that enriched the whole world with its law and justice. They made *ashes* of its ashes! They know nothing of beauty... only ruin. Reckless, purposeless destruction. I hate them! I *hate* them!"

Horus let a silence build. He joined his hands behind his back, leaning in. "So speaks the Vigilant."

Khonshu went to say something, but he could only pant as words escaped him.

Horus slowly turned to go. "We'll have no more talk of putting you on the stand, unless you're quite adamant to repeat this little meltdown in front of the whole court. Like it or not, you're still much better off in my hands."

"I'll never understand why Apep chose *you*."

Horus froze. A tremor ran up his spine. "I'd refrain from using that name, if I were you. I make it very unwise."

"Why? Just because we're in a police station? There're no ears in here but yours and mine."

Even more slowly, Horus turned back. "That still makes two ears where that name holds no honor."

Khonshu snickered. "You hate him. I guess I shouldn't wonder. It's sort of poetic, really. He's everything you should've been. But all the more, it begs the question: Why? Why would he choose you for this?"

"He makes mistakes, you know. Actually, he's quite given to them. The very ethos he lives by is an especially glaring blunder. I had to learn that the hard way."

Khonshu shrugged. "However you have to rationalize it. Cowards *excel* at rationalization. Maybe you can convince yourself of your own superior wisdom, but the rest of us know better. You're just afraid. Afraid to fight."

Horus shook his head. "It takes a special kind of courage to examine one's assumptions... to break away from them when they don't stand the test. Especially when it demands nothing less than starting over. I know it'll only sound like heresy to you... but sometimes, it really does take more courage *not* to fight." Horus nodded solemnly at Khonshu before beginning to back away. "Do me a favor and think about that."

To his own astonishment, Horus succeeded in leaving the cell without so much as a parting jab. There was only the quiet sound of his feet on the concrete, and Deborah's behind him, while she secretly engaged in scratching down one final, gargantuan note to herself. It read:

APEP???

Chapter 10

Art watched in a daze as smatterings of daylight burst through another day of heavy cloud cover. The dance of light through the city squares was just too sparse and fleeting to really improve the mood... it only served to remind him that the clouds were there. Every ray was choked out almost as soon as it escaped. In a moment of relative self-awareness, Art happened to remember back to his brief stopover at Horus' office car. He tried to recall Horus' bit of eloquence. Something about how some people zip their lips because deep down, they care... or whatever. But all Art could remember clearly was when he gave it twenty minutes tops before it wore off, which proved to be about right.

"Ya know, Art..." Steward Jamison said from the seat beside him, as their carriage meandered up and down the tiers of St. Argonsburg. He seemed to take a moment to consider his own words, few though they were. "You don't really mind that I call you, 'Art', do ya?"

Art shrugged. "Nah; it's fine." He searched Jamison appraisingly. "You... you want me to call you 'Stewy', or something?"

Jamison blanched. "Not if you can help it."

Art nodded, frankly relieved. "Alright."

"Art..." Jamison began again. "You'll forgive me sleuthing on a fellow sleuth, but I almost get the feeling that you're not in the best of spirits these days."

"What makes you say that?"

"Just subtle things... here and there. Like the way I just spent the last half-hour talking about the case, and all you did was frown out the window."

Art's ears perked. Not only was he surprised to learn this, but he was forced to realize that Detective Jamison had much more finely honed powers of observation than he expected. "Okay. You caught me red-handed. I've been kinda down and out lately."

Jamison pursed his lips. "Is it lady trouble?"

"Yeah."

"I thooought I recognized it," Jamison remarked with a nod, turning a thoughtful gaze back to the front of the coach. "Strangely enough, I can relate. Ever since I was a young man, I've had this peculiar interest in women."

"You don't say."

Jamison looked searchingly at him again. "Who's the special gal?"

Art sighed, not particularly favoring the notion of hashing out personal stuff with a relative stranger. But at this point, it was easier just to play along. "Blucille Cordon."

"Ah..." Jamison nodded exaggeratedly. "Ya know, I've worked with Blucille Cordon before. I can definitely see why you'd be so long in the face over her. She's smart... dismissive... almost completely aloof." He shook his head, a glisten in his eye. "Why, I'd tie a rope around a great big cheeseball if I could only meet a gal like that."

Art frowned. "That's just stupid. I mean, what would you even do with the cheeseball once you roped it?"

"Well... I'd let it get all old and smelly, see..." Jamison intoned mystically as his big hands set the scene. "I'd wait until the whole outside was all green and putrid. Then, I'd show it to my lady friend. And I'd... I'd carve a great big hunk out of it! Show her the innermost circle of cheese. And it'd still be all fresh, and fragrant, and delicious. And I'd tell her, 'Ya see? It's just like *you*. The real beauty's on the inside.'"

Art eyed him dubiously. "You talk too much, Pal."

"Yeah, I 'spose I do. But the main thing is, Art... you find someone like Ms. Cordon, you don't give her up. Let her have her space, but don't give her a moment's doubt that she's on your miind. Step up and take charge... but don't *ever* force the issue! Be a man of action. Allow *her* to take the initiative. Trust me: If you do all these things, Art, you'll never go wrong."

"If I could do all *that*, I could walk between the raindrops. No two of those suggestions even agreed."

Jamison nodded with a wily grin. "That's how I know I covered all the bases. There's bound to be good advice in there somewhere."

"Well, maybe we should just talk about the case now," Art proposed. "It seemed impossible a minute ago, but you actually found a way to put me in the mood for it."

"Right you are; back to business," Jamison agreed. "It's just like I've been saying... we're deadlocked. Half of me says it must be Captain Alexei. But another half of me says it's the Deputy Constable. And still another half is convinced it's Brocksmith."

"Three halves?" Art ran the numbers with great doubt. "That's 50% more halves than usual."

"Exactly. Nothing about this case adds up."

"Well now, tell me something, Mr. Jamison: In all that thirty-minute spiel I was tuning out, did you happen to ask me about the financial audit?"

Jamison's eyes bugged. "W...why no. Seems I forgot all about that."

"Okay then," Art replied, waxing hopeful. "Maybe I can give us something to work with. The folks at the bank *did* report an anomaly... an anonymous deposit recently made in Brocksmith's account! I mean, it was a relatively *small* deposit... but a shady, suspicious one nonetheless."

"Hm..." Jamison mused, stroking his face. "How much?"

"Three large."

Jamison's look was blank – questioning.

"Three thousand pence," Art explained.

The Human detective's eyebrow rose. "That's not so small, going by department wages..."

Art felt a pang of conflicted excitement. He regretted to point the finger at any one of their suspects... but after all, duty demanded it. And apparently, what he'd found was much more significant than he first realized. "Alright, then," he said evenly. "Does this mean we throw the book at him?"

Jamison waved it off. "No-no-no. We can't get ahead of ourselves, now."

Art hesitated. "But... I mean... we have a money trail. We have evidence."

"Never follow where the evidence leads you, unless you're planning to go a million other places, tooo," Jamison sagely expounded. "At the very least, let's suspend judgment until we've done what we came here to do."

Art looked around uncomprehendingly. "What *are* we doing? We've just been driving around aimlessly for gosh-knows how long. I'm not even sure where we are anymore."

"Then we're getting close," Jamison said. "If you really wanna hit the streets, you hafta get off the beaten path. Streets, after all, just aren't *streets* if you know them by heart, or by name. At that point they're no better than *roads*."

"You lost me," Art admitted. "In more ways than one. I hope we can even find our way back home when we're done here."

"Well, we'll worry about that later," Jamison reassured him, signaling the driver to pull over. "This looks like as good a spot as any. Whatdaya say we scope things out for a spell?"

* * *

The day grew warm... muggy. Naturally, the air would be stifling as the earth continued to wait for relief to pour down in sheets from the sky. But *still*, there wasn't so much as a drop of rain... though Art looked high and low for it. Sitting there, on a wide-open stoop of some fancy building or other, he could hardly think of anything else to do. Whatever they were actually there to 'scope out', Jamison had never said...

"Alright, I give up," Art finally said. "What are we looking for?"

"It's not so much what we're looking *for*, but what we're looking *into* that counts," Jamison explained, narrowed eyes and grim expression slowly scanning back and forth. He shook his head in contempt. "Can't you see it, Art? The black, inky void all around us?"

Art watched as a passing lady and her child caught his gaze, cheerfully waving at him. He waved back. "Nope; can't say as I do. Just a bunch of folks randomly coming and going."

"That's just the inky thing I'm talking about," Jamison explained, gesturing widely. "These are the *streets*, Art! The beating heart of the criminal element. The veins and arteries. The whole circulational system! This is where badness is borrn. Where it lives; where it walks around. This is where it would sleep... if crime ever slept."

Art made at least token effort to see what was in front of him in a new light... to follow along on Jamison's heart-of-darkness dive. He watched a sneering, scar-faced man set down a briefcase... to tie his shoe. He saw another man reach into his long, dark trench coat... to offer a friend a handkerchief. But mostly, the scene remained one big blur of generic men, women and children ambling all about, carefully obeying all traffic laws...

"I don't see any criminal element at work here, Mr. Jamison," he admitted. "I just see people."

Jamison's already serious face sunk into a half-frown. "Yeah, well, if I've noticed one thing about criminals in my day, it's that most of them are people." Art watched as Jamison's eyes soon fixed on a fellow passing them by. Ordinary – unassuming – oblivious in every respect, the man maintained an unbroken happy-go-lucky expression while Jamison tracked him with an immolating gaze. Finally, once the man had gone half a block further down the street, Jamison snapped his fingers. "There's our guuy," he said, whisking himself up on his long, swift legs. Blanching, Art flung himself into the chase...

"Hey, hey," he called to Jamison, straining to catch up. "I'm not sure I like where this is going. What're we doing now?"

"Getting at the heart, Mr. Mallard. We're getting at the heart."

"But... but this is crazy! You're just gonna run some guy down? We don't even know..."

"There's nothing to worry about," Jamison interjected. "Just watch and learn. I'll do the talking."

Art moved his mouth in protest, but nothing came out. Jamison had the lead on this case. Art could only follow... and hope that he wasn't about to charge headlong into a great big social gaffe. This hope was to be short-lived...

"Hey, you!" Jamison called after the man they were pursuing.

The man kept walking, at first, needing a couple seconds to even question whether the call was meant for him. Finally, he turned back. He managed no more than a single incredulous syllable before Jamison came right up and seized him by the collar. He wrangled him into a side alley before throwing him down into a pair of trashcans with a loud crash. Before the poor, unsuspecting guy could even collect himself, Jamison was on him again, gripping his shirt with his pale, shaky fists. Art could only watch dumbstruck from a few yards back as Jamison hauled the man up, fingers clenched so tightly that Art swore he could hear his knuckles rubbing together...

"Wha... what's going on?!" the man pleaded.

"Shut up!" Jamison slapped him one. "I'm the one asking the questions here, Bub. You give us the answers we want, we'll let you off with just a warning this time. Otherwise, we can have this out downtown... at the *station*. Is that what you want?!"

"W-wait! There's... there's been some mistake! I don't know what you think I'm mixed up in, b-but I'm just a carpenter! My name is Hans McAfee; I... I make wooden furniture..."

"I said *shut up*!" Jamison commanded with a fresh backhand. "Don't you think I know *exactly* who you are?" he asked, his voice quavering with rage. Teeth bared, and eyes bulging, his was the very face of horror. "Schembeckler Oligarch... otherwise known as Schemmy the Schnoz... the scummy slime of society, if ever I saw it. You're no carpenter. And I don't have to think... I *know*. You're mixed up in *everything*!"

"No!" Hans insisted, utterly terrified.

"You're a fink! One of the most notorious in all of St. Argonsburg!"

"No, no!"

"You're a dirty rotten *rat*!!"

"No, no, *no*!"

"Yes, yes, yes!" Jamison slapped him yet again, shaking him by the collar. "Now tell us the truth! Fess up! Or so help me...!"

"...Jamison!" Art called. "This... this is crazy! You're going too far. This guy doesn't even know what..."

"Wait!" Hans implored. "Wait. I'll... I'll tell you anything. Just, please... no more. No more..."

Art could only look on silently, unbelieving.

Jamison dropped the man, letting him sink back against the wall beside the toppled trashcans. "Now, that's more like it."

"What... what do you want to know?" Hans – or *Shemmy* – asked, panting for breath.

"I want the straight poop on the Eighth Vigil bombing," Jamison replied. "We need to find out who sold them the classified information on the barge. What can you tell us about that?"

"Well... for starters... that it went for a song," Shemmy said, keeping wary eyes on Jamison. He wiped his lip – checked for blood. "Rumor has it the intel fetched a measly 45 G's. But then, it's generally understood that the Vigil's hard up for cash. Whether it was because of that, or maybe they struck some kind of first-time buyer discount, I couldn't say. All I know is, given the parties involved, everyone was expecting a much bigger price tag."

"45 G's?" Art found himself questioning aloud. "Are you sure it wasn't even less? Like, maybe as low as 3 G's?"

"Ha!" Shemmy exclaimed. "Not a chance. No one sells out for 3. That's chump change."

"But we found three thousand pence on anonymous deposit in Captain Brocksmith's account. He's one of our top suspects. What are the odds that money would turn up mysteriously in the middle of our investigation?"

"Pretty good, when it's frameup money," Shemmy replied. "Even against a pittance like 45, 3 large is a small price to pay for a clean getaway. You're a detective, aren't you? Do the math for yourself. Don't be a patsy."

"Who framed Brocksmith, then?" Jamison demanded, an edge coming back into his voice. "Who was the real culprit? Was it his boss, the Deputy Constable? Was it Captain Alexei?"

"No!" Shemmy insisted. "It wasn't the Deputy Constable or his Captains! I know all about your investigation. You've been barking up all the wrong trees! Oh, you're in the right ballpark... I'll give you that. But you're only looking at the star players."

"Who *should* we be looking at, then?" Jamison pressed him. "The coach? Did Blackforest know something? Or, maybe the owner? The High Constable himself? Come on! It must've been someone higher up the SAPD food chain!"

Shemmy shook his head with fright. "Not higher. It... it was someone *lower. Much* lower. We're talking subterranean."

"But how could that be? How did someone further downstream get a holda that kind of information?"

Jamison got no swift answer. Instead, Shemmy drew himself into an even tighter defensive ball. "Look... I've already said too much. The man you're after runs in some pretty dark circles. The darkest this city's seen in..." He broke midsentence, at a loss for words. "I... I just can't. I can't say anymore."

Shemmy's sudden reticence didn't go over well with Jamison. He reached out and grabbed him again. "The Heck you can't, Buster. If you have a name, you'll give it up... or it's curtains for you. You hear me? *Curtains*!"

"Better than a pyre in the blackest depths," Shemmy replied, practically sobbing. "I'm sorry. Knowing what I know now, I don't dare to cross these people."

"So don't give us a name," Art suggested. "Just tell us how he got the intel. Can't you at least give us that much to go on?"

Shemmy shook his head again. "There's really no way to tell you the how without the who. They go hand in hand. Even to say that much... I'm really pushing my luck." He fixed his teary eyes on Jamison. A more pitiful look was never made. "Please... please let me go. I really can't say another word..."

Jamison turned him roughly, shoving him down the alley. "Alright... get lost! Scram! And don't let us catch you skulking around here again!"

"Tha...thank you..." Shemmy stuttered as he backed away. Then he turned, running full-clip into utter obscurity. "*Thank yooou*!" he called back as he flew.

Jamison sighed, hunkering down in the very spot where he'd cornered his quarry, seeming quite defeated. Feeling keyed up and exasperated himself, Art took out a pipe and soap bottle for the first time in a long time, letting a long string of bubbles waft in the breeze, before finally venturing the obvious question...

"So... now what?"

"I'm not suure," Jamison admitted, puzzling. "He confirmed the one thing my nose was telling me all along... that our mole is in the SAPD. But that's the long and short of what he did for us... besides throw out the only reasonable suspects we had to work with."

They brooded thoughtfully for a while, before Art suddenly scoffed. "You know, it's the craziest thing... I thought I knew all the top snitches in the city. I've never even heard of this 'Shemmy the Schnoz' character before..."

"No... you wouldn't have." Jamison rubbed the back of his neck. "I have a confession to make, Art. There *is* no Shemmy the Schnoz. I made all that up on the spot..."

Art was struck dumb yet again. "You... you made...?" was about all he could say. Finally, he groaned, tossing his arms before letting them fall limp. "That means this whole thing's been for nothing! All we did was scare some random guy into ad-libbing a buncha nonsense he hoped would satisfy us."

"No-no," Jamison contended, waving the idea away. "He was much too frightened to be anything less than completely honest with us. That's what makes this technique so effective."

"You and your *techniques,*" Art lamented, shaking his head. "But alright... let's allow that you produced a cosmic shift in the case ex nihilo. Do you really think Blackforest is going to let us turn the entire department inside-out on the testimony of one snitch... who isn't even *really* a snitch?"

"No... I don't suppose he would. His playbook's a little different than mine."

"Then what in the Undervoid are we supposed to do?"

"We'll figure something out," Jamison assured him. "I've still got a few tricks up my sleeve."

"Oh, boy." Art massaged the small of his head deeply. "I can't wait to see what we try next. A divining rod, maybe? Drawing straws? Or maybe something a bit more scientific? Phrenology? Graphology...?" Art paused, feeling a sudden rush of inspiration from his own wandering sarcasm. Maybe not so much pertaining to the case, as to something else still wrestling for the forefront of his mind. "Hey... wait a minute. Horus used that guy once. What was his name? Creevey! I... I wonder if..."

"Creevey's no good to us right now," Jamison mused a bit absently. "I'd already considered seeking his help, but he's otherwise detained. Guess he's been on loaner to the High Constable for the last few weeks. I don't know when he'll be back."

"Figures," Art huffed. "Just when I had half a mind to cut to the chase and find out what's been bothering her once and for all."

An interval of mutual study broke out between the two men. At length, Jamison broke the silence. "You mean... you wanted his help for your other problem? The Blucille Cordon thing?"

"Hey, don't judge," Art replied, making no bones about it. "If you knew what I was up against, you'd want answers, too. Anyway, it was just a thought. Apparently a useless one."

Jamison kept a steady gaze on him. "Thoughts are a dangerous thing, Art. I try to keep mine to a minimum. But if you learn nothing else from me, I'd urge you not to treat a problem like yours forensically."

Art sighed heavily. "I know. Or anyway, I *thought* I knew. I'm just not sure how much longer I can go on like this."

Jamison came over and patted Art on the shoulder. "I understaand. We all hit those lows in our personal lives. It can get pretty tough to shoot straight – to stay focused. But it's tiimes like these when I find it helpful to bear one thing in mind."

"What's that?"

"If I ever slack off, the Czarina will have my head in a basket."

Art grinned. "I gotta admit, that *does* help just a little. Thanks, Mr. Jamison."

"Don't mention it," Jamison affirmed him with a final pat. "Anyway, I think we'd better get back to Civil Headquarters."

"You go ahead to the carriage," Art said, holding out his bottle of pipe soap. "I'd like to polish this off real quick, if you don't mind."

Jamison nodded. "Alriight. Just don't be long."

Art silently returned the nod, reflexively refilling his pipe, wasting not a moment before falling back into deep thought. For the first time, he'd been forced to reckon with the fact that he was on a very serious caper. But even with that knowledge, he couldn't seem to keep from being distracted. What he needed was resolution... an end to one set of troubles so he could finally concentrate on the other. That graphologist – Dr. Creevey – could still give him that, quick and easy... if only he was around. Art watched his latest series of bubbles with a grimace. Deep down, he knew he was just making excuses to get the answers he wanted. Maybe it was for the best the Doc was out...

...But still, it probably wouldn't hurt to check once in a while, to see when he got back in...

Chapter 11

Horus had no trouble ignoring the scrape of silver on ceramic as he methodically shuffled his food around the plate. What proved more harrowing was the prattle of Guildencrantz and Rosenstern... though at least on this visit to *So This Is Food*, he was prepared for it. In fact, he'd come here at this late hour seeking them out...

"So, you got Ramesses to work with, huh?" *one* of them asked, prompting Horus to immediately regret that he hadn't thought to stop and get confirmation on which of them was which before making this call. He struggled to even remember where he'd left off in his deductions a few days ago. He had a feeling this one was... Guildencrantz? That felt right...

"Man, and we thought we were jealous before!" the other one – most likely Rosenstern – chimed in. "We've done a case or two with Ramesses... a couple of our very best jobs, for sure. That guy is a total pro!"

"He has an even better track record than we do!" Guildencrantz rejoined. But... wait? Guilden*crantz*? Was that right? It could just as easily be Guilden*stern*. Inside, Horus was shaking his head. He wasn't even sure of the names themselves anymore...

"Well, I suppose it's reassuring that the two of you haven't lost your enthusiasm for the case," Horus replied, still fully engaged in picking apart his meal. "As a matter of fact, I've come here seeking your help with it."

Guildencrantz and Rosenstern or Rosencrantz and Guildenstern donned eager looks. "Well, sure, Horus! Absolutely!"

"Anything you need, we've got it covered!"

"But go on – tell us! How can we help?"

"It's quite simple," Horus explained. "I only need you to show up in court in the morning, and stand on my cue. Perhaps rearrange some furniture too, if you're feeling especially helpful."

Their enthusiasm promptly flew away. "That's it?"

Horus shrugged "Yes." He took a moment from watching his silverware to eye them both with amusement. "Could it be you were hoping for something more? Like helping me sort out some forensics, or search for legal precedents?"

They suddenly looked a bit nauseous. "Well, no. Nothing at all like *that*."

"Perish the thought."

"Honestly, Horus, I guess we hoped you'd just turn the whole case over to us."

"It wouldn't be any trouble to button things up for you. We'd consider it an honor... and a privilege."

"Rosencrantz..." Horus responded reflexively. He blanched, looking back up from his food again. "Or... Guildenstern?" His jowls instantly bonded to the flanks of his snout. *Now,* he'd stepped in it. "Ehm..." he covered, searching their eyes for looming outrage. "I'm... I'm sorry," he said, forced to come clean. "Which of you is which again?"

The brothers turned a blank expression on each other. "Well, now... I'm not really sure," one of them admitted, at length.

"We've never actually discussed it," the other elaborated.

Horus grinned, holding in a great sigh of relief. "Well, whoever you are," he segued, returning to the work set before him on his plate, "I can only assure you again that my appointment to this case is far from enviable. Believe me, you're better off on the sidelines."

They both fairly huffed. "Whatever you say, Horus."

"Frankly, I can't imagine what makes you think so."

At just the right time, Horus found what he was looking for in all the shredded slop of food. "Not to be smug..." he said with a smug expression trained on the dinner table, "...but it could be I know a thing or two that you don't about my clientele." Making way with his knife, he used the fork to slide the object of his study out of the slurry and into plain sight, where his comrades could see it. They eyed it quizzically...

"What is that?"

"A little reminder of a passed deadline," Horus said. "Surely the first of many. The old 'sharp rock in the food' trick... courtesy of the Eighth Vigil of Aridos."

Horus took some big, vetted bites while the other two went on staring at the rock with notable discomfiture. *"Mmm,"* he said... and not in the appreciative way. He set down his silverware and took up the napkin instead. "Maybe if my old friends knew what the chefs themselves did to the food, they would've had no need to boobytrap it." He stood up, clapping a hand on one of their shoulders as he began to walk out. "I'll see you gentlemen bright and early."

* * *

"Well, here we go, sports fans," Judge Ramesses announced, executing an expert knuckle-crack before convening court with a stroke of his gavel. "Day Two of Khonshu vs. The State kicks off with the commencement of the defense's case. Everyone is chomping at the bit to see what kind of acrobatics Horus Templar has in store. Let's all hope it's a nose-dive face-plant routine." Ramesses trained his cool shades on Horus. "Take the mat, Mr. Defendo."

Horus stood, taking a brief look at his client. Khonshu had neither spoken nor made eye contact with him since being brought forward. He only stared moodily into nowhere, pitching a childish fit over yesterday's disagreement. Horus wished in the moment he could scold him like a child. The young man was facing a trial that boded his doom, and he went on doing so with no remorse. He wouldn't be bothered to consider for even a moment the gravity of his crimes, let alone the years of his life he'd devoted to reckless hate. He could only pout that he didn't get his way. He could only feel sorry for himself for having a lawyer that he supposed was selling him out. And here Horus was, about to take a major one-two punch at Blackforest's witnesses. It made him sick to do it. But he'd do it now, just the same...

"I call Nora Van Snoot to the stand."

"Now, Mrs. Van Snoot, you claimed in earlier testimony to have positively identified the defendant at the scene of the crime, just prior to its commission," Horus recounted. "I believe it's time to see how your powers of identification bear up when put to the test."

"Ah, yes," she scoffed. "You mean to suggest that we busybodies do not see the world so clearly over the ends of our noses?"

Horus found that old, bitter taste on the back of his tongue. "Well now, that would probably exceed the mandate of this examination, wouldn't it? Although, I admit, as a favored target of unwarranted disapproval, perhaps I wouldn't mind at that."

Van Snoot raised a brow, a strangely earnest question in her gaze. "And what would you deem 'unwarranted', Mr. Templar? Do you see yourself as quite above our reproach? You would hardly be the first. Every man's ways are right in his own eyes. For even what he does that he regrets, he will soon enough rationalize, if given the chance. What, then, is the outlook for a society where disapproval is absent? Will a man train himself to a higher standard, if no one is around to say that he might do better? Nay, but civilization consists in the courage of one fellow to say to another, 'you are making a blemish of yourself'. That is the great charge of all busybodydom. We are tasked to inspire self-examination where none would otherwise exist. To awaken people to the reality that they are all quite boorish clods. So now, I ask you, Sir... would you really prefer to see what the world would be like, if no one did what we do?"

Horus blinked, deeply and unexpectedly moved by Nora Van Snoot's impromptu lecture. Her message hit right on the mark. A man without a voice of dissention in his life was just liable to consider himself wrongly accused in *any* circumstance, no matter how squarely cornered he might be. Especially a man like Khonshu, who had likely spent his most formative years entrenched in an order that specialized in aligning its moral compass with whatever course it found itself on. As frustrated as Horus might be with his client, he was forced to lament the fact that the young man probably never had anyone in his life to so much as insinuate true values and virtues. The world suffered for want of more reliable mentors. Or, failing mentors, at least reliable critics. Horus amazed himself with his next thought. The world suffered for want of more Van Snoots. "No," he admitted, his voice hushed. "No... you're right. I can hardly imagine a more terrifying prospect than that."

Nora managed a bit of a smile that was somewhat less than purely smug, which only added to Horus' overall astonishment. It seemed the two of them had inadvertently reached a most unlikely understanding.

After a few moments of this strange impasse, Judge Ramesses clicked his gavel. "Hey, now," he cautioned. "The two of you were getting along so badly before. Don't go and spoil it now."

Horus shook himself from his relative daze. "Right... of course." He returned to his table, retrieving and scanning a transcript of the previous court day. "Mrs. Van Snoot, I remind the court that you based your identification of the defendant on what you summarily referred to as simply 'height and build'."

She nodded. "That is what I said, yes."

"You also admitted having trouble reckoning the distance from your vantage point to the suspects, is that correct?"

"Regrettably, that *is* correct."

Horus took another look at the transcript. "And when you described the scene, you referred to the suspects as, 'all crouched down and mischievous'."

She blinked tiredly. "Yes. Is there a point to all this rote repetition?"

"Certainly," Horus assured her. "I submit that if you can't be sure of distances, then we shouldn't consider you reliable in gauging height."

"Hmph," she replied. "There is an *appearance* of logic in that, I suppose. Even so, your submission is purely argumentative."

"By itself, yes," Horus agreed. "But as I said, this is a *test*." He turned and nodded at the gallery. On his cue, Rosencrantz and Guildenstern lifted themselves from their strategically-chosen seats, only to crouch down where they stood. Joining them was a third recruit – Wally Ferreter of Ferreter and Finkelstein – giving Nora Van Snoot a respectable battery of options...

"Now I ask you, Mrs. Van Snoot: Which of these three men most closely matches the height of the suspect you identified as the defendant?"

Nora's gaze darted across the courtroom... from side to side, front to back. One was crouched in the front row, the other near the back, the third in the middle, and each was many seats across from the other. Her busy eyes widened as she struggled to feel definite, or even confident, of her answer. "Well... well it's..."

"...Hard to be sure?" Horus interjected into her silence. "But perhaps they aren't crouched in quite the same way as you remember. Could that be the problem? Are they hunkered too low? Their arms spread too wide? You may certainly try to instruct them..."

"I'm... not sure that would..."

"And don't forget... you have the man you identified here as scale reference..."

"But for goodness' sake, how do you expect me to know how tall they are when...?" she demanded, catching herself in her own words.

"Go on," Horus coached her. "When, what?"

She hesitated to answer. "When none of them is upright."

The crowd murmured. Horus grinned. "Alright. Let us for a moment set aside the obvious implications this has on your testimony and oblige you with an easier test." He turned back out. "Would the three of you please stand up straight?"

They did as he told them.

"Now, which of these men is the right height?"

Her eyes went through a similar routine, before she tsked. "Well I hardly call this easier. The cascading of the room... the lateral distances. How do I even know these men are not all the same height? The *wrong* height, at that? Are you baiting me with a trick question?"

Horus was only the more pleased, turning to the court yet again. "Would the three men please come forward?"

Rosencrantz, Guildenstern and Ferreter all gathered in front of the stand, much to the amazement of Van Snoot, and the court at large...

"As I'm sure you can see now, you had a respectable range of options. These men range nearly a foot in height from shortest to tallest."

She shook her head. "Yes... I see that now. Though it is surely too late to redeem anything."

Judge Ramesses snapped his fingers in a flurry at the prosecution table. "Hamilton, old buddy," he called. "How's about a timely objection, eh?"

Blackforest frowned, offering a 'what-do-you-want-me-to-do-about-it?' shrug just as Nora spoke up on her own behalf...

"There is no use, your Honor. I fear I have been soundly impeached." She leveled a glower at Khonshu. "Make no mistake: I still believe this miscreant to be the very fellow I saw on the ship. But apart from that strongly-held belief... I seem to have nothing definite to offer the court."

Everyone – Horus very much included – needed a quiet moment to reflect on this remarkable admission. He spent it looking at Khonshu... basking in the flabbergasted expression that drew his client's entire face back. At last, it seemed he had the young man's attention. Horus could only hope that if the day in court continued to go his way, he might be able to do something with it...

Finally, he turned back and spoke. "Thank you very much for your honesty, Mrs. Van Snoot," he said cordially, before regarding his volunteers. "And thank you, gentlemen. You may return to your seats." He started for his own table as they began to disperse. "No further questions."

Ramesses looked pleadingly in Blackforest's direction again. "You're at least going to cross-examine her, right?"

Blackforest stood. "No, your Honor. Even without her positive identification, Mrs. Van Snoot maintains confidence in her assertion of the defendant's presence on the barge, prior to its destruction. I deem her strongly held suspicion more than plausible, given where we found the defendant *after* the bombing. And I am equally satisfied that her testimony still corroborates the remaining positive identification of Mr. Andrew Campbell."

"Then it is Mr. Campbell's identification that we will next debunk," Horus interjected. "I call him now to the stand..."

* * *

"Now, Mr. Campbell, before we begin, I have to hand it to you: Your part in this has certainly proven an interesting puzzle to piece together, all on its own."

"Well, thank you... I guess," Campbell replied, shifting in the seat he had once again labored to find.

Horus looked up at the judge. "Your Honor, the defense means to put on another demonstration, which will involve a bit of redecorating out here in front of the bench. In order to properly examine this witness, I will need to lay out some visual cues. I only hope this isn't too much of an imposition."

"*Egh*..." Judge Ramesses speculated dubiously. "I don't like where this is going. The last demonstration was bad enough."

"I'm afraid I must insist," Horus pressed him.

"Well, alright. If I could think of a legitimate reason to say no, it'd be a different story. But go ahead."

"Thank you." Horus turned and gave his volunteers their second cue. They promptly converged on the far side of the defense table – an independent section of it that was free to be repositioned. Deborah joined them in placing it perpendicular to the bench. Afterwards, Deborah took up station at the narrow end of the table, closest to the judge, while Rosencrantz and Guildenstern faced each other, each standing behind one of the long sides of the table.

"Now, what we have here is a recreation of the scene you described to the court, Mr. Campbell," Horus explained. "The table represents the diving equipment booth... Ms. Deborah is playing the part of the diving bell itself... and Mr. Rosencrantz and Mr. Guildenstern are standing in for the two men you saw striking the deal to rent the bell out." He gestured to the judge's bench. "Now, let us suppose that the front end of the bench represents the contour of the shoreline. Have we more or less faithfully presented the arrangement of all the pieces here?"

Campbell cleared his throat. "Yes, I suppose."

"Then here is where we begin to drive at the crux of the matter," Horus boded. "Of course, your scene revolves around two men... rent*er*, and rent*ee*."

"Well, naturally."

"I find it strange, then, that you... a mere bystander... were called to introduce this matter to the court. Supposing this scene played out as you say... with my client as the customer, and the unidentified second man as the vendor. Why has this other man not been found, and brought to give *his* account? Would that not have been best evidence?"

Blackforest stood to address both Horus and the court at large. "Regrettably, the vendor in question *couldn't* be found," he explained. "No one has come forward to claim the bell, nor have we audited any inventories that would seem to be missing one. It's our belief that the vendor wants to avoid being implicated as an accessory to the crime. Or, since he was also Mesomela, it's even possible that the merchant is an Eighth Vigil sympathizer himself."

"I see," Horus replied, returning to Campbell. "But then, what of the booth? Did you note which side the sign hung on?"

Campbell shook his head. "There was no sign... only wares on a table, with the bell off to the side. Snorkels, tongs... a magnet on a pole arm."

"And the register? What way did it face?"

"Not many small-time operations along the Harbor have *registers*, Mr. Templar," Campbell explained. "A dedicated shop might, but not a *booth*. Money changes pockets at the tables."

"And whose pockets did the money go to?"

"The vendor's, of course," the man in the beret scoffed. "No one pays out to have their equipment rented."

"You don't seem to quite grasp the question, Mr. Campbell," Horus contended. "Did you see my client pay for the bell, as you allege would have happened? Did you actually *witness* the money change hands?"

"Well... no. I wasn't paying that close attention to what was going on. There was nothing really suspicious in it, until I reflected on it the next day."

"Hm... how very interesting," Horus mused. "No sign... no register... no sight of the money. The bell... neutrally placed off to the side. There's not much to your story with which to orientate ourselves, Mr. Campbell. Except – of course – for the *seat*."

Campbell gulped. "The seat?"

"Yes. Surely, the vendor would be *seated* at his table. A long day of pawning the wares practically demands it."

"...I... I suppose..."

"So that's how you knew, then? Because the other man – the one Blackforest hasn't found – was the one *seated* at his table?"

Campbell fidgeted most uncomfortably. "Well, I'm... I'm afraid I don't..."

"Ah, but I'm forgetting about your condition," Horus interjected.

"My condition?" Campbell attempted to dodge innocently.

"Yes. The one you alluded to, last time in court." Horus reviewed his transcript with a crisp snap. "When called to the stand, you failed to sit. When confronted about it, you said, and I quote: 'What's a man with my condition supposed to think?' Are those your words, Mr. Campbell?"

"They... they are."

"Mr. Campbell, have you ever heard of an affliction known as Fowler's Macular Non-Attribution?"

The witness' eyes bugged. "Um... yes. It's... an exceptionally rare stigmatism..."

"*Why* have you heard of it?"

"Because..." Campbell grinned weakly, cornered. "Because I have it."

The whole gallery was abuzz again. Judge Ramesses was forced to calm them down...

"Very well," Horus pressed on, when the people had sufficiently settled. "Now, would you kindly explain to the court the symptoms of your condition?"

By now, Campbell was mopping his face with a handkerchief. "Uh... it... it affects the nerve centers that differentiate between certain... well... cues of posture."

"And, to what degree are you afflicted?"

"I, uh..." he began. "I have total non-attribution of upright and seated postures in both eyes. I honestly can't differentiate in the slightest between standing up and sitting down."

There were more hushed gasps and whispers.

"Really?" Horus persisted. "Then this booth – without sign or register – had two Mesomelae at it, just as we see here... and you were perfectly oblivious as to whether one or the other was sitting?"

"Yes."

"But the chair? Surely, you would remember where the chair was?"

"No, I'm afraid not. I... couldn't so much as see a chair if it was staring me straight in the face."

"So then, in truth, you had *no* way of knowing which man was operating the booth, and which was just visiting?"

"Objection!" Blackforest called out, amidst a surge of unrest in the courtroom. "Of all the incredible...!" he tried, though for all his outrage he couldn't seem to complete the thought. Horus only watched him, inviting him to continue. "I mean, *surely*, you don't expect anyone in their right mind to believe that all this time, we've been holding the dumb oaf who was running the *rental booth*?!"

"Why not... if neither witness can confirm otherwise?"

"But it's ludicrous! Why would the rental boy be found floating at the scene of the crime?!"

Horus shrugged. "Could be he was looking for his bell, when it wasn't returned on time."

"Returned on...!?!" Blackforest fumed, incoherent. But just then, Judge Ramesses arrested the situation with his gavel.

"Cool your jets, guys," he said. "Both of you," he reiterated, focusing on Blackforest. "Much as I'd like to stick the defense counsel with volunteering conclusions, the fact of the matter is, you haven't even come up with a real objection yet, Hamilton. So just... calm down and think. What have you got?"

Blackforest heaved big, dramatic breaths as he labored to return to room temperature. He looked at Horus, clever eyes prodding for a crack in his bluff. Finally, he spoke again, calm and collected. "The prosecution withdraws its objection, your Honor."

Horus grinned. "That's very gracious. The def..."

"I'm not finished," Blackforest interjected. "While it *is* regrettable to learn that this witness' testimony came with a 50% margin of error, the prosecution is confident that the jury will nevertheless retain the bigger picture. We know that this man Khonshu was at least *involved* in the deal to rent a diving bell recovered from the crime scene... where he himself was later found. Even allowing for Mr. Templar's... *vendor theory*... I think the odds are still very much in our favor. After all, there is no guarantee that the vendor would've known even the general whereabouts of his bell. A Vigilant who had been waylaid by his own act of sabotage, however, would logically be found at the site..."

Horus' brain was suddenly set aglow by Blackforest's little damage-control lecture. For the first time, he found himself deeply perplexed by the facts of the crime itself. A whole barge, blown to smithereens. Why would the Vigil have plotted something so bombastic and reckless in the first place? It would've been much more their style to simply sneak aboard and sabotage the cargo itself. Furthermore, how had the job gone so wrong that one of them only just made it out with his life? To be bombastic and reckless was a hard enough fit... but *sloppy*, too? That wasn't the Vigil at all...

...Then suddenly, Horus remembered: Khonshu claimed to be innocent of sinking the barge. Granted, he'd feigned total innocence to begin with.

But the fact that he'd stubbornly stuck to that specific point made Horus wonder. What besides the Vigil's plot could account for the explosion? What other variables could Blackforest have overlooked? What might he himself have overlooked?

"Your Honor," Horus interjected into Blackforest's ongoing interjection. "What if..." he found himself essentially musing out loud. "What if it could be proven that the Eighth Vigil did *not* destroy the Czarina's barge?"

The courtroom fell utterly silent.

"I'm sorry?" Ramesses ventured. "Come again?"

"It occurs to me, just now," Horus explained. "We've assumed from the first that the barge's destruction was a premeditated act of the Eighth Vigil of Aridos. But what has been done to prove it? We haven't examined the forensics of the crime at all. How does the prosecution posit that the barge was even destroyed? What explosive agent was used? How would they have smuggled enough of it aboard? The witness, Mrs. Van Snoot, mentioned nothing of the suspects being encumbered..."

Blackforest frowned as Horus' train of thought reached an abrupt intermission. "Is there a point to any of these questions, Horus?" he challenged. "The prosecution stipulates that we have no statement from the Vigil claiming responsibility for the attack. That's hardly surprising, if we have one of their operatives in custody. But they *have* taken credit for two other recent attacks on would-be mercenary transports, as we've shown. Three sunken vessels... three cancelled shipments to the Queens of the Berlie Beirels... the hated enemies of the Vigil. If that's not an MO, I don't know what is."

"But the other ships weren't blown to bits," Horus argued. "There are better ways of unfixing a ship... ways that don't rely on planting large quantities of explosives. Ways they've already employed reliably."

"Well, we can argue all we want about *how* they did it... and how they probably *should* have done it. What difference does it make?"

"It might make a great deal of difference, if we simply look into it."

Ramesses sighed. "Does this mean another whole round of examination?"

"Yes, I believe that will be quite necessary," Horus replied, with no thought in the moment as to the potential consequences of continuing the trial any longer.

"Well... alright," Ramesses agreed reluctantly. "We'll recess for another two days. You'll have to have all your ducks in a row by then." He rapped the bench with his gavel. "We're going into extra innings, people." He raised a brow at Blackforest. "Best two out of three better go our way."

As everyone began to quietly and dejectedly disperse, Horus looked back at Khonshu... and what he found immediately alarmed him. No longer astonished, the lad looked unabashedly, deviously pleased. Horus could feel his guts plunge. Today, he had done his best for the interests of his client, as he promised to do. Which meant, unfortunately, he'd given the brat exactly what he wanted...

* * *

"Here he is!" Khonshu exclaimed, a smile growing on his face as he watched Horus march to his cell. "The man of the hour! You came through today, Horus. I mean, you *really* came through! I still don't believe it! I just can't believe it!"

Horus reached the glass, folding his arms.

Khonshu's smile faded as he studied Horus' huffy countenance. "Oh, come on now, don't be like that. You pulled something off in there... it's frankly incredible. Can't we just agree to be happy about it?"

Horus made no sign.

Khonshu sighed. "Alright. What are we going to argue about this time?"

"Did you ever stop to think that if no one was here to confuse the issues for you, you'd only be getting exactly what you have coming?"

Khonshu frowned. "No. No I didn't. And I wouldn't. I already told you: I didn't sink that barge. And I actually thought you believed me for a second."

"Yes, well, I don't suppose you're finally prepared to tell me what *did* happen? So I have something to aim for with this hipshot forensic investigation I've just volunteered to put on?"

"The way you're acting right now? No. Not particularly."

"The way *I'm* acting?" Horus shook his head. "If you could only hear yourself."

"Horus, for the love of mutiny, *why* are you suddenly climbing on my back like this?" Khonshu demanded. "I... I *am* wrongly accused!"

"No, you're *not*."

"I didn't sink the stupid ship!"

"This isn't about the blasted ship!" Horus erupted. His outburst took everyone – including himself – by surprise. He looked down, disappointed with his own lack of self-control, but determined to go on all the same. "I

know – and *you* know – you're in this bind because you *were* there to destroy state property that day. You were there to commit criminal conspiracy with malice aforethought. Maybe you're completely comfortable with the idea of getting off on a technicality, but it's enough that you know: *I'm* not. Do you really expect me to share your excitement? To be happy with myself for having a fair chance of clearing a dangerous criminal of his wrongdoing?"

Khonshu folded his arms. "I call that pretty hypocritical, Horus. You've been where I've been... done what I've done... and you've never even served hard time for it. You think you can just shut the door behind you? That I don't deserve the second chance you got?"

"And what will you do with that 'second chance'... if not go crawling straight back to the Vigil?"

"You're darn right I'm going back," Khonshu huffed. "Not everyone shares your dysfunction, Horus. You seem to think of honor as some obscure thing you keep between you and yourself. Me, I honor my commitments. I honor the man you hate... for teaching me everything I know, and making something of me when I might've been nothing. Everything I've done, I've done for our cause. For our people. I can't be truly ashamed of that. Not even to save my life."

Horus let out a quavering breath, running his hand between his ears, down the length of his head. "Well... if you can't be made to see you're in the wrong, then I'm afraid there's no hope for you. Even if I save you this once. Even if I could save you a hundred times, it would do you no good."

Khonshu shrugged, grinning sarcastically. "What can I say, Horus? Sorry I'm not sorry. But that doesn't change what you have to do now."

"No," Horus quietly agreed. "No it doesn't." He turned and walked away.

Passing back into the corridors of the maximum-security area, Deborah rushed to catch up with him. "Horus," she began meekly. "I'm sorry that..."

"It's alright, Deborah... really," he assured her. "My client is guilty. It isn't the first time. At least there's work left to be done. Quite a lot of work now, in fact. I think it's best we simply set ourselves to it."

"Okay," she went along. "What do you need me to do?"

Horus had to give that some thought. He knew Sergeant Tarkinov had been in charge of investigating the scene of the wreck, supplying what forensic data Blackforest had to go on. His team had recovered the diving bell... analyzed fragments of the ship, even to the point of finding Mesomela claw marks on the rear hull. They'd evidently been impressively thorough, even in the shadow of the internal affairs investigation that currently eclipsed the whole SAPD...

That led Horus to another thought. The Vigil had given him some key insight into that very investigation... insight he should certainly share, in any good conscience. He still needed to tell Art what he knew... that the mole *was* someone in the department. And preferably, he'd have to do it with Deborah absent, lest she learn of his earlier abduction, and be inclined to fret needlessly...

"I'd like you to set up a meeting with Sergeant Tarkinov," he answered. "Find out if he was able to learn the cause of the explosion... press him for everything he knows about the recovered wreckage. I especially need to know if any remains were found."

"Remains?"

"Yes." Horus looked down at her. "Particularly, I'm interested in the presence or absence of *Human* remains."

"Why, pray tell?"

"I have a feeling the biggest variable of this whole equation is the military sergeant... Oregano. We know nothing of his fate except that it *appeared* he returned to the barge before it blew. But *why* do we know nothing more? A thorough sweep should've recovered... *something*... of him, if he perished. Either way, we need to know."

"And you want *me* to talk to Tarkinov about it?"

He nodded. "Yes."

"What does that leave you to do?"

"I'm planning to get caught up with our old friend, Art Mallard," he admitted.

She gave him a questioning look, followed by a dismissive shrug. "Well, suit yourself. But I feel like you're barking up the wrong tree, Boss. He's not exactly on the same investigation we are."

"But the two *are* intwined," Horus replied. "In any case, I'm sure at least one of us will find the meeting beneficial."

Chapter 12

Art stood outside by the dusty broom closets, scratching his head. This is where he vaguely remembered hearing that Dr. Milt Lias Creevey was being put up when they brought him onboard... when was it? A year or two ago by now. And here was his name, right on the door. Clearly, the man himself was still out. But by the look of things, one would think he hadn't been *in* for months. How long exactly had the High Constable been borrowing him for? Surely not *that* long. Art sighed. He was going to have to ask around...

Hardly had he begun to register the sound of small feet approaching as he turned to head back, when the very last person he wanted to catch him calling on Creevey suddenly appeared. He stood in place, shell-shocked, with only just enough presence of mind to hide the little hand-written note he'd brought with him...

"Blucille?" he said, involuntarily styling her name as a question.

"Art," she replied, with all the enthusiasm of a gloomy robot.

His eyes darted around for want of an ingenious excuse to be found down here. There was nothing really to see but the broom closets. Would she believe he was looking for a mop? "I, uh... I was just..."

"Dr. Creevey isn't in right now," she said. "Even if he was, you wouldn't find him here anymore. He's changed offices a few times."

"Ah. Okay."

Silence followed uncomfortably. Art felt many feelings... maybe none so strongly as wanting to avoid any discussion of *why* he was poking around in the basement for Creevey. Finally, it occurred to him to put the ball in her court. "So, what brings you here?"

"I... I had a message for you," she explained. "Seems that Templar's called for a meeting. He'd like to see you as soon as possible."

Another moment passed by without a sound, while Art tried to reckon why he should be getting this vaguely inconvenient news from her. "They sent *you* with a message like that? Isn't that more like Secretary business?"

She shrugged. "I guess... everyone just figured I'd be seeing you around anyway."

Now there was a painful irony. "Oh."

For a while, the two of them engaged themselves in awkwardly avoiding looking at each other. But after about the third random corner Art glanced into, he'd only just begun to consider cutting his miseries short with a wave and a 'well, bye,' when she beat him to the punch...

"So, what did you want to ask Creevey about?" she asked.

"Uh... nothing!" Art replied, as his aching heart suddenly leapt back into panic mode. "I mean, something, obviously, but you know... basically nothing."

"...Alright," she said.

Everything lurched to another agonizing halt. Even after apparently dodging the question he most dreaded with smooth subtlety, Art felt no relief. How had it come to this? Suddenly, they seemed to have become something worse than perfect strangers. It was too much to take. The pain was too sharp not to ask...

"Blucille... is this what we are now? Just two people who might bump into each other in the hall every once in a while?"

She shook her head emphatically. "No, Art. That's not what I want at all. You have to believe that. We can always still be friends. But... to hope for anything more, well... it was a mistake from the start. For both of us."

"But *why*?" he breathed. "Is it... is it because of Bob?"

He could see the question knocked the wind out of her. He hated himself for even asking. But what else could he do? He needed a reason. "No," she surprised him by answering, her eyes thoughtfully dancing in space. "Not really. Not in the way you think. There *is*... quite a lot of blame to go around, actually." She tried to train a steady gaze on him. "But if you have to blame someone, you really ought to blame me, Art. I've been impossibly selfish. I never should've let it get this far."

Art stared, uncomprehending. Even in answering, she hadn't answered. "I don't understand," he admitted.

She deflected to her timepiece. "I really don't have time to tell you," she laughed mirthlessly. "Lieutenant Huxley needs me."

"Will you?" he pressed her. "Will you ever find the time... to tell me?"

She only frowned, slowly stepping away into the shadows. "Creevey will be back soon. I have to go."

Art said nothing more. He only let her walk away, until the sound of her footsteps regressed into utter silence. He let himself collapse against the nearest broom closet door. The dream was over. It was over and he *still* didn't even know why. Once again, she'd given him no answers. Even the hope of *eventual* answers, she'd deliberately withheld...

...Darkly, though, he began to consider that she'd given him the next best thing. *Creevey*. Whether consciously or not, she'd endorsed his mission to get to the bottom of all this, with Creevey's help...

He knew, of course, how shifty it was for him to even think about it that way. But at this point, he was beside himself. He couldn't bear to go on without so much as a reason. He *would* continue to seek out Creevey, until they could finally sit down and hash the whole thing out. He *would*...

Reluctantly, his thoughts returned to present business. He checked his wristwatch. It wouldn't be long before he needed to resume watching Captain Alexei full-time. He groaned, only then remembering the whole reason he'd run into Blucille in the first place. Horus wanted to talk to him... pronto. But there was no time left for a detour like that before his babysitting duty was back on. He was just about to write Horus off for the day, when all at once – and without any great effort on his part – he thought of a workaround...

* * *

The office car was dark. Dark behind the drawn blinds... dark from the ruminating clouds that still hung over St. Argonsburg... dark with Horus' thoughts. His meeting with Art pending, and his own investigations entrusted to Deborah, he found himself sinking deeper and deeper under the gravity of what he'd learned about the mole, the more he considered it. Snatches of what he heard kept playing back in his mind...

***He** reached out to **us**. The bargain we struck was of his initiation... and I daresay it was indeed a bargain...*

Just then, one of his ears swiveled to meet a faint, distant sound. A sound he knew well. It was the door to Deborah's office car, being opened and shut. His pulse quickened. Could she be back already? How incredibly inconvenient...

He collected himself to investigate, quickly rising, opening his own door, and crossing the coupling. Almost too hastily, he threw open Deborah's door, only to find the mysterious visitor just in front of him. His face went blank, trying to make sense of her appearance...

"Greetings, Counselor," Dr. Nokkaeru began tiredly.

"Hello, Doctor," he replied, trying to imagine a reason for her to be here. "I, uh... don't suppose...?"

"Please, don't patronize me with feigned ignorance," she waved him off. "By now, the adept Art Mallard will have pieced the truth together, and relayed his findings to you... his inexplicably close and trusted friend. Well, I won't be the subject of any such intrigue! I would sooner confess the unthinkable. I'm afraid it *is* true, what you've heard. Forasius is my husband."

"He... your...?" Horus stammered, momentarily at a loss to even recall the person she was talking about. "Oh..." he said, remembering. "I see."

"Augh! Confound that man and his shrewd devices!" she growled, commencing to pace the floor. "Of course he could never have been content to leave well enough alone. For years, I've cultivated such a reputation of cold, misanthropic proficiency here as to be the envy of any true Imperial expatriate. He would then have to go and orchestrate this ridiculous *internship* behind my back, purely for my humiliation! The audacity of it! The impudence!"

Horus checked his pocket watch. "Pardon me, Doctor. I'm... sure you have every reason to be quite as upset as you seem to be. Unfortunately, I don't know how much help I can offer on such short notice. As it happens, I plan to be in private conference with Art any minute now." He stepped out of the way, gesturing for the door, a small grin tugging at the corner of his jowl. "I'm... afraid your business will just have to wait."

"*Indeed*?!" Nokkaeru scoffed, temporarily too frazzled to say more, as each of her exposed feathers bristled. "I condescend to admit a personal embarrassment on the same order of magnitude as that which I coaxed from you about your secretary... and what do I get for it? No sympathy... no astonishment. Not even a vindictive word of gloating! My darkest secret is revealed... and you presume straight away to show me the *door*!?"

"Sorry," Horus shrugged, choking back laughter with all his willpower. "There just... isn't time."

"Hey, Horus," Art said all of a sudden, leaning into the open doorway. "I, uh, got your message."

Horus was quick to indicate his arrival to the doctor. "You see?"

Nokkaeru groaned. "Oh, very well! But it's enough that you know: I'm sorely disappointed in you, Horus Templar. I thought we were better enemies than this." She met Art in the doorway. "You cannot imagine how you've stymied me this day, Mallard. But I will endeavour not to let it spoil our friendship."

"Alrighty," he replied, watching her leave in a huff. He turned to Horus. "What was that all about?"

"Apparently, she wanted to let me know she was married to that Doctor Forasius."

"Huh. Well, that's nice, I guess."

"Yes. Anyway, I'm glad to see you made it before the next circuit, Art. I've recently learned some very compromising information, and I've decided it's absolutely imperative to take you into the strictest confidence."

"Compromising, did you say?" another voice called into the office car. Just then, Captain Alexei peeked in. "For the ears of Mr. Mallard? Dear me! Could it be you've made a breakthrough in our case?"

Horus blanched. "You... you brought Captain Alexei?"

"Sure," Art explained. "I have to watch him for the rest of the day, so this was the only sensible thing to do. Hope you don't mind."

"Erm, well," Horus said, clearing his throat. "It'll make what I have to tell you somewhat more awkward, but I suppose that can't be helped. Why don't the two of you come in, since we're already here? The train will be departing very soon."

* * *

They were on their way within minutes, Deborah's office car gently rattling as they put on speed. Horus served both his guests a stemmed glass of juice, hoping it would take the edge off what he had to say. Finally, he sat down across from them...

"There's really no delicate way of putting this, so I'll be forthright," he explained, training his somber expression on the police captain. "I've been given strong indication from parties that shall remain anonymous... that the mole you have been searching for is indeed in the St. Argonsburg police department."

"I know," Art said. They both turned to him, surprised. "Or anyway, I kinda know. It's complicated."

"Creators save us," Alexei breathed. "Surely, it isn't so! Brocksmith... the Deputy Constable..." He stuck his nose up in the air, shaking his head. "No. Though you both agree, still I refuse to believe that either one of them would ever betray his duty!"

"It could still be *you*, Sirens," Art reminded him. "Don't think I haven't picked up on your zany behavior lately. It's a scientific fact: You were the most nervousest on that electrocardiogram test. And how about your wife?"

Alexei's eyes bugged. "My... my wife? Why, whatever about her?" he inquired weakly.

"Well, come on. I've been babysitting you around the clock for days, and you still haven't even introduced us. Every time she comes around, you just herd her right back out the door."

"Ah, yes, well... she's... very busy..."

"And how about the way you jump in front of the door to her study every time I walk down the hall? Even that time you were in the kitchen and had to clear twenty feet and two corners in a single bound? Even though the door is dead-bolted and covered in locks? Huh? Did you think I wouldn't notice that, either?"

"...I..."

"Alexei," Horus interjected, all steely eyes. "Do you mean to say, you never came forward? Even after you assured me you would?"

Alexei snickered nervously, kneading his hands into a sailor's knot. "You know how it is, Sir. Time just... gets away from us..."

"You've had since the Syzygy." He shook his head. "Really, Alexei. I'm quite disappointed."

"What're you talking about?" Art put back in. "What's the big secret?"

Horus shot Alexei another pointed look. "Tell him, Alexei. At least tell *him*. He can't protect you if he doesn't know."

"I... I don't..."

"Tell him. Or I will."

Alexei locked eyes with Art. He hesitated, but eventually shrugged with a squiggly smile. "My wife is a reporter."

"*Bleah*," Art commiserated, his tongue shooting from his mouth. "That's a hard rap, Buddy. But I get it now. I wouldn't advertise it either." Suddenly, a thought struck him, and he snapped his fingers. "Wait. But that could be it! Maybe *she's* the one who sold out! Did you tell her about the barge?"

"Dear me, no," he said. "Since we've been married, we've worked to establish certain ground rules. Particularly regarding classified information."

"But what if you let it slip – I don't know – just accidentally? Like, maybe you talked about it in your sleep."

"Impossible," Alexei answered confidently. "We police captains undergo rigorous anti-sleep-talk training."

"That doesn't fit anyway," Horus volunteered. "I was told in no uncertain terms that the one who sold the information belongs to the department itself."

"Yeah, I guess you're right," Art reluctantly agreed. "That's what we heard, too... among other things."

Horus considered Art thoughtfully. "Curious. When I called this meeting, I didn't imagine I'd only be corroborating things you've already learned. What else do you know?"

"Nothing surely. We didn't get our info from the most... uh... normal kind of snitch. And boy, was he a flighty one. Wouldn't dare give us a name. He only said..." Art looked at Alexei, apparently weighing whether or not to continue. "...He suggested the leak came from someone other than our suspects."

Horus scratched under his chin, absent in his thoughts. "*Very* curious. Perhaps that's what he meant when he said the truth wasn't within the scope of Hamilton's vision..."

Art regarded Horus with perplexity. "Who told *you* all this, exactly? Your source would hold more water than ours, I'm sure. Who was it? Was it your client?"

"Why, no," Horus replied, avoiding eye contact. This wasn't a question he particularly wanted to answer.

"Best not to ask, Art," Alexei said. "Even if it *was* his client, he wouldn't be at liberty to share that with us. We shouldn't press him."

"Now wait a minute... I'm telling you, this could be important," Art insisted. "Come on, Horus. If not Khonshu, then who?"

Horus' mouth hung open, as he deliberated how to answer...

SKREEEEEEEEEEEEEEE!

They all reached up and covered their ears as a horrible screeching sound rent the air, each man curling over as if struck in the gut by the sudden racket. Alexei's glass of juice tumbled from his hand and shattered on the floor. The screech wavered and warbled, so that for a second it seemed to weaken... only to go on grinding again, almost just as hard as before...

"What... what is that?" Art asked over the ear-splitting din.

Horus found himself immediately surprised by the question, knowing the answer instinctually. "The train... it's just the brakes of the train."

"But we aren't slowing down," Alexei observed. And oddly enough, he was right...

Horus willed his hands away from his ears, grimacing as he noted something else. The squeal of the brakes was not just ineffectual... it was localized. He slowly approached the back of Deborah's car to be sure. "It's... it's only coming from *my* car," he explained without a thought. He looked back at the mystified expressions on Art and Alexei's faces. But privately, he already had it pieced together...

"It's sabotage!" Art announced. "Someone musta known we were coming to visit you!" He got up and watched out the small porthole of the back window with dread-fascination. "Man, were we lucky we had this powwow in Deb's car instead. We could be hurtling to our death out there right now!"

"But how?" Alexei demanded. "How could *anyone* know? We threw this entire meeting together at the very last minute!"

"Well, it looks enough like a knee-jerk job," Art reported, keeping his eyes fixed out the window. "Horus' car's still hanging on for dear life! We mighta had time to jump to safety after all!"

"We wouldn't have needed to," Horus replied. "That car's not about to suddenly jettison. This isn't an attack. It's a warning."

They studied him. "How do you know that?" Art asked.

Horus frowned. One more question not to answer. It felt like one too many. "Oh, alright. I suppose it's my turn to explain myself..."

* * *

At last, the train pulled back into the station. Horus and company – bedraggled with shell-shocked expressions – ushered mechanically out of the train, if only to be away from it for a spell. The circuit had been by far the longest one they'd ever experienced. Constrained to schedule, the train hadn't made any stop long enough to affect proper maintenance to Horus' brakes. They'd endured the screech for the entire trip...

"Oh, sweet quietness," Art sighed.

"The sound is gone, yet my skin persists to crawl," Alexei lamented.

"I only hope Deborah doesn't notice the juice stain we left behind," Horus added. "I'd be at a loss to explain it."

They both looked over at him. "How do ya mean?" Art asked. "What's to stop you from telling her exactly what happened?"

Horus shook his head. "There's a reason she didn't sit in on this. I feared from the beginning I might have to explain the deal that the Vigil's trying to force on me. I can ride out their childish threats for a few more days. She doesn't need to know. I don't intend to add to her worries."

Alexei frowned. "You'll forgive me, Mr. Templar, Sir, but I call that rather hypocritical. If you are coming under these assaults, the department can take measures to protect you. Ms. Boulevard would have no need to worry."

"Perhaps," Horus retorted. "But with an unidentified Vigil collaborator in the SAPD, I wouldn't be so sure. Besides, the department has enough on its plate already. I know the Vigil's ways. I can handle them on my own."

Art and Alexei disagreed with their faces, even if they couldn't answer with their words. "Well, good luck with that, Horus," Art said at length. "Let us know if you change your mind." He turned a droopy look on the open road. "Let's stop at the market on the way back, Alexei. I'm fixing to blow through about 30 bottles of pipe soap once we get resettled. It's been a *day*."

"Indeed," Alexei assented as they began to shuffle onward. "I'm not one for the use of recreational soap myself, but I may yet take it up before the day is out..."

Even as Horus watched the men file slowly into the anonymity of the crowd, he saw Deborah emerge from it. He quickly spurred himself to go meet her. "Welcome back," he said, however he privately wished she'd been longer detained. "How was your meeting?"

She extended to him a big, voluminous document. "Here's the CSI report. Tarkinov had about enough time to hand it to me and run."

He absently paged through it. "Looks promising."

"Appearances can be deceiving. There's more pages there than there is information. Mortuary report's negative. No physical remains found... Mesomela, Human, or otherwise. Just a lot of dead fish and barnacles. No explosive compounds found either. The barge was unarmed, so they weren't even carrying gunpowder. No explanation for the explosion; no clues as to the fate of Sergeant Oregano. All we have is two open mysteries."

"Or two mysteries that solve each other," Horus suggested.

"I'm sure I don't know what you mean," Deborah replied, shaking her head. "Unless Art gave you some missing piece of the puzzle I can't fathom."

"Heh," Horus laughed nervously. "Not precisely. Our little parley was ultimately less enlightening than I hoped. Still, I have a theory."

"Care to share?"

"I'm not positive, but I think the magic cargo itself holds the key. We're going to need to talk to someone who peddles in the stuff next... confirm something I vaguely remember hearing once."

Deborah checked her timepiece. "The shops close soon. I think it'll have to wait until tomorrow."

"Well, perhaps we'll just ply the process of elimination on this report in the meantime," Horus proposed. "There may be something they overlooked. In any event, it never hurts to eliminate the impossible. We'll seek out some alchemists in the morning and compare notes."

"Alright," Deborah agreed, as they both began walking back to Horus' office. A few paces along, she turned a quizzical eyes up at him. "Don't look now, but I think the whole maintenance team is swarming your car, Boss."

"Erm, yes. It appears so."

She waited quietly for a moment. "Any idea why that is?"

He shrugged it off. "Just a little case of the squeaky wheel getting the grease."

Chapter 13

Art checked his wristwatch and sighed. He was in for half an hour more of watching Alexei saw logs in his nightcap. By now, light was peeking through the windows, just enough that Art could tell they were in for the umpteenth overcast day in a row. He shook his head. He felt so stuck... so hopelessly caught in his miserable little cycle. Just to hope for the rain to finally come and go didn't seem too much to ask. It was the one thing he should've been able to count on to clear up on its own. But no. The sky was going to be backed up forever...

Suddenly, Art's ear swiveled to meet a knock at the front door. Alexei – not resting soundly anyway – sat up in bed, rubbing baggy eyes. *"Haagh...* gracious," he yawned. "Was that a knock?"

"Yeah, I think so," Art answered.

Alexei threw on his spectacles, climbed into his slippers and led Art out to meet the caller. When he opened the door, it turned out to be a rather frantic-looking young policeman. "Ah, Cadet Buckhanon," Alexei greeted him. "What seems to be the matter?"

"You, eh, better throw a uniform over that nightgown and come with me, Captain," the cadet replied, rending his bobby. "We've been informed by Detective Jamison that he's prepared to close your case."

Alexei and Art exchanged faces of pure disbelief. "He *is*?" Alexei demanded. "Are you quite sure?"

"Well there's no mistaking what he said," Buckhanon assured him. "He's going to announce his findings at the top of the hour."

Alexei looked back at Art again, who threw his hands up. "Hey..." Art appealed, "...I'm just as surprised as you are."

"Very well," Alexei sighed, ambling back to his room to change. "I won't be a minute."

* * *

"Jamison!" Art called across the busy hall of the Civil HQ complex, running the senior detective down the moment he spied him. "We gotta talk."

"Oh! Hello, Art," Jamison greeted him with a lethargic smile. "How're we doing, this fine daay?"

"Groggy, irritable, and downright flabbergasted," Art admitted. "What's this all about? How could the investigation be over? Last I knew, we were all of nowhere."

"Exactly," Jamison said with a nod. He quickly checked his watch before he turned and gestured down the hall. "Walk with me, Art. We're on a tight schedule."

"To do what?" he asked, falling in step. "I mean, what's the master plan here? We can't really be *done*. Not unless you came across some major bombshells since the last time we checked in." He turned wide eyes on the spindly man, only just realizing that it was possible. "Wait. Did you?"

"Nope," Jamison assured him. "Haven't learned a thing since yesterday."

"Ehmstein?"

"Huh-uh. Not him either."

"Well, that wouldn't seem to leave us much. I know *I* didn't make any breakthroughs."

Jamison frowned sympathetically. "I heard you met with Horus Templar. Sounds like he wasn't much help?"

"He more or less confirmed what we already knew. The mole's in the SAPD. It's almost certainly not Miloje, Alexei or Brocksmith. But he had no names – no leads. Same as us."

"Perfect!" Jamison exclaimed. "Er well, granted, if he could've told us who the mole is, that would've been even more perfect. But it helps to have confirmation."

"Confirmation of *what*?" Art despaired. "That we don't know anything?"

"Yes... that's been my point all along. We're not getting anywhere. And we never will, so long as we have the wrong suspects. Think about it, Art. Probably the three best minds in the department are sitting on the sidelines, and there's no good reason for it. They could be leading this thing. They *should* be. It's up to us to see their way clear to it."

Art's jowls drew back tight. "I gotta admit, that actually makes sense." But then, he remembered the problem. "Here's the thing, though. We already talked about this. Blackforest isn't going to be the least bit impressed with your improvised informant technique."

"Yes, that's right."

"Horus' source would get us a lot farther. But you had no way of knowing that when you set this thing up." He looked Jamison up and down, expecting him to leap in with the operative question. But even at length, he didn't. "Don't you even want to know who Horus got the tip from?"

"Nah," Jamison replied. "For what we're about to do, there won't be the slightest call to cite sources."

"What *are* we about to do?"

Jamison grinned as he reached a pair of double-doors. "We're holding a press conference." He pushed through, and Art – after a moment's hesitation – obliged himself to follow...

* * *

"People, citizens, occupants and residents of St. Argonsburg," Jamison began, gripping the podium as he cast his eyes over an enormous mob of journalists. "As you know, I have been tasked with investigating these three men... Deputy Constable Miloje, Captain Alexei, and Captain Brocksmith," he recounted, indicating each man, "for treasonous intelligence brokering. The investigation has been both thorough, and arduous. And now, it is my duty to inform you that my team and I have arrived at our conclusion. We hereby find these three men... to be cleared of all suspicion."

The journalists pounced on this moment of revelation with an onslaught of questions. "Who did it, then?" one asked, managing to call over all the others. "Who actually sold the state secrets?"

Jamison shrugged, pursing his lips. "I really have no idea. I just know these guys didn't do it. That the real mole is still out there... at laarge, and extremely dangerous. He's got underworld connections like you wouldn't believe. And if we don't catch him quick, the cost could be unimaginable." He nodded solemnly. "That is all."

Art watched as Jamison nonchalantly moseyed back into Civil HQ, while everyone else was caught up in silent disbelief. He turned his eyes all over the gathered crowd, hoping to take a cue from anyone who might possibly have an idea what to do next. He quickly spotted Blackforest in the far back, which was about as easy as spotting a raging volcano on the horizon, and for essentially the same reasons. Art instantly decided it was better to turn tail and vamoose himself, rather than linger a moment longer in the courtyard...

* * *

Plunk... plunk... plunk-plunk... plooomph.

Young Horus groaned, turning up his little hands and staring at them with a disowning contempt. He'd been invited to play Sonata Al Dente in H Minor

– a tune he knew by heart, and apparently, one of the simplest. But no matter which key he struck – and he'd tried *every one*, black as well as white – he couldn't get the right sound to come out. Minutes on end, and he was still stuck on the first note. He wanted to blame the piano. He wanted to blame his tiny fingers. But finally, he had to assign the fault where it belonged. "I can't do it," he despaired as he threw his hands down, staring hopelessly at the keys beneath him. "I tried my best, but I just can't do it."

"No... you can't," a voice behind him replied gently. Horus kept his moping expression trained to the fore, making no sign to acknowledge the large form taking a seat beside him on the duet bench. "But, you know what? I couldn't do it either, when I started out."

Horus' ears folded back up straight. He turned, only just enough to see the familiar torso, whose head may as well have been in the clouds, the man next to him seemed so great and tall. "You couldn't?" he asked, in true disbelief.

"Goodness, no!" the voice above him laughed. "Not to save my life! I plunked and plinked just the way you did. I didn't have a clue what I was doing."

Horus shook his head. "You're just saying that to make me feel better. There isn't a song in the world you couldn't play. You're the best there is."

"Well, I don't know about that," he snickered nervously. "But here's the thing, Horus... the real lesson I wanted you to learn from this. The same lesson my instructor taught me, that first day, when he sat me down and told me to play Al Dente." He reached over and set a big hand on Horus' shoulder. "It doesn't matter who you are; you're not going to know what you're doing, at first. You start at zero and you work your way up. Let me tell you: It's a long road. It takes a lot of hard work and practice. A lot of humility. But learning to play the piano, well... it's just like life. No one starts out as a great piano player. No one starts out as a great *anything*. People aren't just born all they should be. They have to grow. They have to work at it. And they have to be willing to learn. To take instruction. To accept help when they can't cut it on their own. Do you understand, Horus?"

Horus looked up with a resolute smile. "I *want* to learn. I want you to teach me how to play just like you do."

He laughed and patted Horus on the head. "I'd *love* to do that! But you know, odds are, this won't be your calling in life. The world only needs so many concert pianists."

"Oh, I know," Horus replied, undeterred. "But I still want to learn. Won't you teach me anyway?"

"Hm..." he mused aloud, followed by a brief, thoughtful silence. "Well, I think I could show you a few things," he said, to Horus' elation. "Anyway, what kind of a life-lesson would this be, if I just left you clueless?" He set his hands on the keys. "First off, let me show you why you couldn't find the first note. It isn't any one key. You have to hit three at a time, like this..."

Horus watched and listened intently as he was introduced to *chords*... the first of many musical concepts to come that completely blew his mind. What his father made look so easy turned out to be unbelievably complex. He could never have figured it all out on his own. It would've been a mistake to even try...

KNOCK KNOCK

A rapping on his door awakened Horus in an instant. He'd dozed off again at his desk. He hadn't exactly been sleeping the best, of late. He stood right up, brushing aside the memory... expecting to find Deborah at the threshold. What he found instead was Art...

"Hey, Horus," Art said. "Hope you don't mind me dropping in again today."

"Not at all; come in," Horus invited him. He cast a look out the door, thinking Alexei would be in step, but the Captain was nowhere to be seen. "You, uh, seem to have lost your tail, Art. Where's Captain Alexei?"

"Back to work, I suppose," Art replied, plopping down in a seat, looking seriously at Horus. "There's been a big shakeup in the case. Jamison abruptly called it off this morning. Declared our guys clear of suspicion, apparently so they could get busy finding the real sellout."

Horus blanched. "That's... well..." he fumbled. "He... he didn't stake his findings purely on what *I* told you, I hope?"

Art shook his head. "Didn't even mention your source. Or *any* source. He just said we were done and walked away."

Horus shook his head. "I'm... I'm rather at a loss. Is Hamilton really going to allow that?"

Art shrugged. "Beats me. I wasn't about to stick around and find out." He looked furtively back and forth before leaning in to comment in a low voice. "Incidentally, I might be lying low for the next coupla days."

"Okay..." Horus replied, not at all sure that was the best idea. "But don't forget... I'm not exactly the safest company to keep these days. I've been giving my car a thorough once-over before every circuit, and I've had a good string of luck dodging flying vegetables of late. But even so, you'd do well to remember that my popularity is currently at an all-time low."

"Eh, good point. Maybe I'd be better off going completely underground. I've got a place, you know."

"I'm not sure I do," Horus admitted. "Honestly, Art, the more I think about it, the more I wonder if so much discretion is really in order. Granted, Detective Jamison's gone and done something... well... rather rash. I can see wanting to sidestep the fallout. But how do you plan to account for your disappearance, after things have blown over? You'll most likely end up in even more serious trouble, if it looks like you've shirked your duties."

"Oh, I'll be working... don't you worry about that," Art assured him. "I'll be looking for the answer to the case of the heartbroken heroine at the bottom of every bottle of juice I can get my hands on."

Horus frowned. "She still hasn't talked to you?"

He shook his head.

"Art... I know I was the one who advocated patience in the first place. But I didn't imagine then that she'd hold out this long. Maybe you *will* have to be the one to take the first step. To initiate the conversation."

"I *tried*, Horus. I tried. But she wouldn't talk. She copped out. She was *busy*. She'll *always* be busy..."

"Well, don't give up yet, Art," Horus assuaged him. "Every storm eventually passes."

Art looked deliberately out the window, into the drear. "Maybe not *every* storm. Maybe not the storm that never really comes to begin with."

Horus only watched him, unable to arrive at any further condolences.

"...Anyway, you're probably right about one thing," Art eventually sighed. "I suppose I oughta split here pretty soon and face whatever music Blackforest is drumming up." He checked his wristwatch. "Day's wearing on," he reported. Then suddenly, he shot a questioning glance at Horus. "Where's Debs?"

* * *

The little jaunt to the nearest alchemist proved to be a bit more of an ordeal than Deborah anticipated. To start with, both the shop attendant and the proprietor himself were a bit star-struck when they realized who she was, and went on to be a tad longwinded in saying so. But even after working through that, she couldn't altogether avoid an unsolicited series of politely injurious comments made about her boss, the now-infamous 'Lawyer to the Ship Blower-Upper'. A bit of groveling at her fame now and then was one thing... Deborah had long since become pretty well accustomed to it. Listening as ignorant criticisms were hurled at Horus did quite a lot more to test her patience. In the end, she wasn't quite as polite as she might've been, getting her answers about magic. She'd have to be forgiven for that.

Anyway, she had a timetable to stick to, and therefore another good reason to give them the quick brush-off. Rather than take the added time to double-back to her house and take her normal route, she resolved to cut through the backstreets that crisscrossed the outskirts of the commercial district. Being a careful study of the city's layout, and a long-time resident besides, she had no trouble finding a different way...

Without conscious expectation of finding such a detour restorative, she soon discovered the fresh surroundings pushed aside all memory of the unpleasantness at the shop. She passed many lively faces on both sides of fruit and vegetable stands, smelling newly-picked strawberries, tomatoes, and earthy rutabagas... all sorts of things she would never *dream* of eating, but that were nevertheless fragrant and whimsical. Even as she passed the last of the market stands and entered the back alleys between rows and columns of small, spartan residences, there were lots of upbeat people coming and going. It could only have helped that for the first time in several days, the light of the sky nearly shown through the very gloomy, very stationary front they'd been having...

But that was about the time a shadow of a different sort began to nip at the back of her mind. Realizing she ought to be a block over, she caught a black shape far behind her, out of the corner of her eye, just as she realigned herself with the next alley. There was nothing particular to alarm her... except the vague feeling that she'd already spied the same silhouette back there, the last time she course-corrected. And suddenly, that dangerous nuance between being merely headed in the same direction – and purposely *followed* – found itself in the forefront of her thoughts. She tried to shake it... to chalk it up to stress taking momentary steerage of her imagination. But then, she realized it would be a simple matter to test it. She could afford to go one block further over...

When she did, a cart passed her by, managing to divert her attention at just the wrong time as she was forced to weave around it. It took a bit of willpower, and more than one try, but she eventually snuck a glance back over her shoulder. Her eyes couldn't dart back to the fore fast enough. The black shape was still behind her... and it took the form of a big, strapping Mesomela...

Deborah composed herself, forcing every muscle to maintain her present speed and bearing. She took a breath... deep, but slow. She had her confirmation. Now was the time to *think*, not panic. She was still in broad daylight... or as close as they'd come in a very long time to it. She was still in public. Though as she looked around, those pleasant faces were quickly thinning out. She needed to get back to a main road. She nonchalantly veered down the first intersection she came to...

Or, anyway, she *would* have. Except that at that very moment, another large and strong Mesomela drew up alongside her from just around the corner, blocking her intended route of retreat, and forcing her back into the straightaway. All she could think to do was try the other way at the next crossing. But just as she went for it, the same thing happened. A third grim figure – as formidable as the other two – cut off her only other escape. She could only continue ahead, sending furtive glances left and right – right and left – at her silent, ominous shepherds on both sides, all the while sensing the one in back was gaining.

They went about five more blocks, before finally, she resorted to her only remaining recourse. "So..." she began, "...where are we all headed?"

"Don't worry, Miss," one of them answered. "We're just here to see you back to your office."

"The city isn't safe, these days," another piped up. "Dangerous vigilantes afoot, they say."

"I... I don't particularly want an escort," she said. "Thank you just the same."

"We insist," the third stranger replied.

And with nothing more said, they continued down the street...

* * *

"Now, calm down a second, Horus," Art said, forming a barrier to the car door with cautioning hands. "Stop and think. We can't just run out into the big city and expect to make everything better. We need a plan."

"How could I have been so blind?" Horus despaired, hardly conscious of Art, even as he began to physically restrain him. "This is what they do! I made it clear that *I* wasn't going to be intimidated. Why couldn't I see that would put her next in line?!"

"Horus, stop!" Art insisted, as he progressed from restraining to wrestling. "You've gotta think this through! Charging out there to find her is pointless!"

"What else can I do?! I can't just sit idly by and do nothing!"

"I think that's *exactly* what you should do!" Art challenged. "Stay here and wait for her. Be here in case she comes back. It could be a false alarm. But even if it's not, we need to be *smart*, not gung-ho. Let me go report this to the police. If they're holding her somewhere, you'll never find her on your own."

"But I *have to*, Art! This is *my* fault! I... I have to make it right somehow..."

"What you need to do is calm down," Art assuaged him, using a gentle voice as they went on tussling. "She'll be alright, Horus. I know she will. They didn't hurt you; they won't hurt her. They'll only try to scare her, the way they did you."

"I don't intend to give them the satisfaction! I won't..." Horus stopped as his sharp eyes caught something in the window. He watched breathlessly as Deborah appeared in the bustle of commuters outside the car. Her pace was a little brisk and her expression notably focused. Yet there she was, apparently none the worse for wear than if she knew she was running a little behind...

But just before Horus could begin to feel truly, overwhelmingly relieved, he spied one or two other faces he knew... *Vigil* faces... and his insides congealed all over again. It was only a fleeting glimpse, as each of them veered away from a wide escort pattern and dispersed, disappearing into the crowd. For Horus' part, he *let* them disappear. He couldn't so much as fix a coherent curse on them for all their dishonor, swept-up as he was in the devastation of his own, towering arrogance. All that mattered now was attending to Deborah...

"Let me go," Horus said.

"Nothin' doin', Horus," Art replied, shaking his head. "I'm not about to..."

"She's *here*, Art!" Horus explained.

Art immediately surrendered, but Horus had only enough time to meet Deborah in the doorway. His heart and body froze as he watched her calmly shut the door behind her. She looked up at him, pasting on a thin façade of normalcy with a weak grin. Slowly, he reached out to her, taking her by the shoulders. "Deborah..." he said, a lump forming in his throat.

Her grin cracked momentarily, a flash of resignation in her eyes. Clearly, she wasn't going to be able to sweep the whole matter of her unwanted followers under the rug. Horus already knew. "Horus," she began calmly. "I'm fine," she said, even as she began to tremble. "I'm... I'm just f... I'm..."

He didn't let her try for another word. He wrapped her in a tight embrace.

"...Oh, alright..." she went on at length, a quaver in her voice. "So maybe they spooked me just a little."

"Oh, Deborah. How can I ever...?" Horus choked. "This is my fault. It's all my fault."

"I... I just don't understand," she lamented. "You're already handling their case. You're doing everything they wanted."

"But I'm not," Horus admitted. "They've been strongarming me into a plea deal. I didn't want you to know. I didn't want you to worry." He shook his head over the top of hers, the two of them still locked together. "Every time. *Every* time I hold something back, I convince myself I'm protecting you. Well, I certainly didn't..." His words escaped him again. "Deborah, I'm sorry. I'm so sorry."

Art could only sink dejectedly against the wall, feeling powerless to articulate anything meaningful. What could he say in a moment like this? Deborah was shaken up, and Horus... Horus might never forgive himself. Art didn't know what to do for any of it. Making light of the situation... doling out idle threats against those honorless Vigilants... offering clunky expressions of sympathy... it all struck the wrong chord. It all fell short. But they were his friends. He had to do *something*...

Suddenly, it dawned on him... a real way he could help. He didn't like it much, at first. But after a little shouldering through a thin hedge of selfishness, he piped up...

"Hey, uh, guys," he began, unsure. "Not ta butt in or anything, but... well, I just had this thought."

They both looked over at him. "What is it, Art?" Deborah asked.

"Well, there's this place, see..." he explained. "A secret place I know about. A place you guys could hide out until this whole thing blows over."

They silently considered this for a moment. "You don't mean *your* secret place, do you?" Horus asked, in disbelief.

Art scratched his head, folding his ears back. "Kinda. Yeah."

Horus drew back enough to consider Deborah's reaction. "What do you think?"

She rallied another slight grin. "What do I think? I think it's not every day Art Mallard offers to show off his secret place. We better take him up on it."

* * *

Horus shot another glance over his shoulder, into the gathering dusk, as they wove through the cobblestone jungle of St. Argonsburg. The three of them had just hopped their train after it pulled out of the station on the evening run. It was a rather dramatic gambit to be sure their goings went unnoticed, perhaps, but there was no sense taking any chances. Having been too shortsighted to spare Deborah from the Vigil's intimidation tactics, Horus was filled with deep apprehension for the first time in this entire misadventure. Fortunately, the streets were growing barren as the night approached. The uproar from Jamison's inconclusive investigation had spread by this time; the ubiquitous odor of doubt in the air revealed that much. Only those who had to were venturing out. But every face Horus came across was a cypher he couldn't read. He knew the Vigil had retained its *old* informants, but that didn't preclude them from signing-on *new* ones as well. He had no way of knowing. All he could do was watch. Watch for any sign of being watched...

"Hey, Boss..." he heard Deborah say from just beside him. "Don't take this the wrong way. I do appreciate the gesture. I just hope you know: I'm not going to suddenly evaporate if you let go of me."

Horus looked down, surprised. Apparently, he still had an arm around her. "You'll understand if I'm not in a hurry to take that chance," he replied. "I'm... still reeling to think how careless I've been. If only I hadn't been so recklessly defiant. I made this out to be strictly between me and... well, *him*. I signed you on for dangers you weren't even aware of. I don't know how I ever got it in my head that I was taking all the risk."

"That's just how you think, Horus. You're always trying to shoulder everything yourself."

He regarded her with pained eyes. He made a brief, stuttering attempt to answer for himself, but she stopped him...

"Now, don't misunderstand me. I'm not angry with you. I'm not even particularly disappointed. But, well... we're a *team*, Horus. And a team has to be able to trust one another. So... if I've ever done anything to make you feel like you *can't* trust me... if you don't think I'd gladly help shoulder your burdens... then I'm sorry."

"Please, Deborah... don't you go and apologize to *me*," Horus implored her. "The fault is mine. All of it. I... I promise to be more honest with you from now on. More forthright." He swallowed hard. "Ask me anything. Anything at all. And I'll answer... here and now."

She looked up at him. "Did you read your letter from Mo yet?"

He winced. Of all the questions he tried to steel himself to answer, this one hadn't sprung to mind. "The letter? Is that really your question?"

She nodded seriously. "Yes."

"Well... no," he replied, studying her. "I'm afraid I haven't yet."

"That's too bad," she said.

"Yes... I suppose it is. I especially regret it now. I'm sure I've already let you down enough for one day."

"No chance you grabbed it on the way out?"

He shook his head. "I've had other things on my mind. This little getaway, for one." He checked their surroundings again. "It'll all be for nothing, if we can't come and go unnoticed."

"You let me worry about that," Art put in, slowing to match their speed. "If I know one thing, it's disappearing. You guys are in good hands."

Deborah nodded at him. "I'm grateful, Art."

"Sure thing, Debs," he replied, giving her a thumbs-up. "Wouldn't want your face showing up on a milk carton now, would I?"

She grinned a wry grin. "Or better yet... a *cereal box*."

Horus sighed. "It's still too soon for any jokes like that. Are we getting close, Art?"

"Not hardly," Art answered, springing back to his lead a few paces ahead of them. "We've got a long ways to go yet..."

* * *

Their collective worries eased as the city and all its eyes eventually began to regress, with Art leading them ever further into the cover of night, and the wide-open anonymity of a strange old desolation. With their keen low-light vision, any tag-alongs they might've amassed in the city proper would have been easy to spot out here, where they were the only creatures left prowling about on two feet. But as they came to the end of a wide clearing and reached a few long rows of great, desiccating warehouses, Art went the extra mile by performing a few double-backs, just to be extra sure. In fact, Horus was about ready to appeal Art's thoroughness in the interest of retaining any earthly idea how to keep his bearings, when finally, Art pointed far ahead, beyond the tightly-clustered old buildings to one standing by its lonesome near a bend in a disused rail track...

"That's the place," he said. "The old Ecre Point Warehouse. One of the first to go up in this area."

"And one of the first to cave-in, it would seem," Horus remarked, noting a significant deficiency in the roof.

"Yeah," Art agreed. "But ya see, that's the beauty of it. Out of all the abandoned warehouses I could find, this was definitely the dumpiest. It's the ultimate camouflage for a chic mancave."

"It certainly could've fooled me," Horus admitted with a nod. Ecre Point was indeed a harrowing sight. What little remained of their exodus to it passed in a breathless unease. Sentinel crows flapped and cawed angrily at them for disturbing their haunt. The churn and moan of a distant train echoed off the crumbling walls. Even Art appeared cautious about opening the rusty door, as if what was left of the place might come crashing down on them if he gave it too much shoulder. Naturally, the hinges made a point of gracing his efforts with an eerie creak, before they all slowly ventured in...

To Horus' surprise, the view from inside was no improvement. Actually, with so much of the building compromised, it was a lot like still being *outside*, if not even spookier.

"Goodness... Art..." Deborah gasped at the darkness, covering her muzzle. "Is this... is this the warehouse where you were taken by the Digit Cults?"

"Nah," he assured her. "They just had the same idea as me. I've had this place since long before all that. The one you're thinking of is miles from here." He looked around with a grim expression. "I gotta admit, though... coming here gave me the willies for quite a while afterwards. Still does, a little bit."

"I can't imagine," Horus said, doubling down on his disbelief. "I have to say... this isn't at all what I pictured when I thought about your secret stash."

"Ditto," Deborah nodded her agreement. "Landslides of frivolous junk, sure... but not bricks and broken glass. Art, this isn't camouflaged as a dump. It *is* a dump."

"Don't write the place off just yet," Art replied, before waving them onwards. "Wait 'til you see the basement."

* * *

CLICK

With the mere flip of a small switch on the wall, a world of total darkness in the bowels of urban decay transformed instantaneously to a surreal little dimension of pure, sophisticated fashion sense. Blinding in its initial intensity, Art's hidden penthouse was above all striking for its stark, spotless white walls, so evenly lit that they almost seemed to have their own luminance. But even after their eyes adjusted, the scheme of monochrome prevailed triumphantly everywhere they looked, with both furnishings and decorations being sparse and stygian. Horus was forced to admit... it was probably the greatest tribute to the simple aesthetic of ivory and ebony that he'd ever laid eyes on...

"Wow," Deborah summed it up.

"Nice, eh?" Art asked.

"Nice? Art... this... this is even less what I pictured than the entropy upstairs. It's so... so *clean*. *Orderly*. Subtle, yet tasteful. How any bachelor could ever pull it off, I'll never understand."

"I'm frankly just as astonished," Horus agreed. "You had us thinking this was where you hoarded piles of expensive knickknacks. This place is ritzy, to be sure. I can clearly see the *expensive*. But where are the *knickknacks*?"

"Mostly stuffed in closets in the back," Art explained. "Honestly, I'm a little hurt you guys thought I'd have such a weak handle on the high-rolling lifestyle. If you're gonna be urbane, you need to understand the value of negative space."

"Spoken like a true fashionista," Deborah remarked, absently letting her gaze wander over those select trinkets which Art had chosen to put on display. There was a chaise lounge of black, buttoned-down leather, resting on twisted silver legs. Farther back was a bar whose unusual doors came to a point at the top – white-sided with a shiny, dark board and knobs. A sleek little display shelf shown off a bizarre but nonetheless swanky sculpture of a melty-looking clock. And off to the right, she found a grand piano of lustrous onyx. Her eyes lingered there the longest, watching Horus seat himself on the bench, while he studied the keyboard solemnly...

"Art..." he began at length. "This is a priceless Steinwyk. It's like... it's just like..." He looked questioningly back at his friend. "What on earth would possess you to buy one of these?"

Art shrugged. "Just seemed to complete the ensemble. Pianos are a staple of classiness. I gathered from the price tag that I was getting a good one. Why do you ask? Was I wrong?"

"No..." Horus answered in a low voice. "No you weren't, Art. You chose the very best."

For a while, he just sat there, overshadowing those keys... drawn across the wide gamut of all they once were to him, and all they'd come to be. A son's ingenuous aspiration – a father's legacy. Broken dreams, squandered purpose. Harmony, and joy. And ultimately, tragedy. He looked away, only for his glance to fall on the old, hickory weapon in the display case directly across from him. *How poetic*, he thought. *How apropos...*

Quietly, Deborah sat herself on the bench next to him. "You want to talk about it?" she asked gently.

"I'm certain I'd be darned if I didn't talk about it *now*, after everything that's happened," he replied, without so much as a hint of playful sarcasm. He commenced to look right through the piano, down at his hands as they wrang each other out. "He had one just like this, of course. My father. Not that he ever could've afforded one on a concert pianist's wages. But the finest tools have a way of ending up in the deftest hands, just the same. I can still remember the look on his face the day the Double Flat Philharmonic had one of these delivered to our parlor. They earnestly felt that the best should have the best. Because that's who he was. Who he was obviously meant to be." He fixed a look of remorse on Deborah. "I wish you could have met him. The *real* him."

"Horus..." she said, reaching out to his hands with one of her own. "Would you forgive me if I ask you a very direct question?"

He nodded. "Of course. You already have my permission."

"Your father. Did... did he really die? Or, well... is he just dead... to *you*?"

Horus blinked. He slowly grinned, despite himself, shaking his head. "Well now, that *is* the shrewd question to ask, isn't it? Yes. He really is dead."

"Then who is Apep?"

Now, Horus went *really* blank. If the first question impressed him, the second fairly astonished. He didn't answer, at first. For as much as he tried, he *couldn't...*

"You understand why I have to wonder, I hope," Deborah went on, compelled by the silence. "If your father was dead, then how did Khonshu note the family resemblance? I noticed the effect the name has on you. You don't take its use lightly. It's a name you seem to hate... perhaps as much as you cherish the memory of your father... the *real* man he was. I honestly don't know how else to make all the pieces fit together. All I can think to do is put it to you again. Can you honestly tell me that Apep is *not* your father? The man your father is *now*?"

Finally, Horus came back around to being rather amazed with Deborah... even if she'd ultimately drawn the wrong conclusion. "Remarkable," he said. "I can see it now. This is just my way of dealing with my father's descent into darkness... to pretend that he's dead, and to hate the man who goes by his name as an imposter. Is that it?"

She shrugged. "Near as I can figure. Yes."

"As if I could regret my secretive tendencies any more in a single day," he remarked. "I know I've been evasive on the subject of my father. It appears all I've accomplished is to make him look like more of a villain than he ever truly was. You're close to the mark, Deborah... very close. Apep and I... we *are* related. But he's not my father. He was my father's brother."

Deborah's eyes searched his as she began recalculating everything she'd come to believe about his inner conflict. "Ah... I see." She rubbed the back of her neck. "I guess I'd forgotten there was an uncle involved in all this. Well, that changes things. It's not quite the story of paternal betrayal I thought it was."

"No. It's decidedly more *fraternal* in nature." He pivoted slightly toward her. "But Deborah, it isn't enough to understand Apep as merely a part of the family. My earliest memories of him are still mythic. He was like the wind, coming and going as he chose – unexpectedly, enigmatically. But when he was with us, everything revolved around him. Making him feel welcome, and secure. Endeavoring to meet his every expectation. He was, a *sage* – unmatched in his wisdom – unquestionable in his judgments. That's how my father saw him. And that's how I learned to see him, too."

"He was the one who convinced your father to join the Vigil?" she asked.

"Yes. It took a lot of insistence – years of wearing him down. Much as my father hated to deny him anything, he wasn't quickly sold on the idea of upending our entire lives to join Uncle Apep's cause. Deep-seated hate for Berlie Beireldom simply didn't foster in him. All the emphatic appeals to vengeance in the world failed to move him. But given enough time, Apep always finds the means to his ends. When everything else fell short, the steady application of guilt and shame eventually won out. Because of course, father's reticence to join made him a 'coward'. The day finally came when he couldn't stand to bring so much disgrace to the family any longer. To his brother, most especially."

"And you... you just got brought along for the ride, huh?"

He frowned. "To a point. It's true: I wasn't yet old enough to be on my own when father answered the call. I'm sure that was a deadline Apep always intended to meet... to bring in two new Vigilants for the price of one. But honestly, Deborah, I can't place all the blame on the Vigil, or even Apep himself, for my time there. I knew well enough what I was doing. I even made an honest effort to adopt their views as my own." He looked off silently into space for a moment. "Lately... I've been forced to reckon with the fact that I may have gone over to them entirely, if not for my father. He was both my reason for joining up... and, ultimately, my reason for leaving."

She shifted in her seat uncomfortably. "What's the rest of the story? What was the end of it all? Will you tell me?"

He nodded. "We both adjusted to the Vigil as best we could. It was easier for me. I was younger. The frustrations of starting life over were channeled into my training. It was a rigorous curriculum, mentally and physically. I came to enjoy the challenge. But for Father, I got the feeling it was all he could do to grin and bear it. He tried to apply himself. He rode out the ideology they foisted on him, and even managed to regurgitate it at need. But his heart was never fully in it. I could see that. We all could. But none of us more than Uncle Apep. His brother's half-heartedness was a constant embarrassment to him... one he wasn't going to suffer forever. Father proved to be even more of a thorn in his side after he'd joined than before."

Deborah hesitated to ask, but Horus left her little choice. "What did he do about it?"

"What he always does," he replied with a shrug. "He'd invested too much in Father not to get something out of him. So, he simply dreamt up a new way he could serve the Vigil. Apep's every bit as cunning as he is unscrupulous. He... he reasoned that even a lukewarm acolyte could win outstanding honor as..." Horus faltered. For all his practiced powers of calm, rational discourse, he came abruptly to words too horrible to say...

"...What?" Deborah coached him.

"...As a martyr."

Deborah was aghast. "He... sacrificed his own brother?"

"Sent him on a suicide mission... yes. He had the audacity to call it a 'bold raid'. Well, it was bold, alright. Father didn't have a chance. But of course, he was never meant to succeed. He was of far greater use as a fallen hero."

He blinked at her with moist eyes. "Apep achieved everything he set out to, Deborah. Or anyway, almost everything. He used my father up. He tarnished his memory forever. And me... he taught me something I pray he never got through to Father. He taught me how to *hate*. The only problem was, I didn't wind up hating the right people." He turned his gaze back on the Steinwyk. "How can a man's legacy be so completely destroyed, Deborah? How can he be given such an obvious destiny... only to have it stripped from him and replaced with something so contrary... so false?"

She reached up and gently rubbed his shoulder. "Who can say? It's a world of Will and Purpose, Horus. Your father's legacy... it's a messy one. But no one's is ever quite what it should be."

"But it's so much worse than that," he despaired. "How can I remember who he was, without also remembering what Apep made him out to be?"

"I think..." she began. "I think you need to find it in yourself to embrace the whole picture. Learn to see the value in all of it. Your father *did* save you from a life wasted on the Vigil, Horus. You had the memory of the good man he was to pattern yourself after. But perhaps most of all, you had his tragic end to force you to see the road you were on – to make a change before it was too late for you, too. Everything he was – the good, and the bad – all of it worked together to make you who you are today. A man who's decent; a man who chose a better path than the one set in front of him. And if your father was only here to see that, I know he would be proud of you."

Horus closed his eyes a moment, feeling a weight he'd carried for many years suddenly ease in a way he never imagined it could. Deborah was right. His father's sacrifice had achieved *one* end that Horus knew he would've celebrated. It had redeemed his *son*...

"How is it you always seem to know exactly the right thing to say?" Horus asked, a warm smile forcing rogue tears from his eyes.

She looked down – rather bashfully, it seemed. "I guess I just think of it as part of my job."

He shook his head. "Small wonder you're the best there is."

For a little while, they just sat in contented silence, loath to spoil a moment like this with any more words. But too soon, Deborah sighed...

"I don't know about you, Boss, but I could just *collapse*."

"I feel the same," Horus replied, running a hand down his head... checking his watch. He suppressed a groan. "It's not even a suitable hour for dinner yet."

"As far as I'm concerned, food can wait for the morning. I just need to know where I can sleep."

"I'm not hungry either. You might fit well enough on the chaise. I'll make do with something. The floor, if necessary."

"There's a fold-out bed hidden in the wall over here," Art unexpectedly chimed in. "And a loft in one of the back rooms. Plenty of meat stashed in the kitchenette drawers for tomorrow, too. I can show you everything you need."

They both looked over at him with wide eyes. "Thank you, Art," Horus said. "I... sort of forgot you were here."

"Yeah, that's my bad," he said, scratching the back of his neck. "Guess I kinda went quiet when you guys launched into that spontaneous heart-to-heart, there. Didn't really know what else to do. I'm not always so eloquent when it comes to the heavy stuff." He shrugged apologetically. "Sorry about your dad, Horus."

"That's alright, Art. And thank you... for *all* you've done today."

"No problem." He pointed vaguely to the side. "I'll show you the beds, if that's what you really want. I'd like to give you the whole proper tour some time, but I guess it can wait."

"That would probably be best," Horus answered. "Tomorrow promises to be another big day."

Chapter 14

Puhloof

As his briefcase gently rapped the defense table, Horus watched Khonshu turn a bit of a startled look up at him. "Where have you been?!" his client demanded in a curt whisper. "I more than half thought you'd deserted again!"

"My apologies," Horus replied, none too apologetic. "We may've misjudged how far we had to come this morning. It's a longer road now, to be sure."

Khonshu slow-blinked, having little patience for such a vague answer. "Why would you be coming from somewhere else?"

Horus sat down, keeping his eyes trained on the latches of his briefcase as he uncoupled them. "Do you really want an answer for that?"

Khonshu only studied him in perplexity.

"Your heroic band of Mesomela avengers seems to have lost any compunction against targeting its own brothers and sisters. They've been strong-arming me for the better part of a week now. From the beginning, really."

"Well... you did kind of betray us," Khonshu retorted. "That sort of makes you fair game."

Horus turned a face of steel at him. "Yesterday, they extended their threats to Deborah. Is that also fair game?"

Khonshu was momentarily dumbstruck. His mouth worked for a reply, but it was some seconds before any began to formulate. "I... the Stentor, well... maybe he does overplay his hand, sometimes."

Horus nodded. "That he certainly does."

The distressed look on Khonshu's face intensified. "What are you going to do about it?"

Suddenly, a bit of pomp and fanfare broke out as Ramesses began his approach. Horus readied to stand back up. "Just you wait and see."

* * *

"Here we are, folks... Khonshu vs. the State... day 3. For those of you just tuning in, the bad guys have been hitting way above their weight class. A shadow of a doubt has been cast over all the principal witnesses. Now, everything comes down to a good, hard look at the forensic evidence. The hopes of a nation – and the track record of one seriously swank judge – rest on what we're about to find." Ramesses turned anxious shades to Horus. "Call your next witness, Mr. Templar."

Horus rose. "I call Doctor Nokkaeru to the stand."

* * *

"Now, Doctor," Horus began, as all attorneys invariably do. "It was you who oversaw the effort to plumb the harbor's depths for remains, is that correct?"

She nodded. "It was a chore that demanded considerably more scrutiny and careful orchestration than is customary among Humans. You will at a glance understand the overlapping complications of trying to identify sapient organic residue on the ocean floor after a bomb blast."

"And you're quite satisfied that your search was exhaustive?"

"Yes. We left no barnacle unturned."

"And what, pray tell, was the fruit of all your meticulous efforts?"

"In a word, nothing. The explosion appears to have been without fatalities."

Horus paused in his pacing, grabbing hold of the stand. "But isn't that rather strange, Doctor? Isn't it understood that the injured Sergeant... Mr. Oregano... must have gone down with the ship? Wasn't a blood trail found that led from where he was shot, up the ramp?"

She nodded again. "It is true. Some of the planking of the ruined vessel was also stained with the same blood."

Horus' ears set. "How then can you say you found no remains?"

"Hm... perhaps I have been somewhat negligent in defining my terms. Cursory blood staining is not quite the same as finding *remains*... bone and tissue. A trickle here and there does not suffice to confirm the man Oregano's death. But even had we found *buckets* of it, I would hope it is understood that people do not merely evaporate into a pool of blood when caught in an explosion. There would be... pieces. We found none."

"Are you positive?" Horus pressed her. "That there would *have to* be physical remains, that is? Is there no way that an explosion could be sufficiently intense to actually *vaporize* someone?"

"I can't rule out the hypothetical possibility that *some* explosion could be sufficiently intense," she retorted. "I do know that *this* explosion would not have been. It was a blast of comparable force to a mishap with a moderate ship's supply of black powder."

"*Comparable*, you say?" Horus pivoted and took a few paces back toward the gallery, before returning his gaze to her. "Why should it be *comparable*? Do you have reason to believe it wasn't a black powder explosion?"

"I'm certain it was not," she revealed. "We tested for such things, of course. For the cause of the blast."

"And... what did you find to be the cause?"

She hesitated, all in a twitching disquiet. "...I'm ashamed to admit, I don't know," she answered at length. "There doesn't seem to have been *any* traditional explosive agent at work."

"Fascinating," Horus framed it. "An apparently immaculate explosion... a man – injured and on the lam – found to have been on the scene, but having left no sign of his demise there. How are we to account for this?"

"Frankly, it escapes me, Counselor. It has been a maddening riddle. The more so now that I am forced to recount it publicly."

Horus returned to the stand, leaning on it. "Tell me this, Doctor: What do you know about magic elixirs? From a professional standpoint, of course? What effects do such things have on the body?"

She shook her head. "You really mean to put me on the spot, don't you? I confess I have given very little professional consideration to the foolhardy imbibement of so-called *elixirs*. I am no expert on the subject of magic."

"Oh! But I am!" an exuberant voice called out from the gallery. "I have read copious peer-reviewed journals on the subject and even been party to a few high-profile experiments myself! Call on *me*, Mr. Templar! I will be most happy to supplement our dear Doctor Nokkaeru's testimony with my own!"

Horus grinned, finding the source of all the commotion. "Very well. I also call Doctor Forasius to the stand."

Nokkaeru sighed deeply, as if giving up the ghost.

* * *

"So, let me see if I understand what you're saying," Horus recounted, pacing before the witness stand, where two birds of a feather now perched together... one following Horus with an eager visage, the other slouching unconsolably. "The more elixir one consumes, the more magic power he or she is granted. Is that correct?"

"It is," Forasius nodded.

"So, then..." Horus segued, "...what is to stop anyone from drinking so much elixir, that they begin to wield unimaginable elemental power?"

"That would be the ASP," Forasius explained.

"ASP?"

"Arbitrary Saturation Point. That's what I like to call it. It is the point at which an individual's entire quantity of inborn *stuff* – that being the technical term – has been transfigured into elemental *stuff.* At this point, the individual has no remaining Purpose of his own. He becomes merely an extension of whatever element he was been trifling with. He is transfigured to a *spirit*, able to do only what his chosen magic allows. This is why magic is considered quite dangerous, you see. One would naturally seek to maximize his effectiveness, but he does so at his own peril. To date, we have no way of determining how much *stuff* any one person possesses, and it varies widely from person to person. That is the 'arbitrary' bit of the Arbitrary Saturation Point. If you have great Purpose, you might down a whole flagon and be a potent sorcerer. Conversely, a single swig might make a ghost of you! There's no way to be sure ahead of time. It is all rather daring."

"*Ludicrous*, more like it," Nokkaeru quipped.

"Very interesting," Horus mused. "In light of this, I have to ask: What of the supply of magic elixir that the barge was to be carrying? *Fire* elixir, to be precise. Is it possible that Sergeant Oregano consumed a sufficient amount of the elixir to become a Fire spirit? Could that not account for the absence of his body?"

"*Why am I even still perching here*?" Nokkaeru puzzled aloud.

"...It could indeed, yes," Forasius went ahead and confirmed, paying no mind to her. "Quite unlike the traditional explosions my beloved colleague expounded so sweetly, magical transfiguration leaves nothing of the original body."

"Could that not also account for the explosion itself?" Horus went on.

"That would depend somewhat on the unfortunate Sergeant's ASP. But yes... if he was a strong enough spirit, it is certainly possible he could have caused such an explosion. In fact, given our inability to determine any other source of ignition, I would even say it is the *most likely* cause."

"Objection!" Blackforest called. "The defense counsel has volunteered a conclusion!"

"I inquired as to a *possibility*," Horus corrected. "If the expert witness has identified a possible cause – and even, by his own account, the most probable cause – that is hardly any fault of mine."

"But this can't go on record as the most probable cause! It's ridiculous! Why would one of our own soldiers raid the cargo he was supposed to be protecting, only to blow himself up... and the barge along with him!?"

"Far be it from me to offer any conjecture. But we can place Oregano definitely on the scene at about the time of the explosion. What we *cannot* otherwise do is account for how neither he – nor any part of himself – has since been found... let alone for the source of the ignition. This is the only theory that explains all of that."

Blackforest angled a knowing glare at his opponent. "Small wonder if you don't want to speculate on his motive, Horus. Accepting your theory, I can think of only one good reason for what he did. He was on his way out. And if he couldn't stop the Vigilants, he at least meant to take them down with him."

Horus shook his head. "That won't do, Hamilton. Now *you're* the one offering conclusions."

Blackforest made a toothy scowl. "Now wait just a minute! I'm... I'm not..."

"Not what? Speculating on Oregano's state of mind? Trying to shift blame back to the Vigil because you're forced to admit the likelihood of his culpability for the blast? For the *actual crime* with which my client has been charged?"

"That's... that's not what I...!"

"...Because the fact of the matter is, you can't prove that the Vigil destroyed the barge, or even intended to destroy the barge. Furthermore, you can't prove that my client was there as an actor in any Vigil conspiracy, or even that he's ever knowingly affiliated with the Vigil."

"That's patently absurd!" Blackforest fumed. "It's *painfully* obvious that...!"

"...It's not a question of what's obvious! You have to *prove* it! *Prove* the Vigil – and not Sergeant Oregano – destroyed the barge! *Prove* my client is the one at fault! Prove it, Hamilton!"

"If you would just...!"

"***Prove it***!"

The court fell silent. Horus drew in quick breaths through his nose, daring Blackforest with an unblinking intensity. Until finally, after a truly withering stare-down, Blackforest was obliged to return to his seat. Horus stared on for a moment or two longer, only to join him in sitting dejectedly. "The defense rests its case."

"This... this can't be happening," Ramesses despaired, holding his ears out. "C'mon, Hamster... you gotta have *something* left in the tank."

Blackforest made a show of roughly smoothing down his hackles. "Apparently not, your Honor." He snuck another side-eye glare at Horus. "If all it takes to acquit the defendant is the *possibility* of his innocence, then I guess I'm finished. After all... anything is *possible*."

Ramesses sighed. "Your snide remark is well-taken, my good man. We'll, um... we'll take closing arguments tomorrow. Then... we'll proceed to *sentencing*," he said, practically whimpering the final word. He struck with his gavel. "Think long and hard on this one, dudes and dudettes of the jury." He stood somberly. "Court is dismissed."

With great wealth of disheartened muttering, the members of the gallery began to shamble out. Horus only busied himself with his briefcase again, while Khonshu looked on incredulously...

"I don't understand..." he said. "For as much as you hate them... after everything they did... you *still* came through."

Horus hurriedly shut the latches and stood. "I didn't do it for *them*."

* * *

The first hour spent back at Art's private sanctum was a quiet one, as the return trip had been. Even with plenteous time set aside for it, Deborah hadn't rested very soundly the night before, and she resolved to eat merely out of necessity. Her appetite revived somewhat once she actually sat down to some good, wholesome carnage... but she spent most of the time at the bar silently brooding about Horus' silent brooding. He hadn't joined her. He'd simply withdrawn to some back room...

Following a slow, small meal, she ambled lazily in the direction she supposed Horus had gone, trying to be nonchalant as she absently browsed more of Art's classy digs. She took her time... as much to make herself believe nothing was wrong as to project an image that she wasn't concerned. But it was obvious. Something was eating at Horus again...

Sure enough, she found him in the very backest of the back rooms. He had a pipe. And he was blowing bubbles...

"Hey, Boss..." she called out quietly. "I, uh... I'm a bit surprised to find you like this," she admitted. "I guess I didn't take you for a soaper."

He grinned half-heartedly, offering a weak shrug. "I've been known to indulge in a bottle or two, on special occasions," he explained.

"What occasion would we be celebrating right now?" she asked.

"Isn't it obvious? We've done it again, Deborah. We pulled victory from the jaws of defeat. We beat all the odds. What's not to celebrate?"

She took a seat by him, offering no answer. "Khonshu hasn't been acquitted yet. Maybe there's still hope he won't be."

He looked at her blankly.

"...But I take it that's no comfort, either."

Horus turned his gaze down at his feet. "I don't have any particular malice for Khonshu. Much as he resists the idea, he's more than just a Vigilant. He *could* be more."

"He reminds you a lot of yourself, doesn't he?" Deborah ventured.

Horus chuckled. "Yes, I suppose he does. So headstrong. So driven to prove himself. I... I hoped that it would help. Our similarities. I actually thought for a while that I could get through to him. Make him see that he could change. That he *should* change. But all we've done from the start is butt heads. I guess, in the end, we're just *too* much alike. I can't be any help to him." He sat back up just enough to blow another thoughtful string of bubbles. "Of course, it was always going to be a no-win scenario. If we'd lost the case, as we should have, he would've proudly joined my father as a martyr of the Eighth Vigil. But now that we're about to win..." He looked back at her again with empty eyes. "He's going to pick right back up where he left off, Deborah. He said he would. He learned nothing from this. It redeems nothing. I... I've redeemed nothing."

Deborah sat silently for a moment, considering all he had said. A gambit began to arise in her mind... a desperate one. But as she watched him work his pipe morosely, she knew... of all the cases that had gone against him in the past, this one was sure to leave the deepest scars. Winning was no consolation. He'd always feel that he'd been used. Used by the forces of corruption he most reviled. Used by the Vigil. Used by his *uncle*...

Yes... his uncle most of all...

Gently, Deborah reached out for his shoulder. "Horus..." she began. "I'm going to turn in again. I didn't sleep a wink last night," she exaggerated. "I... I think you should do the same."

He nodded. "I will. Just as soon as I finish this bottle of soap."

"Alright." She slowly began to withdraw. "Good night, Horus."

"Good night... Deborah."

* * *

Blackforest sat heavy-eyed in his warm, woolen robe, passing a rare evening at home, where he could grumble venomous nothings at the fireplace from the comfort of his favorite wing-backed chair, all the while chain-soaping his way to an early grave. And after all, why not? Between Detective Jamison's surprise announcement and the shocking turn in the Khonshu case, there seemed little doubt he'd be starting his dirt nap soon regardless...

Suddenly, there was a knock at his door. "That's probably the firing squad now," he said, smiling an ironically unironic smile to himself as he got up to answer it, feeling steeled against all comers. But as he turned the hinge, and opened the door, he blanched... looking at the last person in the world he was prepared to find on his threshold...

"Ms. Boulevard..." he said, astonished.

"Hamilton," she acknowledged him.

With a delayed reflex, he clutched at his robe. "I... I wasn't expecting company; please forgive my appearance. Let me just go throw something less comfortable on..."

"I'll only be a moment," she called before he could quite dash away. "I've risked a lot just coming here. If Horus finds out I've gone... it won't be good."

Blackforest did his best to regain his composure. "Alright. What's on your mind?"

"I'm going to give you... a *name*," she said. "What you choose to do with it is entirely up to you. I'd give you a rank, serial number, and home address too, if I had them. But the name will have to be enough."

"What sort of name?" he asked, his sharp features scrunching up now, as dramatically as they'd drawn back.

"An Eighth Vigil name. A prominent one. The man who calls the shots."

He hesitated. "How... how did you come across this name?"

"How do you think? Khonshu used it. *Horus* has used it. They've chatted about him quite openly."

Blackforest shook his head with renewed disbelief. "Deborah... you have to realize... what you're proposing is the ultimate breech of client confidentiality. Of *Horus'* confidentiality. If... if it's found out... your reputation as the greatest Secretary in the world..."

"Hang my reputation," she replied, folding her arms. "Horus needs this. He would never do it himself. So, I guess I have to do it for him."

Blackforest drew a deep, quavering breath. "Alright. If you're sure this is what you want."

She nodded. "I'm sure."

"Very well. What's the name?"

Behind her, the night sky rumbled its latest false promise of a storm. The rumor sank away into the dark recesses of the horizon. And then, she spoke the name...

Chapter 15

The hour was late when Art got the news. Creevey had returned. It was a fact which he made an honest effort to meet with ambivalence. But of course, he had to be real with himself. He'd spent every hour since he'd brought Horus and Deborah to safe haven with nothing else to think about… nothing to even pretend to engage his investigatory mind with. At around two hours past sundark, he had to concede there was just no recourse. He couldn't stay couped up in his house another minute. Even as the hollow boom and bluster began to pick up outside, he simply *couldn't*. And, if he happened to amble in the general direction of Civil HQ, maybe he could chock it up to a fit of absentmindedness. Presently, he found himself unable to think of a single other place in the whole world…

The long, dark road to the station was no help. The farther he went, the more he expected – and even, perhaps, counted on – something to leap in his way. After all, circumstances had prevented him from seeking the help of the graphologist a time or two before. Why should this time be any different? The only problem was that tonight, he just couldn't seem to find anything remotely hindering him. The streets were barren… silent, and emptied. With little apparent hope of the law catching up with the Eighth Vigil, or even their own secret sellout anytime soon, there was currently very little public enthusiasm to be found on the wrong side of a locked door after dark. Everyone that didn't absolutely need to be out was in, and everyone that had somewhere to be had made a point of already being there. No matter how deep into the city he ventured, Art was nearly alone…

As he finally cleared Headquarters security, however, he found himself quite suddenly immersed in an altogether different but hardly less unsettling world. Whereas Civil HQ was customarily sparse after hours, tonight the place was hopping. The whole police force was set aswarm, with every individual officer auditing the personal effects of every other officer in a seemingly endless sequence. *No one* could be trusted… and the only remedy Miloje and Blackforest could contrive on short notice was to have every hand watching all the rest. It was the most dramatic contrast Art could imagine to the city that – not two weeks ago – could be entrusted to a mere skeleton crew of lawmen during the night hours. The great metropolis of St. Argonsburg seemed to be steadily losing its innocence…

Here again, though, Art's hope to be distracted was rekindled. Surely in all the bustle and commotion, there would be *something* to pull him off the rails to Creevey's office. Perhaps he'd be swept up into the audit... or sent to Blackforest for a bit more haranguing over his part in the abridged Jamison investigation. But no. Everyone was so tensely engaged in their current business that as Art passed through the crowded corridors, he felt as much a phantom to them as if he was pulling his newspaper trick. Until, at last, someone simply bumped right into him at high speed...

Quickly collecting himself and brushing down his suit, Art wasted no time seizing the opportunity this little foible afforded him. "Hey, sorry there, Buddy," he said. "Didn't mean ta get in your way."

"That's alright, Mr. Mallard; the fault was mine," the officer replied, all in a flurry as he gathered his own spilled effects. He suddenly paused and looked up questioningly. "What brings you this way? I'd think you would know the best route to Ms. Cordon's office by now. Though I'm sorry to say, she's not in at the moment. The whole DA's office has been turned out for the audit. The Deputy Constable thought it best."

Art felt a pang. "That's alright. I'm, uh, not here to see her anyway."

"No?" the officer inquired, looking even more confused. "Is there something else I can help you find, then?"

"Well, I..." Art stopped up. It occurred: Between the late hour and Miloje's apparent list of absentees for the audit, perhaps Creevey wouldn't even be in the office! As a civilian consultant, he hardly qualified as part of the department anyway. "I was, er, looking for Dr. Creevey – the graphologist. But he's probably just touched base and gone home by now, so..."

"Oh no, he's still here!" the officer elated. He pointed vaguely behind him. "You take the stairs over there all the way to the top and hang a couple sharp lefts; it'll be the door at the end of the hall! Can't miss it!"

With the beaming smile of being such a great help, the officer left Art behind to contemplate the insufferable convenience of it all...

At last, Art stood with his nose to Creevey's door. His finely-honed eye for fashion told him this was a door of special niceness. Nicer, even, than any other door to be found in Civil HQ... and probably half or more of the doors in the office wing of the Palace itself. He tried to find that interesting. He tried to waste some time musing about it. But ultimately, he didn't care.

With perhaps the last deliberate sloth he could muster, he began to reach out for the handle...

...When suddenly, the door was opened from the other side. And Art found himself face-to-face with a man whose strikingly confident smile was only to be matched by the sketchiness of his perfectly groomed goatee...

"Well hello there... Detective Artimus Mallard, isn't it?" the doctor said in warm, reassuring tones. He shuffled various effects under his armpit, so he could reach out again and shake hands. "Milt Lias Creevey. Pleased to meet you."

"Heya, Doc," Art replied. "Nice to meet you, too."

They shook... a perfectly firm shake... and Creevey laughed. "No need to call me 'Doc'. I'd like it if you call me Lias."

Art nodded. "Okeedoke."

They reached a beat of silence, but 'Lias' filled it with a searching look. "I take it you're not here by accident, Artimus. Eh, you don't mind my using your first name, do you?"

He shrugged. "I go by Art. You're free to call me that if you like."

"Well, Art, if you've brought me business, I'll be happy to have it. Why don't you step into my office for a bit?"

Again, it was all too easy. Things were lining up for Art where they should've been jackknifing. "Alright," he agreed at length, turning his eyes down to all the papers Creevey had nestled under one arm. "...I mean, if you're sure you're not too busy. I know you folks've got a lot on your plate right now."

"Yes," Creevey chuckled – almost a bit nervously. "Wouldn't you know? I'm gone for a few weeks, and the whole department comes unbolted! I'm not too humble to admit: I have every confidence my services will be instrumental in setting things right again. But I can spare a minute for the city's best Private Eye! Come in!"

"Well... okay..." Art went along.

* * *

Looking around at Creevey's office, Art was quick to note one thing: There was quite a lot to look around at. The second thing he noted was that all of it was expensive. He let his gaze wander to every little knickknack, pursing his jowls in respect at more than a few trinkets that he himself had passed over for their price tag. Finally, it would seem he'd found a bit of diversion. But even this didn't quite foot the bill of what he'd been hoping for all along...

"You strike me as a man who has an eye for the finer things, Art," Creevey interjected at length.

"You could say that," Art admitted, eyes still roaming.

"How would you rate my decor? From one discerning consumer to another."

"Pretty good," he answered with an obligatory nod. "Very choice merch, to say the least. Though I gotta dock you a few points in the negative space department."

Creevey inclined his head. "Fair enough."

For a little while, they just sat quietly on opposing sides of the great big bocote desk.

"...So..." Creevey finally rebooted the conversation, leaning forward with a drumming rap on the board. "How can I help you?"

Art frowned at him. He was finally going to have to speak the words. "It's, uh... kind of a personal problem." He reached for his vest pocket. "Actually... it's even worse than that. I'm hoping to stick my nose into someone *else's* personal problem. Do you do that kind of thing?"

"Maybe more often than not," Creevey answered, undaunted. "So long as I get paid, Art, I don't find it necessary to agonize over the finer points of ethics. You give me something to read, I'll read it." His eyes glinted as they probed the note in Art's hand. "Is that what you've brought me?"

Art nodded. "Yup. This is it."

From there, nothing much really happened for quite some time. Art just sat still... holding the note up, but not out. Having reached the final, paralyzing crossroads, he found himself unable to do anything besides watch Creevey's face slowly contort in much the same way as if he'd just seen someone turn to stone before his very eyes...

"...Art...?" Creevey eventually inquired.

"Yeah?"

"Is there a reason you're not handing the paper to me?"

"I'm waiting for something," he answered, remaining stock-still.

"Waiting for what?"

"I dunno," Art admitted. "I figured I'd know it when I saw it... but now I'm beginning to think I must've missed it somewhere."

Creevey shook his head. "I'm afraid I don't understand."

"There was supposed to be a sign," he began to explain. "Some sign from the universe to say, 'Hey there, Buster. You're lousing it all up. You're breaking trust... going behind her back. You're folding the minute things get rough. Yes, sir. You go through with this, and you'll only prove you care more about yourself than you do about her.' So now, I'm waiting. Because once I hand you this note, it'll be too late for the universe to say any of that."

Both men let another lengthy interval pass silently by.

"...Well..." Creevey got around to saying, gesturing out, "...it appears to me that the universe has nothing to declare. So how about that paper now?"

One more moment was all it took, and at last, Art mustered the willpower to fold the note back over his finger and replace it in his pocket. He stood. "You know what... never mind. I don't care what the universe has to say. I told her I wasn't gonna be a snoop. And by golly, that's exactly what I'm not gonna be..." He turned and strode powerfully out of the office, leaving a deeply perplexed Dr. Creevey far behind...

"...Alright..." Creevey replied, both weakly and belatedly. "Suit yourself."

* * *

Another dry thunderclap rolled in the distance as Art plopped down on the park bench, letting one arm rest across the back. It was only a few moments before he found himself mesmerized by the swaying of the trees across the open field, recalling the night some months ago when he'd shared this bench with Blucille. Of course, everything was different tonight than it had been. No light from a once-in-a-lifetime planetary alignment... no unearthly droning noise. The world around him was roiling and booming ineffectual threats – a far cry from the eerie calm he remembered. Even the smells had subtly shifted with the seasons. But this was still the place. This was where the trust had run both ways, however briefly. Art sighed, and for the first time in as long as he could remember, it was a sigh of relief. If nothing else, at least he could feel good about himself now, knowing he'd kept up his end of things...

After a good long while of just sitting, though, he began to feel a disarming reality come over him again. He had no idea what to do next. He wasn't hungry, and sleeping was out. Bringing his baggage to the Ecre Point place didn't grab him. Horus and Deborah obviously had enough going on. But returning to the solitude of his house didn't sound any better. It was a decision made impossible by how incredibly much it didn't matter. Finally, he could only reach the vague resolution to simply keep moving...

Extracting himself from the bench, Art stuck his hands in his pockets and began to stroll away in whatever direction he happened to be pointing...

But he only got a few paces before a whiff on the breeze froze him in his tracks...

Lavender...

Instinctually, he turned in just the right direction. And there she was, standing under a streetlamp with her hands folded, returning his gaze as the wind gently ruffled her hat and dress. He watched in stunned disbelief as she began to close the distance, until she joined him under the pool of light by the bench...

"Howdy, Poopsy Pook," Art said, calling on his signature charm to mask the fact that he was going to pieces. "What brings ya to this neck of the woods?"

Blucille grinned... an act her eyes told him must've taken some courage. "I was looking for you, Art," she explained. "I didn't find you at home. I couldn't find you anyplace. I quickly got where I didn't know where else to look. The only thing I could think to do was... retrace our steps."

Art chuckled. "I guess that makes two of us."

She gestured at the bench. "I think we should sit down, Art." She flashed an apologetic look up at him. "I hope you don't mind if we have this out here."

Art had to work past a big lump in his throat. He was really about to get his answers. "I can't think of a better place for it."

They sat down, turning to face each other... joining hands, with no sense at all of who had initiated the action.

"Art... there's no other place to start but to tell you how sorry I am. I only wish what I have to tell you would make it any better." She swallowed, and he was conscious of her breathing. "I... I know you think this is all Bob's fault. And I guess it's just as well... because it's helped me come to grips with what I have to do here. I owe this explanation to him, almost as much as I do to you."

Art studied her, unblinking. "What happened, Blucille?"

"Well... what happened is... we made it *this far*," she explained, turning a hand up. "He and I did. We were going steady for a long time. And, then... then we took the next step. We got engaged."

Already, Art was met with news he didn't like. But he resolved to take it in stride. "You did?"

She nodded. "It was always going to happen. Everyone knew it... even before we knew ourselves. We'd been inseparable from childhood."

"I remember," he confirmed with a quick bob of his head.

She turned her downcast eyes away as she spurred herself farther into the nettle patch of her memories. "I... I even overheard my parents forecasting it a time or two, back when I was still just a little kid. It's funny the way you think when you're small. The idea of... of getting married one day... it just seemed silly. At the time, I thought they'd shut themselves up in a back room to talk it over so they could spare me some embarrassment. It *was* embarrassing to think about. Until... one day... it wasn't anymore."

"So, what kept you from... you know... going through with it?" He managed a sincere look of sympathy. "Did he... did he bite the dust?"

"No," she answered with a sniff, a few small tears already rolling down the sides of her face. "No, nothing like that."

"Then... what?"

She shrugged. "Everything was moving forward without a hitch. Just like we were living in a storybook. The date was set. The guests and... the jurors were rounded up. Court was convened."

"You made it all the way to the *ceremony*?" he marveled.

"We did. To... and *through*. We spent those three days of court in a haze... starry-eyed, and dreaming. After all, it was a sure thing. We *knew* it was. Our case was air-tight. The witnesses called against us didn't have a leg to stand on. It was just one last stuffy formality to sit through... and then begin our lives together." Her jowls quivered as her tear-filled eyes searched the sky. "But when the verdict came back..." she whimpered, faltering. "They'd... they'd found our marriage unsuitable. Our application was revoked."

Art shook his head in disbelief. "*No...*" he said, breathless. "You can't mean...? Your own closest friends and family...?"

She nodded through it, quietly sobbing. "They did. They ruled against us."

"But *why*?" he demanded. "I mean, how? How could they just...?"

She changed over to shaking her head. "You'd have to have *them* explain it," she replied, a bit of venom mixed in with all the hard and fast misery. "Near as I could ever figure, they thought we were a distraction to each other. That he was undercutting my professional advancement... or else I was undercutting his." She withdrew one hand and cupped it over her head. "The whole sentencing phase is just a blur to me. It was a living nightmare..."

Art rubbed her remaining hand in his, trying to untangle all the daunting thoughts and feelings he was left with. He couldn't imagine her grief. All the most important people in her life had apparently conspired to deny her the one man she'd loved most specially of all. Art had no way to process a betrayal like that. He was heartbroken for her. He was even heartbroken for *Bob*...

...But before long, it also dawned on him that her sorrow was more than just the drudging up of a repressed tragedy. He began to see what it meant for her future. For *their* future...

He took her in his arms...

"I'm sorry, Art..." she cried. "I'm so sorry."

"Hey... come on, now," he coached her gently. "Don't you go and apologize to *me*. Blucille... I'm the one who's sorry for *you*. I understand. I can see, now. I see why you didn't want to tell me."

"But I did so much worse than not tell you," she insisted. "All this time, I've been leading you on. I... I wanted to be happy again. And when I saw the chance I just *took* it. I had no right to do that. I should've driven you off. That was the only honorable thing to do. I should never have given you a chance to think we could have a *future*."

"That's crazy talk," Art said. "You can't let them keep you sad and alone forever, Blucille. You can't just accept defeat. You're the strongest person I know."

"But I'm *not*. I'm *not* strong." She pulled away, locking eyes with him. "What can I do, Art? The moment they see that I've found someone as special as he was – someone who makes me so happy – it'll only happen *again*." She quaked at the very thought. " I... I can't go through it *again*..."

Art moved his hands up to her shoulders. "Look, Blucille. If all you ever want to be is friends, then I'll live with that. I'll find a way to live with that. But... if you *do* want a future with me, then please: Don't throw it away without even trying. Think for a minute. Think about everything we've been through. We've already beat all the odds just to get where we are now."

"I know that. But Art: This is different. This is trying the same thing twice and expecting different results."

"But at least it's *trying*," he encouraged her. "I know you think your family is only gonna shoot us down. And I have to admit: You could very well be right. But the only way to be absolutely sure is to *try*. I don't know about you, but I think that beats the alternative. If they're really warped enough to break your heart all over again, then that's their issue. But please: Don't choose the heartbreak for yourself."

"But what about *you*, Art?" she asked. "Don't forget: They'll be breaking your heart, too. I... I can't ask you to go through that. That's one thing I *really* can't do."

"But I would," he said. "I *will*... if you'll let me. You're worth the gamble, Darlin'. For you, I'll bet the farm. I'll take the longest odds they can dish out." He set one finger gently under her tiny chin. "I love you, Blucille Cordon. And it would never be my choice to let you go."

The faintest glimmer of hope tugged up at the ends of her jowls. "Are you sure, Art? Are you absolutely *sure* you don't want to back out now, knowing what's ahead of us?"

"Darn tootin'," he replied. And then, still cradling the end of her face, he leaned in, determined to follow through on what he'd started the last time they were sitting here...

He licked her.

And, after a moment of gleeful amazement, she licked him back.

Drawing into a firm embrace, this continued for some time... until a sudden, mighty thunderclap startled them out of their reverie. Blucille pushed back and laughed. "When is this ridiculous storm finally going to hit?" she asked.

Art turned a palm up to the sky, conducting a mock survey for rain. After a moment, he shrugged. "Maybe it just won't this time."

Blucille appeared quite pleased with his answer, snuggling her way under one of his arms, and removing her big hat to rest her head against his chest. Art grinned down at her, then traced her view out across the field. And for a long while, they just sat quietly in the night, watching the dance of the trees...

Chapter 16

Horus rested his head on one hand, blinking with saggy eyes. On a morning like this, there didn't seem to be any point in concealing his general malaise, when it was so obviously shared by everyone... everywhere. Deborah was quiet – almost strangely reserved. The gallery was somber. The jury was sweating bullets. The judge was fit to be tied. Even Khonshu himself didn't seem greatly enthused about his impending acquittal. Horus huffed to himself as he glanced side-eyed at his client, knowing that whatever shadow of reverent remorse the boy might be feeling at the moment, he'd soon enough get over it. The Vigil would make sure of that...

Lethargically, his gaze pivoted back to Judge Ramesses. And suddenly, it struck him... there hadn't been any fanfare today. No trumpets, no heraldry. Not one confetti popper. The man had simply walked in at some point and silently assumed his place. Horus shook his head. He actually felt a little sorry for him...

Even as he pondered at this, he watched Ramesses check his timepiece... straighten some papers on the bench. Then something else struck Horus. The Judge wasn't just ruminating over the black mark that was about to blemish his career. He was *waiting* for something...

Horus blinked. As he reviewed his inventory of all the miserable countenances in the courtroom, he realized that one especially bellicose face was indeed missing from his tally. He winced. Where the devil was...?

CLACK

Blackforest aggressively set his briefcase on the prosecutor's table, causing Horus a start. Or anyway, a fellow who *should* have been Blackforest – and in many ways answered to his general description – set his briefcase on the table. But to Horus' wondering eyes, it seemed impossible that this man could *actually be* Blackforest. After all, the man he was looking at was *smiling*. Horus blanched at a most horrific thought. Perhaps he'd finally driven his old counterpart off the deep end...

"Good morning, your Honor," the happy Mr. Hamilton Blackforest called out with inscrutable sincerity. "I do apologize for cutting it so close to the wire, here. The duties of a District Attorney are forever in many places at once, you understand."

Ramesses seemed to be at a loss for how to respond. *"Oh-kay..."* he intoned at length, before he checked his watch again. "Well, nothing to worry about anyway. You aren't late. Just not very early."

"Excellent," Blackforest replied. He made a gesture, much like a butler welcoming in a house guest. "Shall we convene court, then?"

Ramesses openly frowned. "Must we?"

The DA nodded. "Yes, I'm afraid so." He didn't look a bit afraid...

"Alright." Ramesses struck his gavel against the bench. "Court is back in action. We were just coming to closing arguments." He raised a very conspicuous brow at Blackforest. "I take it from your weird behavior: you must have a pretty good one."

"Not at all, your Honor," Blackforest replied, the picture of glee. He took a moment to unlatch his briefcase, while the whole court regarded him with breathless incredulity. "The State has no closing argument whatever. Nor any plan to directly contest acquittal."

The judge was frozen. "You don't?"

"No. I don't. As a matter of fact, the State intends to make a preemptive motion to dismiss the case against Mr. Khonshu entirely."

Finally, the tension in the room was just too great for any more silence. The crowd commenced its murmuring...

"Hey-hey-hey," Ramesses warned, clicking his gavel a few times. "We don't need that right now." He turned his shades back on Blackforest. "Hammy, I hate to be the one to tell you this, but you're not a well man. You're talking complete nonsense. I know things have been going the wrong way for a while. But you can't just let this guy go!"

Blackforest shrugged. "I don't see why not." He leveled a particularly villainous smile directly at Horus before continuing. "The defense counsel has to be given his due: Our choice to pursue Grand Demolition of State Property was, shall we say, a tactical error on the State's part from its very inception. I'm obliged to admit that the evidence indeed supports Mr. Templar's theory that the barge's destruction was actually perpetrated by the deceased Sergeant Oregano. Our failure here, then, is two-fold. We pressed the wrong charges." Here, he fixed a deadly glare on Khonshu himself. "And what's more, we tried to make them stick to the wrong man."

"Hmm..." Ramesses sunk back into his seat, striking a thoughtful pose. "I think I begin to see where you're going with this. A retrial, perhaps?"

"Yes. New charges... brought against a new defendant."

The Judge nodded. "Alright. Sell me on it. What are the new charges?"

"Conspiracy... plain and simple," Blackforest revealed. "We *know* – and have demonstrated – that a two-pronged assault with intent to infiltrate the barge was carried out by Mesomela agents – ostensibly members of the Eighth Vigil of Aridos. That much has been proved, and can be easily proved again."

"So far so good," Ramesses assented. "But what's this about a new defendant? You lost me on that part. Why not simply retry Khonshu here as a conspirator? That much still seems plausible to me."

"Plausible, perhaps, but frankly irrelevant. You see, it *all* has to be recalibrated. Whereas we set our sights too high with our original charges, the fact of the matter is – in terms of dealing meaningful damage to the Eighth Vigil – we now know that we set our sights far too low..." He reached into his briefcase, rolling a folder up into the tight grip of his sharp claws.

"So... you've zeroed in on someone else to charge? A real high roller in the Vigil?"

"The highest." Blackforest slowly began to march on the defense table. Horus could only watch as if in a trance. "You see, we've been building a dossier, ever since that first mercenary transport was sunk," the DA went on. "And – thanks to a series of breakthroughs in our internal affairs investigations, which we hope to announce by day's end – the State is now poised to arraign the very orchestrator of this conspiracy himself..."

He set the folder down on the table. To Horus' final astonishment, he found the loathsome name typed out officiously on the manilla tab...

-APEP-

Scarcely had he even begun to process this impossible turn of events, when another sprung up next to him with a great rattle of chains...

"I confess!" Khonshu exclaimed.

The people gasped. Ramesses – socked flat against the back of his tall chair – was too lost in the flood of joy and relief to notice or care about the crowd noise. Blackforest himself had to coach them to settle down...

"Now, now," he said, raising a commanding hand over the gallery. "Let's hear the man out." He turned back to Khonshu. "I'm afraid you'll have to be a little more specific, Sir. What exactly would you be confessing to?"

Khonshu needed half a beat just to mull the question over. "I... I orchestrated the conspiracy! I scuttled the ship! I did it all! I confess!"

"Objection!" Horus shot off as he pushed up from the table.

"Oh, no!" Ramesses replied, waving a finger. "I don't think so, Horus. You can't object to this kind of thing anyway."

"Then I implore the court to give me a moment to confer with my client before his statement is entered into record."

"There's nothing to talk about, Horus," Khonshu fired back. "You know and I know: I'm guilty."

"Oh, are you now? And just what pray tell would inspire you to come forward about it *now*?"

"How about a sudden attack of conscience? You were always calling for one of those anyway."

"Who do you think you're fooling? Certainly not me. I know *exactly* what this is, and I won't stand for it."

"Look, I'm doing what you wanted, aren't I? I'm accepting responsibility for my actions."

"I'm not going to let you sacrifice yourself for *him*!"

"Order!" Ramesses shouted, backing himself up with his tiny wooden hammer. "Horus, the kid confessed. I'm sorry, but that's all she wrote. There's nothing left but to move on to sentencing."

"*Sentencing*?" Horus demanded. "Sentencing comes at the *end* of a trial, your Honor! You know that. But as it stands, we are currently *between* trials. There hasn't even been an official arraignment on these Conspiracy charges Hamilton alluded to. And as for the charges of Grand Demolition, he himself just motioned to throw them out! He dismissed the case!"

"I believe my exact words were that the State *intended* to dismiss the case," Blackforest qualified. "I was still in the process of explaining why, when we were suddenly interrupted."

"Well, it's official then!" Ramesses elated. "Khonshu is found guilty as charged on one count of Grand Demolition of State Property. And the sentence *iiiiiis*... death." He clacked his gavel.

"But your Honor..." Horus appealed.

"*Death*, Horus," Ramesses insisted, pointing with his impediment. "*Death*." After delivering his stern warning, he stood up, clapping his hands together as he looked out. "Anyway, that's a wrap! Court is adjourned. Thanks for a real show-stopper, Hamster; you're one cool cat. Cue the victory music, Mr. Williams!"

As the overbearing melody began to play, all the people energetically collected themselves to go, exuding nothing less than a refreshed outlook on life. Khonshu was swiftly unbolted and corralled away. Horus didn't even look at him. His eyes were transfixed on the floor, darting in a vain attempt to make sense of everything that had so abruptly unraveled. No matter how he fit the pieces together, it left him with a question he couldn't answer. Or at any rate, a question he could only answer *one way*. But surely, it couldn't be as it seemed. The only answer was out of the question...

"Sorry, Horus," Blackforest said, a bit more somber now as he collected his folder. "At least now we'll have one less Vigilant to worry about."

"How did you do it, Hamilton?" Horus asked, slowly looking up to meet his gaze, alternating a glance at the folder. "How did you get that?"

Blackforest grinned. "You mean, you didn't recognize the oldest trick in the book?" He opened the folder, revealing a healthy stack of totally blank pages. "That's what we've got for a dossier. And as for the breakthroughs in the internal investigation, we can *hope* all we want for something to announce by day's end."

"That's all well and good," Horus deflected. "But the *name*, Hamilton. How did you get the *name*? I'm certain I never gave it to you."

Blackforest frowned. "I'm afraid you're going to have to puzzle that one out for yourself," he answered quietly... solemnly. With nothing more said, he turned and walked away.

Horus' gut managed to sink even deeper into his little feet. Hesitantly, he turned to face Deborah. She only avoided his gaze. That was all the confirmation he needed. But even still, he couldn't believe it...

* * *

Once again, the time passed very quietly back at the Ecre Point Warehouse. Horus had immediately retired himself to a moody, chin-scratching meditation on the Vigil warhammer in the weapons display case. Deborah reacted to this by pretending to read a case book across the room from him. The silent tension built and built between them, until finally, it broke...

"I don't suppose it would help anything if I apologize," Deborah inquired.

"I only want to understand what made you do it," Horus replied, never breaking eye-contact with the hammer. "What you thought there was to gain by giving that name to Hamilton. What would possess you to venture out from here alone on a false pretense and..." He cut himself off, cradling his head as he at last turned to face her. "Well, never mind the details. But *why*, Deborah? What did you think was going to happen? What did you *want* to happen? Did you get anything like the outcome you were hoping for?"

She shrugged. "Well... I certainly didn't have any delusions that Blackforest could go out and *find* Apep with nothing to go on but the name. That was an obvious longshot. So... yes. I guess I hoped he could devise a bluff like he did. That he could find a way to trick Khonshu into implicating himself."

Horus shook his head in disbelief. "And *how* in the world did you think that would make things better?"

She offered no answer.

He turned back to the glass, and the weapon within it. "Khonshu's willingly added himself to Apep's collection of martyrs. Maybe that *is* better than going on to serve the Vigil for a lifetime. But right now... it's proving very difficult to convince myself of that."

Deborah closed the book she wasn't reading, standing up with a barely-audible sigh. "I did something else while I was out," she admitted, slowly coming up behind Horus. "I swung by and got that letter Mo wrote you. I only wish I could've convinced you to read it earlier. I think it would've saved a lot of grief." She retrieved the letter from a pocket, holding it out to Horus as he returned to her, his eyes uncomprehending. "Please read it, Horus," she implored him. "I *could* just tell you why I did what I did. But I honestly believe you'll like it better if you get to figure it out for yourself."

As soon as he accepted the note, she walked away. She left him alone. He looked at the note, and then at the empty doorway. He didn't understand. But however mystified he felt, she'd certainly managed to impress one thing on him. It was high-time he sat down and read the letter...

* * *

After just a little wandering, Horus found a back room with an actual work desk. He struck a match... lit a lamp. He sat down in the low, wavering light with the letter, reaching with extended claw to lance through the envelope, forgetting it was already open. He reached in, took it out and unfolded it. And then, he began to read...

Dear 'Orus,

'Ope you don't mind much, my callin' you that, Sir – 'Orus. I 'aven't any mind to pay you disrespect – cross me 'eart, if I 'ad one! I don't mean any presumption. If you want me to be more formal-

like in future correspondence, I'll 'appily oblige! I only settled on your first name so's to let you know: I consider you me friend.

Horus looked up for a moment with his face drawn back. *He certainly managed to capture his own vernacular in print form*, he thought. He returned to the letter...

Anyway, I shan't blather on an' on like this. I'll bring you up to speed. I've put in me deaths and been discharged! I'm settled back in at me same ol' Dronehood office! The other lads send their regards. They seem to find it right favorable to 'ave me back. An' as for me scatterplot... Ah! you should see 'er now, Sir! Blimey, but she's grown so much. No Clerk was ever so proud as I am.

Horus grinned. Despite his own trials, he found himself getting a bit misty-eyed...

But well, 'Orus – Mr. Templar, Sir – I've got to be quite frank with you. I 'ave to 'ave the 'ole ugly thing out at least once, or I'll be sore. I don't put pen to paper 'ere to make out like there wasn't grim days and 'ard-going in the armies. It tried me, Sir – that it surely did. The war. 'Aving enemies – an' brothers-in-arms. The rhapsody of victory. The ashes of defeat. A cause the other lads 'ad been givin' their lives for, over an' over again. A jealous love for one Queen – and an even deeper 'ate for the other. It was a saga, Sir. It was a lot to take in. I couldn't 'elp bein' a mite swept up in the camaraderie – the special bond between fightin' men – even when it was poison. Even when it demanded me to share in the 'atred. An' I'm ashamed to admit: I nearly got lost in it, 'Orus. It almost claimed me, more than once...

But you see, Sir – that's the equal part of why I 'ad to reach out to you like this. I never forgot what you said. I never forgot you warned me ahead o' time. You warned me about all of it. That was the only thing what prepared me, Sir. That was all what saw me through to the end. If it weren't for your words to me, I fear I would've re-upped, an' still been fightin' a war what has no point, even now. I would've lost sight o' the better things in life, such as I already had. I only 'ope my decision to go 'ome 'ad some effect on the fellows. They were me dear friends, before long – the southern lads, and the northern, too, in their turn. I pray for their sake the war doesn't use them up to the end o' their days. I shouldn't be the only one with the good fortune to escape it all. But for what I 'ave, I'm grateful. An' I owe my thanks to you.

Very Best Regards,

Lucky

Horus put the letter down, overcome. It would've been enough for him to know that Lucky was well... that he was happy. But his old client had shared so much more than that. To say that Horus felt validated would've fallen short. Frankly, he felt *humbled*... humbled to have been more help to a dear friend than he ever could've imagined...

But even in that thought, his present dilemma pressed back in on him. Why had Deborah been so insistent that he read this? Surely, she didn't mean to simply distract him from how grievously he'd failed Khonshu by shifting his attention to a previous success...

He scanned back through the letter, regarding it now as if it was a sypher. But even on a third read, and a fourth, all he could really seem to do was marvel at Lucky's account of his time in the service. On the one hand, it paralleled his own experience in the Vigil... the feelings of camaraderie and brotherhood being distorted into vehicles of infectious hatred. But what was most amazing to Horus was the way that Lucky's experience was *different*. Having first been made to serve in the Southern army... and then, the North... it blew Horus away to know that Lucky had learned to think of drones from *both sides* as his friends. How could he first learn to hate the North, and then to love it? But then, in a way, it made sense. It was easy to hate what was far away... what was against him. But the moment the tables were turned – the moment he was given a new band of brothers – it was only a matter of time before he was forced to see what he could relate to in them. It wasn't hidden any more by distance or rivalry. Immersion inspired empathy every time...

Horus' heart skipped a beat. Finally, he could see it... a chance for Khonshu. A gamble of long odds, to be sure, but undoubtedly, Khonshu's *only* chance. It would take some careful negotiating on Horus' part... and more than a little flexibility and longevity on Khonshu's part. But it was still a chance...

*   *   *

"Deborah," Horus called, as he stepped quietly into the room.

She turned up from that same casebook she still wasn't reading and searched him. "Yes?"

"I'm going to be stepping out for a while," he explained. "It would seem I have some business at Civil Headquarters that needs attending to."

Deborah grinned. "Really? I don't suppose it has anything to do with reading Mo's letter?"

"As a matter of fact, I *have* quite recently drawn inspiration from a bit of personal correspondence," he admitted, grinning back at her. "Incidentally, you wouldn't happen to have a sentence appeal form, would you?"

She smiled more broadly. "I think I've got one lying around somewhere."

*   *   *

The department was still buzzing when Horus got there. He frowned, catching sight of so many bloodshot eyes – frankly finding the odor of Human sweat overwhelming. He went to check in at the front desk, but Muriel the receptionist was being grilled by one of the police officers, answering his questions tiredly, in a voice that said she'd already had this interview many times before. The effort to turn the whole department inside-out was ongoing, and ever-broadening...

"Are you lost, Templar?" the voice of Stenya Miloje called out. "I'm surprised to see your face here again so soon."

"Milo... good to see you back in action," he replied earnestly, overlooking the horrible bags under the Deputy Constable's eyes. "How are things with the investigation?"

"Horrid, obviously. I've already begun to miss being on the sidelines. At least then, this wasn't my affair to botch. I'll give Jamison this: He got farther than we can seem to get on a lot less. After all this time, I confess: I still don't even know enough to clear *myself*. How *he* ever did it, I may never understand." He frowned even more, if that was possible. "But surely you're not here for me to list my grievances. What do you want?"

"To appeal my client's sentence... and propose one of my own."

Miloje huffed. "Ridiculous. After everything the Czarina lost, you think the courts would ever be persuaded to spare him?"

"Well, maybe there're things worth more to the Czarina than his death."

Horus extended the form, which Miloje took, studying it doubtfully. But after a moment, he grinned. “Ah… clever, Templar. Most clever.” He winked. I’ll send someone out with the decision, the minute it’s made.”

Horus nodded. “Thank you, Milo.”

Chapter 17

Art opened the door with one hand, gesturing suavely with the other. Blucille stepped in, already awed by what she saw.

"So this is Art Mallard's famous hoard of treasures..." she said, turning her head with amazement in every direction. "I can't believe how organized it is."

"Yeah, that's what they keep tellin' me," he sighed. "Don't let it fool ya, though; there's still boatloads of cool stuff to see. Check out this melty clock thing over here..."

"Well hello, Art," Horus called, turning back at the sound of their voices from a couch off to the side. His ears swiveled with special attention to Blucille's presence. He stood up. "And, Ms. Cordon! How nice to see you *both*."

Deborah poked her nose in from a back room. "Do I detect visitors?"

"Hey, now," Art chuckled. "Let's not forget: This is still *my* place."

"I'm beginning to forget already," Deborah admitted. She turned and gave the Assistant DA a nod. "Hello, Blucille."

"Hi," Blucille replied, with a bit of a stifled nervous laugh. This was – unavoidably – the first Horus and Deborah would've known about her and Art patching things up...

"Okay, look," Art volunteered. "I don't want this to be awkward, so let me just pounce right on the elephant in the room. You guys know that Blucille and I... well... we were kinda on the outs for a while. And I'm sure she probably knows that you guys knew that. You might even know that she knows that you knew... but just so you know, we've got things all figured out again. I mean yeah, okay, not to get too deep into personal stuff, but there's gonna be challenges still ahead of us. Which isn't to say that we're unsure about each other or anything. Far from it. But I guess what I'm trying to say is..."

"...It's alright, Art," Horus interjected. "We can plainly see the two of you are getting along again. I couldn't be happier for either one of you. But if you want to avoid making things awkward, I'm afraid you might be headed in the wrong direction."

"Took the words right out of my mouth," Blucille said, through a bout of nervous lockjaw.

"Alright, then," Art replied. "In that case, why don't we just try shaking hands and moving on?"

Horus nodded. "I'm sure that sounds sensible by comparison."

They all shook hands.

"So," Horus segued, "I take it this is Ms. Cordon's first time seeing your secret lair."

"Yup," Art explained. "I'd been on the fence about showing her the place for practically forever. But now that you guys have been here, the lid's blown off." He turned to Blucille with a cutesy smile. "I just didn't have any excuse left not to show my little Baluga Buttons."

"That's very sweet," Blucille said, and they rubbed snouts. "But I'm here on business, too." She set her eyes on Horus. "I was recruited to tell you that your appeal of Khonshu's sentence has been processed... and approved. The State will be most pleased to get back even a small fraction of the revenue they lost to the Vigil attacks."

Horus and Deborah exchanged a smile. "That's wonderful news," Horus replied. "I... really don't know what to say. This was one case I just couldn't see coming out the right way, no matter which way it went. But now, with hope – and perhaps a contraband prayer or two – I think it might."

"Imagine Khonshu's surprise," Art put in. "No sooner than they get him penned up in Grufthoffen, they'll be shipping him right back out."

Everyone turned scrunched-up faces at him. "Grufthoffen?" Horus questioned. "That local Despotopian stalag?"

"Yeah, you remember the one," Art confirmed. "Course, it's not really a Despotopian stalag anymore, ever since you got all our guys out of it. But still, that's the place."

"Art, what on earth are you talking about?" Blucille pressed him. "Khonshu isn't being held in *Grufthoffen*. Not now, and not ever. We wouldn't *dream* of transferring a maximum-security inmate."

Art shook his head. "That's not what I heard. And I got it straight from the horse's mouth. I overheard a couple guys who work the detention center, on their way down from the top offices. They were ruminating over their orders to 'move the Vigilant'." He paused a moment in his reflections. "Come to think of it, they sounded just as surprised as you two."

"Art..." Horus said, taking his big friend by the shoulders, searching him with piercing intensity. "You're not serious. Tell me you're not."

Art frowned. His ears folded back...

* * *

The wall of night drew up like a cosmic spectre over the city of St. Argonsburg, poised to collapse at a moment's notice. Shackled and under heavy escort, Khonshu made a convincing show of being led around placidly. Cooperation was key. Everything about the art of escape favored the patient. It gave you more time to read your opponents – to plan your best play. And the people guarding you enjoyed more time to grow complacent. Unfortunately, this particular group of policemen wasn't giving much on that front, appearing perhaps no less nerved-up than when they'd first set out for Grufthoffen Stalag. It was little wonder. No one in the group had the faintest idea why they'd been ordered to transfer him. Khonshu, on the other hand, knew exactly why. It had been arranged for him to escape. Granted, even *he* couldn't speculate the reasons he should be gifted the opportunity. But all that could be figured out later. The main thing was to not miss the chance...

The real and only trick was to decide on a winning first move. After that, the training would kick in, and everything else would work itself out. All Khonshu could think about were the two policemen with bayonets at his back. They'd already demonstrated a willingness to use their blades as prods, having poked him once in the back at the journey's onset. Finally, he decided he'd get them to do it again...

And now – in the low light of dusk – was as good a time as any...

Gradually, he started slowing down. Once the cops picked up on his sloth, he watched one of them make the wrong move, electing to shove him in the back with the blunt of his long gun...

"Keep moving," the officer said.

Khonshu dramatized his fumble, trying to appear more hurt than he was, though the officer had been far from gentle anyway. This was a very bad start to his plan. Now they were all back on high alert. "Sorry," he said quietly, doing what he could to pass it off like he hadn't meant to be uncooperative. He waited another block. Then, he started slowing down again...

"Hey!" the same man exclaimed. "What'd I tell you? Get a move...!"

Just as the officer went to back up his tough talk with the business end of his bayonet, Khonshu lunged to the right and backward, holding the crook of his shackled arms out where his torso had just been, catching the gun barrel and promptly wrenching it from his opponent's grasp. He extended the barrel in his right hand and spun around, staggering both officers directly behind him with glancing cuts. With the half-second he bought himself, he tossed the musket out from under his arms, getting it out in front of him where he could maneuver it.

From there, the attacking officers fell one by one as he clubbed them down with the stock, until all seven were sprawled out on the ground. He took a moment to breathe, and recenter. Then, he retrieved the keys, and disappeared into the darkness...

* * *

"Templar, don't be rash," Blucille said as Horus whirled for the door. "I know your mind is with your client, but we have to keep the bigger issue in mind here. We need to get back to Civil HQ and find out who gave the order! We need to focus on catching the mole before he does any more damage. As for Khonshu... I'm sure the officers entrusted with him know what they're doing."

"They'll never make it to the stalag," Horus revealed, complying with her at least enough to stop a moment and talk it over. "Certainly, the three of you should get back to Headquarters at once. Catch the mole red-handed, if you can. But it's up to me to stop Khonshu."

"Horus, she's right – it's useless," Deborah said. "If they *don't* reach the stalag with him, he'll vanish right off the face of the earth. Even *you* won't be able to find him."

Deborah had a point. Horus didn't know where the Vigil was put up these days. But he did know of *one* location they were currently watching – a secure stopover Khonshu might make on his way back to their true base of operations. He knew they had eyes on the Greyson Estate, where he'd been instructed to leave a sign for them after arranging their proposal with Blackforest. He could only hope that Khonshu also knew this, and that the Estate was actually somewhere on the road back to Apep. He knew it was quite a lot to hope for. But to Horus, it was a chance well worth taking. He would do his utmost to make it there first. And he'd have to make good and sure he was ready for a fight when he got there...

"I know one place he might go," Horus explained, marching deeper back into the room. He stopped in front of the weapons cabinet. "Art... I may need to borrow this for a bit."

Art nodded. "It's yours, Horus."

* * *

Sheltering along walls and darting between buildings, Khonshu heard one last roll of thunder far off before the distant moan of police horns took sonic dominion over the city. He looked up into the sky, where searchlight beams began to sway. It was rather a lot of melodrama for one simple message: The SAPD knew they'd been had. For Khonshu, this changed nothing. It had only been a matter of time. And by now, he was very near a place where he could lie low, and find some welcome aid for the rest of his flight from the city. The drop-off was just ahead...

For a moment, he skittered out to the edge of a precipitous shelf in St. Argonsburg's tiers, looking down on the sharp spires of an otherwise forgotten edifice from of yore – just one of many grand old homes that owed its continued existence to a moldering decree in the Dronehood archives that dubbed it a historical site. The Greyson Estate...

Passing without a sound into the third-story parlor, leaving behind a rickety drawbridge that met one of the signature long stairs of the urban side of Mt. Norvein, Khonshu was slow to abandon any pretense of stealth. But a sniff, a careful sweep of night-sensitive eyes, and a long pause to listen with keen, swiveling ears began to ease his mind. He roamed a bit more freely, up into the old Greyson sitting room. Once there, he set a shoulder into a false panel, opening a trap door in the wall beside the bookcase. He reached in and retrieved one of the warhammers they'd stashed, and a short cloak to go over his prisoner tunic. As he threw the garment on, his gaze swept over the vast wet spot on the ceiling, and the ruined canvas draped over the furniture below. He took the hammer back up and nearly left the room, when he caught just a whiff of something besides the rot. He grinned...

"Well, how do you like that?" he spoke aloud. "I didn't think I'd have the good luck to meet a brother here."

"And you were right," Horus replied, standing up from the shroud of the high-backed chair in front of the mantle.

Khonshu recoiled. "*Horus*? How did... what are you...?"

"I'm bringing you in, Khonshu," Horus explained. "I've made big plans for you... plans that don't include slipping silently into the night. I've worked much too hard to let that happen."

Khonshu scoffed, rallying a half-smile. "Well… I've got to hand it to you, Horus: You always keep me guessing. I'm still not even sure if I respect you or hate your guts. But frankly, at this point I'm tired of the whole question. I think maybe it's about time we both move on to bigger and better things. Don't you?"

Horus nodded sternly. "I couldn't agree more. As a matter of fact, that's precisely what I'm here for. To give you one last chance at something better."

"Like what?" Khonshu laughed. "A quick drop? Sorry; not interested."

"They're not going to execute you, Khonshu," Horus explained. "Not anymore. You see, I've made an appeal on your behalf – changed your sentence." He reached into his jacket and retrieved written permissions.

"What are you talking about? What is that?"

"Draft orders, conscripting you as a State Mercenary," he answered, holding up the papers. "This is where you'll begin to pay off the damages the Vigil has done. Considering their recent antics, it's more than a little apropos. Your skills are going to be put to a better use… or at least, a more profitable one. You're going to be shipped out immediately. Right to where the demand is highest."

Khonshu was incredulous. "What? To the Queens' War?" He shook his head tiredly. "You see, this is just the kind of thing I'm talking about. I never know what's next with you. First you condemn us for hating the Berlie Beirels. Now you've got me all signed up to go fight them?"

"Yes," Horus answered solemnly. "I've had to accept that you'll be fighting them. But, on the other hand… you'll also be fighting *alongside* them. You'll be among them. Getting to know them. And it won't be long before you learn things Apep never told you. Before you have something more for them than just your prejudices."

Khonshu groaned. "Do us both a favor and spare me your delusions. You talk about all this as if it's actually going to happen. But Horus – it's a fantasy. I'm not going back with you. I'm getting back to my *life*. I suggest you get back to yours."

Horus replaced his papers. "Very well," he said. Then, he reached beside the chair, taking up his father's warhammer from its resting place. "I hoped it wouldn't come to this. But I'm prepared to bring you in by force, if I must."

Khonshu snickered. "Now, that's a good one. Come on, Horus. Put that thing away before you hurt yourself."

"This is no joke," Horus warned him. "I can bring you back on your feet, or on a stretcher. The choice is yours."

"Look, how can I put it modestly?" Khonshu retorted, hefting his own weapon. "Picking a fight with me would be rather ill-advised for a – *domesticated* – old fellow, such as yourself." Whether consciously or otherwise, they'd already commenced circling each other. "But then again... who am I to discourage you, if this is what you really want? I've been itching to teach you a lesson since we met."

"Well before you go and try it, there's something you should know," Horus replied. "Something the others certainly wouldn't have told you about me, in the interest of saving face."

"Oh? And what might that be?"

"I'm the best fighter they ever had."

Khonshu huffed. "That makes two of us."

It was on in a flash. Khonshu initiated with a feint step followed by a delayed clearing stroke. Horus almost took the bad cue but had time enough to duck. He came back with a shallow swing. Khonshu stuck the haft-end of his warhammer in like a spear, blocking Horus' attack and nearly wrenching the weapon from his grasp. But Horus held firm, and the two of them tussled back and forth for a while in a hold. Khonshu tried a few kicks at Horus' legs, but he deflected every attempt to trip him up. Finally, they leapt apart... but Khonshu didn't miss a beat. He flew back in with two more swings like lightning. Horus dodged more than blocked, and spun out of the way of a downward stroke altogether. Khonshu's hammer sunk into the floorboards with a hollow crunch, flinging a cloud of dust from the whole carpet. Horus raised a brow, drawing heavy breaths...

"Well, you've got moves," Khonshu grudged him, gently panting himself. "But come on – this is child's play." He wound up for another overhead swing. Horus caught it, holding his long hammer up like a staff. Khonshu followed up with another swift kick, this time aimed at the torso. Horus kept it to a glancing blow, not quite getting out of the way. But Khonshu already had the other end of his hammer lined up on Horus like a pool cue. He gave him a stinger to the gut. It sent Horus to the ground. "You see now? It's pointless."

"On the contrary," Horus grunted, picking himself up and dusting off. "I think that was just the thing to break the rust loose." He rolled his shoulders. "What else have you got? Anything I haven't seen?"

Khonshu shook his head, reassuming his stance. "I guess we're going to find out."

He threw a long series of blows at Horus, who nimbly dodged and parried, resolving to be economical in his movements – conservative. Khonshu's technique – he had to admit – probably had the highest marks he'd ever come across for both speed and execution. He was swift – he was flashy… almost impractically so. He seemed determined to prove he knew every move there was. So, Horus did the sensible thing and fell back on the sturdy fundamentals. After all, there was nothing quite so infuriating to a flashy fighter as a sturdy fundamentalist…

Finally, Khonshu took a step back. "Come on! Fight me if you're going to fight me!"

"What's the matter, Khonshu? All those flourishes tiring you out?"

Khonshu lunged in for another assault. Horus took this as the perfect opportunity to change gears. He interlocked their weapons and used his leverage to shove Khonshu across the room, right into one of the musty canvas-covered couches. Khonshu didn't quite topple it over as he bounced off the arm, onto the ground. But he leapt back up in a flash. "Now that's more like it," he said with a chuckle, undaunted. Regaining defensive footing, he tapped on the end of his own hammer with his palm. "Let's see something else."

Horus took slow, purposeful strides forward. "You're sure this is where you want to make your stand?"

Khonshu nodded. "Any time you're ready."

"Alright," Horus obliged him. Then, with a great deal of space still between them, he made a huge downward stroke… right into the rotten floorboards under the leaky spot. He caught the horrified look on Khonshu's face only momentarily before the entire corner of the room collapsed under his feet…

The crash was long and loud – the dust was slow in clearing. But as Horus gazed down into the mirk of the third floor, he finally found Khonshu on his feet. Harried – with sharp tufts of fur sticking out of shorn spots in his cloak. Panting – hopeless to pretend any longer that the battle wasn't pitted. And above all, seething. His eyes were ablaze with rage, and his teeth were bared, as Horus stood tall, calm, and composed on the edge of the ruined floor. Until, at length, he turned for the nearest staircase…

They watched each other unblinking as Horus descended the stair, crossed the parlor, and made his way round the ruins. The air remained thick with churning dust as the two men squared up for what seemed sure to be the final exchange of blows.

Just as before, Khonshu initiated, but quickly began to give ground. He baited Horus into the role of the attacker, probably hoping to turn the game of endurance around in his favor. Either that, or he meant to catch him in a slip-up. Horus was determined not to let either one happen...

They fought until Khonshu had himself cornered by the doorway. He backed right up into the door itself, faltering at the surprise impact. Horus seized the moment. But it was another feint. Khonshu juked out of the way as Horus smashed a gaping hole in the door. He had only just enough time to duck under his own handle as Khonshu came back with a heavy swing. With desperate strength, Horus levered his hammer free from the smashed paneling, catching Khonshu with the length of the weapon and sending him through what was left of the broken door. He fell headlong onto the stone balcony that met the bridge to the city stair. Horus stepped out as Khonshu got his arms back under him and traded a quick look over at the bridge. There was indecision in his eyes. It appeared he might give up the fight entirely and bolt. Horus made a few fast strides to get between him and his escape route as Khonshu shot back up to his feet.

"You're not just going to run away now," Horus said.

"Alright then. Let's finish this."

Khonshu drove Horus to the bridge with a furious onslaught. The battle took on a whole new complexity as they lost their sure footing. Old, worn, and quite without rails, the only safety feature of the bridge was its width. The ropes holding up the wooden planks moaned under their weight, and the whole length swayed beneath their feet...

Finally, the two of them were caught in another hold... and all at once the footing became the sole determining factor of life and death. Horus was in trouble. However beat up he might be, Khonshu was still younger, stronger, and certainly more enraged. He drove Horus back... and what was worse, kept steering him towards the edges. Fortunately, Horus found a good spot to plant his feet, and dug in. The two of them strained in place for a long time. Horus' reserves of strength were quickly depleting. He could feel his foothold begin to slip. And for a moment, it appeared inevitable. There was nothing left but a bit of stumbling, and a long fall...

Just then, he heard a *crack*. The board Khonshu was standing on gave just enough to unsteady him for a split second. Horus leapt at his one chance. He reached out, grabbed Khonshu by the back of his neck, and drove his face right into the head of his own hammer. Khonshu went down flat...

Horus drew a cleansing breath... slowly forcing it through his snout. He watched Khonshu struggle to collect himself, fumbling for his hammer. Horus gave it a kick and sent it careening off the bridge, into space.

"It's over, Khonshu," he said. "Don't fight it anymore."

Khonshu sneered with his swollen eye and bloodied fangs. "You'll never get your way, Horus," he spat. "You may beat me down; you may bring me in. But you'll never *change* me. I'll always hate them, forever. I'll always be a Vigilant."

Horus frowned. "I'm afraid that might be so. But you have a *chance*, now. A chance to learn a better way. I wish there was more. But that's really all I can give you."

Khonshu only eyed Horus as best he could. There was nothing left to say. At length, he let his head drop, panting on the bridge where he'd fallen, vanquished for now.

As the adrenaline began to subside, Horus became aware of his various bruises... his exhaustion. An inconvenient reality set in. Actually bringing Khonshu back to Civil HQ was... *impractical*, to say the least, if he could get no help. Back at Ecre Point, he'd realized at the last moment that he was making the same mistake he'd made with Arcadian Tweed: He was rushing off with no one the wiser as to where he was going. He'd remedied that by sharing his destination with Blucille, and appealing for her to send police reinforcement, if she could. But given the more pressing emergency of catching the mole, he understood there might be no one to spare...

Just as he was about to resign himself to the task of devising a way to singlehandedly drag Khonshu from the bridge – let alone halfway across the city – he spied motion along the edge of the tier above them. And sure enough, as his eyes zeroed in, he found a small team of policemen making their way down to the Estate...

Horus sighed, and sat down. He'd done his bit...

Chapter 18

Art was a little taken aback as everything Horus had earlier boded began to bear out before his very eyes. Another quiet night of virtual house arrest for the city of St. Argonsburg suddenly erupted into a massive production while they were on their carriage ride back to Civil HQ. Searchlights and sirens filled the sky with alarm. And as they drew near their destination, they found themselves riding upstream against seemingly endless waves of policemen. The department was out in almost unprecedented force. Art shook his head. It seemed like a lot of heat for one fugitive. But even so, given the background of the man they meant to find – not to mention the enormity of the city he had to hide in – it might not be enough...

"We're close, now; I'm going to hop out," Blucille announced, taking Art's hand and shoving a bunch of coins into it. "Pay the cabby off, would you? There isn't a moment to waste..." Before he could answer, she was gone...

Art regarded the pile of shillings in his grip for a beat or two. Then, he hurriedly foisted them off on Deborah. "Could you get this for us, Debs?"

"Well, I..."

"Thanks." He took off like a shot, escaping just in time to avoid Deborah's huffy squint...

"Miloje!" Blucille called, picking the Deputy Constable out of the swarming crowd in the lobby. "Miloje, over here!" Her call stopped him, and she quickly closed the gap.

"Ms. Cordon," he replied, inclining his head as he regarded her with grave eyes. "I'm grateful to see you respond so quickly to our latest little emergency."

"You took the words right out of my mouth," she panted. "Evidently you've learned of Khonshu's escape on your own."

Her comment seemed to puzzle him. "We've learned he was *transferred* without my authorization. If he's since escaped, I suppose I shouldn't be surprised. Perhaps you'd better tell me what you know."

...Around this time, Art came hoofing up to them...

"About the same as what you know," Blucille answered. "Khonshu was being moved to Grufthoffen."

"I overheard a few of the guys talking about it," Art explained. "Drucker and Kimball, I think. They were part of the team assigned to the job."

"Beyond that, we're sure of nothing," Blucille went on. "Templar *believed* Khonshu would find a way to escape on the road. All this uproar in the department seemed to confirm it." She returned Miloje's quizzical look. "But you don't know for sure that he's gone, either…?"

He shook his head. "As I say, that would just about figure. But right now, he isn't our principal concern. We need the man who gave the transfer order."

"Do you know who it is?" she asked with bated breath.

Miloje nodded, reaching into his breast pocket. "We have the order in writing." He showed it to them. "It's Brocksmith."

"Gadzooks," Art breathed. "I can't believe it. Jamison was so sure…"

"I'm not yet convinced he was wrong," Miloje replied. "A bonified saboteur should be more discreet. And besides that – anything less than a Captain's orders would never have got Khonshu out the door. This smells of a frameup job to me – a desperate maneuver to divert our suspicions, and perhaps to liberate a co-conspirator in the process." He hung his head. "Nevertheless, we're constrained to follow up on the evidence. We need Brocksmith back here for questioning. It doesn't particularly help his case that his whereabouts are currently unknown to us. He wasn't on duty when all this came to light. And he's not at home."

"That's sketchy, alright," Art commiserated.

"What's our master plan?" Blucille asked. "And how does raising the alarm like this fit into it?"

"It's a calculated gambit," the Deputy Constable admitted. "If Brocksmith was framed, we expect he'll be drawn back to Headquarters, being none the wiser that he's the one we're looking for. But if he *wasn't* framed… well… in that case it seems almost certain he meant to disappear regardless."

Finally, Deborah joined them.

"Well, we're all here now," Blucille said. "What can we do to help?"

Miloje wrinkled his mustache. "You didn't bring Templar with you?"

Blucille clapped a hand on her hat. "Goodness, I nearly forgot! He's gone to hunt down Khonshu. He thought he might find him at the old Greyson Estate. Miloje, if he's right, I'm afraid he's going to need our help."

"I scarcely have anyone to spare right now." Miloje sighed. "But very well. The last thing we need is to compound this mess by letting a public menace get away."

"Deputy Constable!" a voice called out. "Deputy Constable, Sir! Thank goodness I've found you!" A frantic policeman flew into their huddle.

"Corporal Dawson," Miloje acknowledged him. "What is it?"

"Sir, I know where the Captain is! Or anyway, where he should be." He showed his superior a small letter. "This is what we found in his wastebin at home. He's gone back to where it all started, Sir – the shipwreck – in answer to a summons from Lieutenant Carbine!"

"Carbine?" Blucille repeated. "That's Amadeus' new PSO, isn't it?"

"Regrettably, yes," Miloje answered. "What would the High Constable's right hand want with Captain Brocksmith? Does it say?"

Dawson shook his head. "I'm afraid not, Sir. The letter merely instructs him to report to the dock by 20-hundred hours."

Miloje looked back at Blucille. "You asked how you might be of assistance. Come with me – all of you. We're going to the docks." He returned to Dawson. "You've done well, Corporal, but I'm afraid I'll have to reward your success with a new task. I need you to assemble a team for a raid on the Greyson Estate..."

The Deputy Constable commenced with the details of the mission as he turned to lead them all to the stables. But Deborah, having arrived quite in the middle of things, just stood in place for a moment, looking perplexed at Art. "Mind telling me what on earth I missed?"

He nodded, setting a hand on her shoulder and bringing them into step with the rest of the group. "Come on; I'll explain on the way."

* * *

"Stop right here!" Miloje commanded. His driver tugged the reigns and quickly pulled the break lever. Fully steeped in the relentless mood of a dogged investigator hot on the trail, Miloje hopped from the carriage with the swift sure-footedness of a man forty years his junior. Blucille, Art, and Deborah were right on his heels, with no need for anyone to stay behind and settle-up this time. Their feet were a flurry of *thunks* on the boardwalk as they waded into the endless maze of docks that ran the whole of the Great Harbor.

Privately, Art was at the mercy of his various senses, none of which could currently be bothered to portend anything good. Even here at the coast, where trade was continuous, the watchful night had reduced the everyman's comings and goings to a vague rumor. No matter which way he turned, he was met with stillness and silence. Those few still to be found moving their goods to and fro managed to keep their business to the shadows, behind manifold curtains of fog, and always at the edges of his field of vision. In essence, he saw nothing. He heard nothing. But worst by far was what he *smelled*. He recalled Steward Jamison's comment some days ago: that if he could only get his snout on straight, he'd be sure to smell something rotten. Art was left to wonder how he ever could've missed it before. The air was rank with it now...

"I've got a bad feeling about this," he admitted, as they passed straight through a stagnant patch of fog. "Do we even know where we're going?"

"I've been to the scene a few times – I'm confident I can find it again," Miloje encouraged him. "*Reasonably* confident," he hesitated to add.

"*Great...*" Art intoned.

Miloje shot a gruff look over his shoulder before pointing vaguely off ahead of them and to the left. "It should be..."

BANG!

A loud disruption echoed off the water all around them. They all froze for a moment in their tracks...

"Was that a...?" Art inquired.

"Yes," Miloje anticipated him. "Gunshot. Hurry!"

In one final burst of speed, they found themselves arriving at the exact vague spot the Deputy Constable had indicated. Through the mists, they made out the silhouette of a big, hulking figure... and immediately thereafter a shorter, bald man in a long, regal overcoat. The former had his left hand tucked in his military uniform – the right hanging by his side, knuckles veiled in a metallic shell. The latter held a smoking pistol...

And at their feet was a corpse...

"Wha... what is the meaning of this!?" Miloje demanded, breathless... for more reasons than one. Drawing near the whole ghastly ensemble, he confirmed his worst fear. It was Captain Brocksmith lying there, dead on the ground. And, his *killers*... they were none other than Lieutenant Carbine... and the High Constable himself. "Lord High Constable!" Miloje appealed. "What has happened?"

Amadeus slowly turned to meet the newcomers, his square features arrested in a haunted stare. At first, he said nothing. For a moment, it even appeared beyond his capability to do so. But at length he blinked, and made his answer. "I've done what you apparently couldn't, Miloje," he said... his calm, stern voice contrasting uncannily with his astonished face. "I've concluded your investigation. The mole is dead."

"But *how*, my liege?" Miloje pressed him. "How could you be sure that...?"

"It's a tale as old as time," the surly, oversize Lieutenant Carbine interrupted. "The perpetrator always returns to the scene of the crime."

Miloje glowered. "I beg your pardon?! That's pure farcical nonsense and you know it! Brocksmith only came here on *your* request, you...!" Art had to physically restrain the old man.

Carbine shook his head, tsking. "You really ought to keep your little compsognathus on a tighter leash, Amadeus," he said.

Blucille stepped forward. "But the Deputy Constable isn't wrong. This is no chance meeting. There must've been *something* to point the finger at Brocksmith, or none of us would be standing here now. What was it? As one of the State's duly appointed District Attorneys, I demand to know."

Carbine looked back at his boss. "You seem to have an entire department of upstarts." He tiredly massaged the bridge of his nose. "Handle this."

Amadeus turned his puffy lip up at Blucille. "Your demands *are* a bit high-handed, *Assistant* District Attorney," he admonished her. "But if it's proof you want, I can oblige. I don't suppose you were aware... it seems your dear Captain Brocksmith was accepting bribes. We found 3000 pence in his account – anonymously deposited. Every red shilling of it."

Art joined Blucille, folding his arms. "*I* knew about that. Detective Jamison knew. He passed it off as frameup money."

"Then he's an even bigger fool than I thought," Amadeus retorted. "If he was any kind of detective, he would've at least confronted Brocksmith about the money. *I* did... and he tried to kill me for the trouble. *Me*. It's... only lucky I was faster on the draw."

"I... I don't believe it," Miloje dared admit, in a broken voice. "Brocksmith... after so many years of exemplary service. He could... he could never be..."

"But he was," Amadeus cut in. "And that's the necessary end of it. The answer was right in front of you the whole time. You were just too sentimental to see it." He shook out his overcoat before wrapping it tight, passing Miloje by. "Be sure it doesn't happen again."

"But..."

"The case is *closed*, Miloje. ***Closed***. That's not just a fact. It's an order."

Amadeus resumed his long march back to the coast. After a short, smoldering stare, Carbine fell in step with heavy boots. For his part, Miloje was by this time almost oblivious to them. He knelt by the spot where

Brocksmith lay. He removed his bobby, silently paying his respects to a fellow officer of great distinction, powerless to even imagine a reality in which he was undeserving of them. Art looked on – solemn, and bewildered – putting an arm around each of the ladyfolk. He hadn't known Brocksmith well. But even so, it was as clear to him as anyone. No justice had been served here tonight...

That rotten smell was just as pungent as ever...

* * *

KNOCK KNOCK KNOCK

Removing his hand from the door, Art sighed in the pre-dawn darkness. It had taken long minutes to wind-up the courage to knock... and now, a mere instant to regret it. He knew that most people at least *tried* to sleep on a regular basis, and even for the better part of the night. Coming here at this hour was selfish. He quickly resolved to hope his rapping had gone unnoticed and buzz off. But just as he was turning to go, the door began to open...

...And there was Steward Jamison, fully dressed and hatted...

"Well hello, Aart," he intoned in his kindly voice. "What brings you to this crummy old shack?"

Art was a little surprised at the harsh adjectives Jamison assigned to his own home, just then. After a moment's reflection though, he had to admit: The place *was* a little spooky. But he shook it off, refocusing. "I, eh... I brought you some news about the case." He rubbed the back of his neck. "It would seem... we finally caught up with our perp."

Jamison nodded gravely. "I know."

Art raised a brow. "You do?"

"W'll sure, sure." He gestured out at the sky. "What with all those bells going off, I had ta know *something* was up. Well, I wasn't just going to sit by and let my mind race, was I? No, Siir. So, I got someone to tell me all about it."

Art's face drew back as he contemplated the plight of whatever poor, unsuspecting someone Jamison ran down to get his answers. "I see."

Jamison made a study of him. "You... y'don't seem too thrilled with the way things turned out."

Art shook his head. "Not particularly."

"Could it be that's the *real* reason you're here?"

"...Could be."

Jamison grinned. "Come on in, Art," he said with a wave. "We'll talk."

* * *

"So, it was Brocksmith after all, eh?" Jamison called over his shoulder, pouring a hearty glass of some inscrutable, odiferous liquid for himself.

"That's what the High Constable would have us believe," Art replied.

Jamison held the pitcher out. "Yak's milk and ginger ale?" he asked, before Art could even begin to untangle his embattled olfactory signals.

"No, thank you."

Jamison came into the living room, joining Art in relative darkness, seating himself in the opposing chair. "You don't really believe it was Brocksmith, do ya?"

"You tell me, Jamison," Art said as he leaned in, resting his elbows on his knees. "We already knew everything Amadeus had to say about it. We knew all about the bribe money... and we wrote it off. Is there any chance we were wrong?"

Jamison set his jaw, and looked down.

"Yeah," Art sighed. "That's what I thought." He ran a hand over his folded ears. "What am I gonna do about this? What *can* I do? The whole thing's been sealed off by the High Constable – the second-biggest big-wig in the country. Not you, not me... not Blackforest himself can go against *him*."

Jamison reflected on Art's plight for a spell, taking a long, refreshing draught of his concoction. "Art... do you want to know what I do every night? And I mean, every *single* night for the last twenty-five years?"

Art shrugged. "I suppose you're going to tell me either way."

"Every night, I alphabetize my sock drawer, put on a four-piece suit and go straight ta bed. And *then* do you know what I do? I *look baack*. I look back on all the old cases. *All* of them, Art. I go over everything I can remember. And when that fails, I get out the notes. I solve the same old mysteries over, and over, and over again. And y'know, most of the time, they come out the same way in the end. And that's good! But every so often, I thinka something I didn't before. Something that – occasionally – changes everything. There's been five... six... no! *Seven* cases I've come forward and reopened. Seven cold, dead cases where the verdict had to be overturned!"

"Wow..." Art marveled. "That's, um... that sounds like a horrifying way to go through life."

Jamison nodded enthusiastically. "Yes. It is!"

"But how does that help with this?"

Jamison made a pointing gesture at his head. "The trick is to keep your eyes open... even when everything tells ya to shut them. To not lose your focus. Because the case is never *really* closed. That goes double for a case like this. Because you and me – we already know the truth, whether we can prove it yet or not. The *real* bad guy's still out there. He can thank his lucky stars for now, but that kinda luck never holds out. Even the smartest bad guy can only help himself so long. By and by, he'll start up again... doin' his dirty deeds. And when he does, we'll still be watching. We'll catch him with his hand in the cookie jar. And there won't be any hasty assumptions from the High Constable to help him out a second time."

Art nodded his agreement with a half-smile. "Play the long game, eh? Sounds like a winner ta me." He raised an imaginary glass. "Here's to keeping our eyes open."

Jamison joined the toast. "I'll drink to thaat."

Chapter 19

The day was clear and bright for the first time in ages. The fresh smell of a gentle sea breeze affirmed Horus' alert optimism as he watched the proceedings unfold beneath him from the highest fastness of the bell tower. At the signal of a whistle, pairs of blue-coated Mercenaries commenced to board the transport, row upon row. Until, finally, a late addition to their lineup was personally escorted in chains up the ramp by an extremely healthy entourage of policemen. Horus watched as a sergeant handed the keys to Khonshu's restraints off to a bosun before leading his squadron back down the ramp. No sooner than they'd returned to the dock, and the ramp was promptly retracted. The captain gave the order, and all the mooring lines were cast off. Before long at all, the ship was off and away. Horus felt a wash of relief...

"Well, there you have it," said Miloje, just then. He must've noticed Horus loosen his grip on the railing. "I'd say your work here is quite thoroughly done, Templar. I've every confidence that Captain Christophe and his new compliment of Mercenaries have the situation well in-hand. Just as I assured you that my own, hand-selected team of men did."

"You'll have to forgive me if I'd just as soon stay until the ship is out of sight," Horus replied, eyes still fixed into the Harbor.

Miloje huffed. "I suppose this is your way of rubbing it in."

Horus looked back at him. "Rubbing *what* in?"

"Oh, come, come. You know very well what I mean. Your single-handed defeat of a rogue who incapacitated his entire retinue of armed guards, seven men strong. You'd have us all believe you're the only fellow in all of St. Argonsburg who can take a Vigilant in mortal combat. I half suspect you're convinced of it yourself."

Horus grinned wryly. "Well, there's no use taking any chances, is there?"

The Deputy Constable returned his wry expression. "In any event, it would appear you can back up the claims you made after the Tweed case was closed. You *aren't* helpless after all, Counselor. Far from it, it seems." He raised a brow. "It gets an old sleuth to wondering. Wondering how and why an *attorney* would acquire such a particular set of skills."

Horus shrugged it off. "You have your secrets. I have mine."

"But you *know* mine."

"Sorry, Milo," Horus replied, shaking his head. "I simply don't share your open-book policy."

"Indeed. I've known many prominent lawyers in my day, Templar, and I do believe you keep things tighter to the chest than any of them. That may be the ruin of you yet."

"Deputy Constable, Sir," Captain Alexei called up the ladder, even as he ascended it to their level. "You'll pardon my interruption, I hope... but of course, we mustn't linger." He removed his bobby, taking a forlorn study of the floor. "There is much work to be done, back at Headquarters."

Miloje frowned, and nodded. "Yes... of course. Lest I forget for a moment."

Horus felt a pit form in his stomach. He cleared his throat. "I suppose I've gone long enough without really acknowledging the dark side of all this. I don't have the words to tell you both how sorry I was to hear about Captain Brocksmith."

"Perhaps it's for the best if you never find them," Miloje quipped, looking off distantly. "Brocksmith's passing alone would've been a heavy blow. But worse by far, we're forced to subscribe to the ludicrous idea that he was a traitor, and a villain." His mustache twitched. "Officially, we can't even grieve for him."

"It's a travesty," Horus sighed. "But you know, Milo... the truth always comes out. Brocksmith's good name *will* be cleared one day... even if it isn't until the Great Looking Back. All we can do now is our best to take this in stride."

They eyed him rather doubtfully. "And how, O tireless oracle, do you advise we do that?" Miloje challenged.

Horus shrugged, smiling apologetically. "Alright, so I don't have all the answers. I confess. But of course, you're going to have to *try*, Milo. You're going to have to carry on one way or the other. Sometimes you just have to stop and remind yourself that things aren't always as hopeless as they appear." He gestured out. "Look around. That storm we never got has finally passed. It's a beautiful day."

"That it is, Mr. Templar, Sir," Alexei agreed, glumly replacing his cap. "Though, I daresay, we could've used the rain."

* * *

"You know, I'm really going to miss this place," Deborah said, gathering her effects from the back room as they both prepared to depart the refuge of the Ecre Point Warehouse.

"Don't worry," Horus assured her, folding a case book under his arm. "I suspect Art can be persuaded to let us visit now and then."

She turned a questioning look at him. "You're sure the Vigil won't give us any more trouble? After all, you didn't quite do what they wanted."

Horus shrugged. "I guess I can't say for certain the danger has passed. Vigilants *are* spiteful creatures by nature. I'd like to think they'll leave us alone now, seeing there's nothing more we can do, whether for or against them. But I'm not positive." He scratched under his chin. "Would you prefer to stay here a bit longer?"

She shook her head. "We'll have to resume business as usual sooner or later. We have to be out there where our next case can find us. The Vigil's one thing, but I know the Czarina won't give an inch, if it looks like we're shirking our duties."

"Agreed."

They both resumed packing for a few beats, until Deborah broke the quiet by clearing her throat. "Speaking of, well... 'professional misconduct'..." She turned back to him. "Horus... I hope you're not still angry with me. For going to Blackforest, I mean."

"I don't think I ever got around to being *angry*," he replied. "There was too much disbelief to make room for any other feeling."

"Well, that sounds about right," she sighed. "Even the worst Secretary in the world doesn't go around scuttling her boss' cases on purpose."

"No, I should say not." His deliberately stern expression melted into a grin. "Only the very best would do something like that."

She returned his warm expression. "Thanks, Boss."

For a moment, they were both quiet, until Art suddenly peaked his head in the room. "Knock-knock," he said. "How's the packing going? Surely you guys didn't smuggle that much stuff in here."

"We were just finishing up, Art," Deborah answered.

"Okay, well, I got a cab upstairs."

"Why don't the two of you go ahead?" Horus proposed. "I'll follow on foot later on."

Art winced. "Why would you wanna do a thing like that?"

Horus turned up his palms. "Honestly, after a case like this, I think I could use a little time to clear my head."

"Fair enough," Art went along. "C'mon, Debs. Blucille and I'll get ya settled back into the old office."

Horus made a quick stopping motion with his hand. "Only if you're sure you can spare the time until I get back," he interjected.

"No problem," Art assured him. "I'm between cases right now too."

"Alright," Horus nodded. "I won't be long."

"Take your time."

Deborah made for the door, turning back at the threshold. "See you later, Boss."

He nodded. "Soon."

* * *

Despite his promise to be not long delayed, Horus was very slow even making his way back to the front room of Art's private holdout. In truth, it wasn't so much the walk back through town where he planned to do the balance of his head-clearing. It was right *here*... alone with his father's keepsakes. Nonchalantly, he sat down at the piano bench, facing out, looking around at nothing in particular. They'd left the room dark anyway. He didn't mind. They wouldn't have expected that he meant to linger here. But as he let his thoughts and gaze wander, he realized he was just stalling... putting off the task at hand. Before he could turn and 'face the music', though, he heard footsteps in the hall again. He swiveled to meet the door...

"Did we forget something?" he asked. "I was sure we..."

"Hello, Horus."

An altogether different apparition darkened Art's doorway. Horus shot up to his feet...

The Mesomela in the shadows gently laughed. "How gracious of you to come to attention in my presence. You did learn how to show *some* respect, after all."

Horus remained silent... frozen.

"What's the matter? Aren't you going to invite your old uncle in?"

"How...?" Horus stammered. "How did you...?"

"Oh, come now," Apep retorted. "With all the trips you've been making back and forth, did you really think you could keep this place a secret from us forever?"

"I..." Horus began. "I had high hopes."

"*Hm...*" Apep replied doubtfully. "Well, never mind the formalities. I'll let myself in." He strode into the room, his confident gait untouched by age.

At last, Horus began to move past his initial shock, into a briny contempt. "What is it you want this time? I did everything I could for Khonshu. I saved his life. If that's not good enough for you, then I hope you've at least come to take it up with *me*. Leave my associates out of it."

"And, if I've come for a *truce*? What then?" Apep stood there grinding his teeth a moment, then looked away. "You never could relent your pugnaciousness... your ugly presumptions."

I've never made a presumption so ugly that you couldn't find a way to behave even uglier."

Apep sighed. "I can't imagine what would make you want to rehearse all this *again*. This conversation has a *point*, Horus. Let me make it." He took a moment, apparently trying to coach his face into something warmer than a scowl. "We are... *grateful*... for what you've done, Nephew. *I* am grateful. I didn't trust you to come through without careful handling. But I see now that was a mistake. It was much as you said: You succeeded despite me. And how fortuitous that you did. Khonshu is very much the auspicious young man that the future of the Vigil depends upon."

"That future may yet be in doubt." Horus folded his arms. "Khonshu's gone beyond your reach for now. There's a distinct possibility he may never return."

Apep nodded gravely. "It's true. He's consigned to the very den of our accursèd adversary. It may yet be the death of him."

"It may. But there're other reasons he might never come back."

The Stentor slowly turned an accusatory look at Horus. "You don't mean to suggest that you've influenced him? That's one thing I would find *very* disappointing."

Horus shook his head. "Not nearly as much as I meant to. Suffice it to say, if he *does* one day break ties with the Vigil, it won't be because of any great persuasiveness on my part. He's as far beyond my reach as he is yours. Whatever choice he makes will be his own."

Apep gave him the side-eye. "A choice you bought him deliberately, no doubt?"

Hours made no response.

At length, Apep turned aside dejectedly. "There's nothing quite so unfortunate as a *choice*, when it's the wrong one..." he rued, taking a few deliberate paces toward the weapon case by the piano. "I admit... I've made a few that I regret."

The bile in Horus' mouth turned sickeningly sour. "You're not seriously going to try and apologize for what you did to Father?"

"What *I* did?" Apep fired back. "What about *you*, Horus? *You* were the one who deliberately turned his back on everything he was. Everything he stood for."

Silence prevailed as the two men's eyes traded icy darts, exchanging accusations that transcended words. After a few withering rounds of this, though, Apep was the first to avert his gaze...

"But then, I suppose it was my own fault," he went on. "Clearly, I misread the situation. *Badly*. I thought your father's brave sacrifice would only serve to galvanize you, in turn. That was assuredly my greatest error." He reached out and set a clawed hand on the glass barrier between himself and Tanis' old hammer. "You had such promise, Horus. You should have been the ideal Vigilant. For the life of me, I've never understood how anyone could turn aside from his calling. From his perfect destiny."

Horus swallowed. It affected him, somewhat, to hear his uncle recite the very same question that had haunted him for years. "Well..." he began. "If you ever get to the bottom of that one, be sure to let me know."

"That may prove difficult..." Apep withdrew his hand from the display case, looking back at his nephew. "There's something else I meant to tell you. The Vigil is pulling out of St. Argonsburg. There's no room left to maneuver here."

There was another short, tense silence, as Horus tried to figure how he was supposed to react to the news. "That's probably wise," he said finally.

Apep cleared his throat, appearing somehow disappointed. "Yes, well. It would seem this is goodbye, again. Now, and for the foreseeable future..."

As Apep began to turn away, Horus called after him. "You weren't also planning on taking his hammer back, were you?"

Apep stopped, apparently giving the question some thought. "No. It should remain with you."

"Just as well. I intended to keep it anyway."

"Really?" Apep intoned. "Good. Then let it be a reminder to you. A constant reminder that he gave up everything – his very life for the Cause."

"He gave his life for the love of his brother," Horus answered him.

Apep only stared, his eyes shifting as he strove to comprehend Horus' statement. But finally, after a few prolonged moments of fruitless calculations, his face hardened. "You remember him your way, Horus... if you must. And I'll remember him mine."

"Naturally," Horus replied. "But for my part, I don't intend to delude myself any longer. We both had our ideas of who he *ought* to be. At the end of the day, though, he was neither one, nor the other. He was a little of both."

With that, Apep turned away silently – thoughtfully – and disappeared back up the stairs...

When he was satisfied his uncle had quite gone, Horus turned back to the bench behind the Steinwyk. He felt a lump forming in his throat – a rush of second thoughts. But he pushed through. This was something he'd made up his mind to do. He *had to* do it...

So, he sat down.

For a while, he could do no more than vacantly roam over the keys with his eyes and hands, like he didn't know where to start. But finally, he chose a few that looked promising. He pressed the keys. *Dissonance*. But wait... of course... it was the next fifth *over*. He tried again. *Flat*. What now? He had his fingers too far apart. They'd been shorter when he was little...

At last, he struck the right first chord... and then, the second. The third was off again, but he realized his mistake more quickly than he could even explain it to himself. He started over. He got midway through the third bar before the next little slipup. He started over again...

...And before he half knew it, he was playing a lively melody right along...

Acknowledgments

I should really thank Christopher Nolan for providing a convenient muse to help me navigate through the challenging opening scene. His movies provided much inspiration for this phase of the story in general. And I should probably apologize for the lazy jabs taken here at some of our most enduring soap operas. I feel like I don't know enough about the genre to get great mileage out of lampooning it, since the only soap I really watched very much of was Carol Burnette's "As the Stomach Turns" ... unless you count the episodes of "Heartland". Restyling Jimmy Steward as Steward Jamison was also questionable, I'm sure.

A special thank you to John for suggesting Rosencrantz and Guildenstern... like you said, a perfect pair of attorney handles if ever there was one. The Bard, of course, gets some credit for the names themselves.

It would also be irresponsible not to acknowledge my hijacking of the ending to that Mr. Rogers movie from a few years back.

For More from E.L. Ward...

Visit his personal site, at:

https://www.booksofelward.com

His vast arsenal of backlist titles includes the following:

TITLES IN THE ORPHAN UNIVERSE

HERON PROPHECIES SERIES

The Chocolate Prophecy

HORUS TEMPLAR – PUBLIC DEFENDER SERIES

Horus Templar and the Case of the Wimpy War-Criminal
Horus Templar and the Case of the Iniquitous Inquisitor
Horus Templar and the Case of the Draft-Dodging Drone
Horus Templar and the Case of the Dubious Decedent
Horus Templar and the Case of the Vengeful Vigilant

E.L. Ward is proud to partner with:

MALOB ARTS

Check out his and other creative works at:

www.malobarts.com

Made in the USA
Monee, IL
04 November 2026

67386534R10125